FRETBOARD BIOLOGY
COMPREHENSIVE GUITAR PROGRAM

"The Knowledge without the College"™

LEVEL 6

This textbook accompanies the Level 6 course at Fretboardbiology.com

©2024 Joe Elliott. Please do not distribute or reproduce this material. This program represents a lifetime of work teaching guitar players like you how to be better musicians. If you think this program is great, please encourage your friends to sign up for the course and go through it with you. They will get more out of the program, and you will feel better knowing that you aren't hurting fellow artists by just giving away their work. Thank you.

©2024 Fretboard Biology • Fretboard Biology.com

Music Biology Publishing

Copyright © 2024 Joe Elliott

All rights reserved. Except as permitted under the U.S. Copyright Act of 1976, no part of this book may be reproduced in any manner whatsoever without written permission from the publisher, except in the case of brief quotations in critical articles or reviews.

The paper used in this publication meets the minimum requirements of the American National Standards for Information Services - Permanence of Paper for Printed Library Materials,
ANSI Z39.48-1984.

ISBN: 978-1-7362942-5-3

DEDICATION

I would like to dedicate this to all the great teachers out there who are passing along their knowledge and experience.

ACKNOWLEDGMENTS

In any project like this, it is hard to thank all of the people who have been instrumental in its development and success. I've been fortunate to have the support and friendship of many people along the way. I've somehow been wise enough to listen to those who know more than me, too. I encourage everyone to live that way.

I would like to start by thanking my wife, Eileen, for all the support, encouragement, and freedom to take on this monstrous project—and the faith that it would be a success—as well as all the years of putting up with the stresses of being married to a professional musician. My interest in music was fostered and supported by my parents, Jack and Marian Elliott, who always had a house full of big band and classical music, and my older siblings, Dave, Mary, and Dan, who exposed me to a lot of great music growing up like the Trashmen, The Beatles, The Stones, Sergio Mendes, Chicago, Sly, and Crosby, Stills, and Nash.

There were several people who were very influential in my development as a musician and educator that I would like to acknowledge: Fred Brush for showing so many great musicians to me in my formative years. Glen Johnston for exposing all of us "Montana Boys" to the real musicians in person at Montana State. Kent Erickson for drilling me on theory on our long road trips. Carl Schroeder for your unique way of getting your points across back in the day when I was in your classes in LA. You certainly shaped my way of teaching and managing a classroom. Keith Wyatt for the steady example of professionalism in guitar education. Combining great guitar talent with an organized mind is a great combination for any student. Scott Henderson for your relentless intolerance of mediocrity. You still scare me into working harder. Don Mock for being such an egoless sharer of your knowledge and gifts. You'll probably never know how many lives you affected with your pragmatic approach. Howard Roberts for all the lives you changed teaching guitar players real-world skills and shaping the most innovative guitar program that's ever existed. Bruce Buckingham for feeding me the right information at the right time. Eric Paschal for always finding the best in all your students. And Dan Gilbert for the energy you pumped into every class and the motivation to practice more than I've ever practiced.

For this project I was very fortunate to be surrounded by a team of amazing and intelligent musicians and specialty experts such as Ricky Peterson, Sean Nilson, Eliot Briggs, Bill Lafleur, Luke Elliott, Carter Elliott, John Krogh, Harry Chalmiers, Kevin Sullivan, Tony Axtell and the McNally Smith College of Music "guitar department in exile"—Tim Lyles, Paul Krueger, Chris Olson, Mike Salow, Dave Singley, and Eva Beneke—for test-driving this Fretboard Biology method for seven years.

None of this would have happened without the dedicated work of my former business partner in the Fretboard Biology program, Todd Berntson, and his wife, Monique. There's a lot of skill and talent in that duo and it was only through Todd's insistence that this project was launched.

Lastly, I would like to thank all the great musicians and students I have had the pleasure to work with over the past 40 years.

CONTENTS

LEVEL 6 INTRODUCTION — 1

UNIT 1 — 3
- Theory – Avoid Tones
- Fretboard Logic – Avoid Tones of all Chords of Harmonized Major and Minor Scale Patterns
- Rhythm Guitar – Review of Reading Chord Charts
- Chart Writing – Definitions of Sections, Creating a Form Chart
- Improvisation – Playing and Hearing Avoid Tones
- Practice – Solidify all Unit 1 Information

UNIT 2 — 25
- Theory – Methods of Viewing the Seven Modes, Mode Qualities, Mode Key Signatures
- Fretboard Logic – Reassign Numbers of Scale Degrees to Learn Modes
- Rhythm Guitar – Creating a Rhythm Guitar Part for a Blues Song
- Chart Writing – Creating a Crude Chord Chart
- Improvisation – Sounds of Lydian, Mixolydian, Dorian, and Phrygian Modes
- Practice – Continue Practice Routine Development

UNIT 3 — 63
- Theory – Harmonized Modes
- Fretboard Logic – Major Modes and the Major Pentatonic Scale, Minor Modes and the Minor Pentatonic Scale
- Rhythm Guitar – Creating a Rhythm Guitar Part for a Folk Song
- Chart Writing – Figuring out the Chords of a Song for the Crude Chart
- Improvisation – Sounds of the Major and Minor Pentatonic Scales
- Practice – Continue Practice Routine Development

UNIT 4 — 85
- Theory – Dorian Scale Construction and Progressions
- Fretboard Logic – Five Patterns of the Dorian Scale, Adding a Major 2nd and Major 6th to the Minor Pentatonic Scale Patterns
- Rhythm Guitar – Creating a Rhythm Guitar Part for a Classic Rock Song
- Chart Writing – Figuring out the Rhythm Figures and Riffs of a Song for the Crude Chord Chart
- Improvisation – Soloing over the Most Common Dorian Progressions
- Practice – Continue Practice Routine Development

UNIT 5　　　　　　　　　　　　　　　　　　　　　　　　　　　　　107

- Theory – Composite Minor
- Fretboard Logic – Visualizing Parallel Minor Scales within the Same Octave Shape
- Rhythm Guitar – Creating a Rhythm Guitar Part for a Reggae Song
- Chart Writing – Using One-Bar, Two-Bar, and Four-Bar Repeats on a Chart
- Improvisation – Improvising over Progressions with Chords from Parallel Minor Scales
- Practice – Continue Practice Routine Development

UNIT 6　　　　　　　　　　　　　　　　　　　　　　　　　　　　　129

- Theory – Harmonic Analysis and Scale Application for Progressions with Composite MInor
- Fretboard Logic – Visualizing Parallel Minor Scales within the Same Octave Shape
- Rhythm Guitar – Creating a Rhythm Guitar Part for a Country Song
- Chart Writing – Using Start and End Repeat Brackets as Endings
- Improvisation – Improvise over Progressions with Chords from Parallel Minor Scales
- Practice – Continue Practice Routine Development

UNIT 7　　　　　　　　　　　　　　　　　　　　　　　　　　　　　151

- Theory – The Most Common Progression Fragments in the Mixolydian Scale
- Fretboard Logic – Deriving Patterns of the Mixolydian Scale from the Major Pentatonic Scales, Common Mixolydian Progression Fragments
- Rhythm Guitar – Creating a Rhythm Guitar Part for a Funk Song
- Chart Writing – Using Jump Marks Like DC, DS, and Coda Signs
- Improvisation – Using the Mixolydian Scale
- Practice – Continue Practice Routine Development

UNIT 8　　　　　　　　　　　　　　　　　　　　　　　　　　　　　177

- Theory – The Most Common Progression Fragments in the Lydian Scale
- Fretboard Logic – Deriving Patterns of the Lyydian Scale from the Major Pentatonic Scale, a Common Lydian Progression
- Rhythm Guitar – Creating a Rhythm Guitar Part for a Classic R&B Song
- Chart Writing – Placing all the Information on the Page
- Improvisation – Using the Lydian Scale
- Practice – Continue Practice Routine Development

UNIT 9　　　　　　　　　　　　　　　　　　　　　　　　　　　　　201

- Theory – The Most Common Progression Fragments in the Phrygian Scale
- Fretboard Logic – Deriving Patterns of the Phrygian Scale from the Minor Pentatonic Scales, the Most Common Phrygian Progression Fragments
- Rhythm Guitar – Creating a Rhythm Guitar Part for an Afro-Latin Song
- Chart Writing – Adding Helpful Information to a Chart
- Improvisation – Using the Phrygian Scale
- Practice – Continue Practice Routine Development

UNIT 10   229

- Theory – Different Kinds of Modulation, Various Ways Modulation is Used in Songs
- Fretboard Logic – Deriving Patterns of the Locrian Scale from the Minor Pentatonic Scales
- Rhythm Guitar – Creating a Rhythm Guitar Part for a Song in 5/8
- Chart Writing – Write a Complete Chart from Start to Finish
- Improvisation – Improvising When There is Modulation
- Practice – Continue Practice Routine Development

APPENDICES   251

LEVEL 6 INTRODUCTION

Fretboard Biology Level 6 builds on the material in the previous levels. If you haven't completed those levels, go back and make sure that you are confident in all the material. In Level 6 you continue your study of Theory, Fretboard Logic, Rhythm Guitar, Improvisation, Chart Writing, and Practice. Work at the pace that fits you.

What's in Level 6

- In the Theory modules, you will learn about avoid tones, the modes, Composite Minor and modulation. This includes harmonizing each mode and the harmonic analysis of progressions in each of the modes as well as progressions which mix minor modes.

- In the Fretboard Logic modules, you will learn five patterns of each mode and learn to adapt them from the major and minor pentatonic scale patterns. You will learn to play the arpeggios from the common composite minor progressions in-position. You will learn common progressions in each of the modes.

- In the Rhythm Guitar modules, you will learn to read chord charts and use style-appropriate parts.

- In the Chart Writing modules, you will learn to build a chord chart and organize the content of a song on the page in a way that helps the reader perform comfortably.

- In the Improvisation Modules, you will learn to improvise in each of the modes as well as progressions that mix minor modes.

This is a progressive course. Each module in each level builds on the information from the previous one. You'll get the most out of the program by staying with the sequence.

In each unit, you will find references to tracks for you to listen to and play over. All of these tracks can be found at the link below:

https://fretboardbiology.com/book6

UNIT 1

Learning Modules

> **Theory** - Avoid Tones

> **Fretboard Logic** - Avoid Tones of all Chords of all Harmonized Major and Minor Scale Patterns

> **Rhythm Guitar** - Review of Reading Chord Charts

> **Chart Writing** - Definitions of Sections, Creating a Form Chart

> **Improvisation** - Playing and Hearing Avoid Tones

> **Practice** - Solidify all Unit 1 Information

The tracks for this Unit can be found at the following link:

https://fretboardbiology.com/book6/#u1

THEORY

The Modes

Level 6 focuses on modes, which is a topic that most developing musicians hear of and wonder about. The goal in the Theory modules in this Level is for you to have a clear grasp of the modes and how they are used. We start learning about the modes specifically in Unit 2. Before we do, we need we need to discuss the concept of avoid tones. Avoid tones affect the use of modes so it is important to study this topic first.

Avoid Tones

An avoid tone is a note which is a half step above a chord tone. This minor 2nd interval between the chord tone and an avoid tone creates dissonance that can be uncomfortable for the listener.

An avoid tone can be in any octave relative to a chord tone in the chord voicing. For example, against a C major triad, F is an avoid tone because it is a half step above E, the 3rd. If you sustain an F in any octave against the C triad, it's dissonant and therefore an avoid tone.

The term, avoid tone is a bit of a misnomer, or perhaps better said, an incomplete description. It's not that you should never play avoid tones, but more that you should know the effect on the listener when you do. A more complete description is something like: Avoid holding this note against the chord if you want to avoid dissonance. Obviously, that doesn't work well as a name, but it does suggest that there are notes in scales that cause dissonance and notes that don't. Chord tones don't cause dissonance. Avoid tones do, when sustained against the chord, because of their proximity to a chord tone.

Your goal may be to make the listener feel uncomfortable in a particular spot in a solo, and nothing does that like dissonance. Think back to Level 1 Improvisation when I said that music is emotional manipulation. Think of all the different emotions you've felt listening to music. You've felt excited, calm, happy, sad, stressed, and so on. If you want to play a note that makes people really uncomfortable, play an avoid tone and hold onto it for a musical moment. Your listener will feel uncomfortable.

Every musician has unwittingly played and sustained an avoid tone and wondered why it sounded so dissonant. They wondered why a note that's diatonic to the key sounds so dissonant and undesirable.

Let's look for avoid tones in two scales you know very well: the Major and Natural Minor Scales.

Here is the C major scale and a Cma7 chord side by side. Look at the chord tones of a Cma7 chord. Are there any notes of the C major scale that are a half step above a chord tone of Cma7? Yes, the 4th of the scale, F. It is a half step above E, the 3rd of the Cma7. Therefore, it is an avoid tone when played over a Cma7.

Avoid Tone on a Cma7

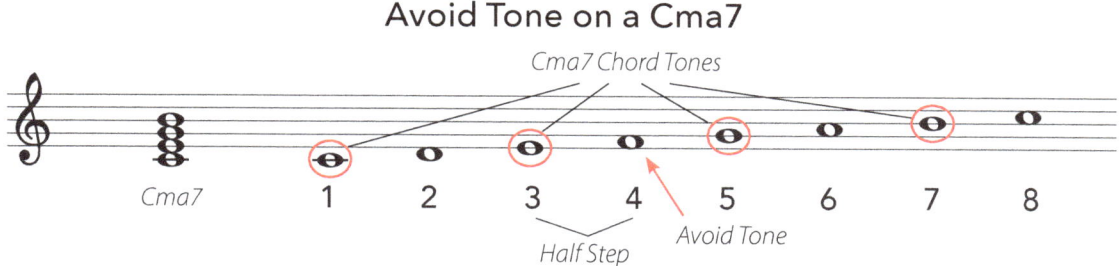

So, if you play the C Major Scale slowly over a static Cma7, and dwell on each scale degree for a moment, you get a good sense of how the 4th conflicts with the major 3rd of the chord. I suggest that you create a static Cma7 vamp and try this to hear what the avoid tone sounds like. Obviously the 4th of the scale would not be an avoid tone played over any diatonic chord that contains the 4th, such as the II, IV, V, and VII chords. They contain the 4th scale degree of the Major Scale.

Next, here is a C Natural Minor Scale and a Cmi7 chord side by side. Are there any notes of the C natural minor scale that are a half step above a chord tone of Cmi7? Yes, the ♭6th of the scale, A♭. It is a half step above G, the 5th of the Cmi7. Therefore, it is an avoid tone.

Avoid Tone on a Cmi7

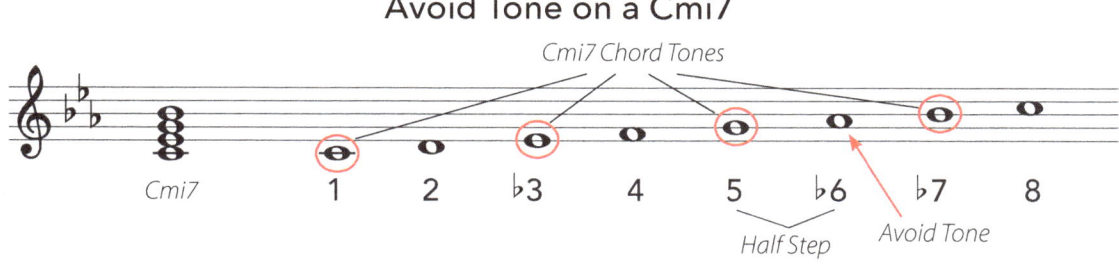

If you play the C minor scale slowly over a static Cmi7, and dwell on each scale degree for moment, you feel how the ♭6th conflicts with the perfect 5th of the chord. Like with the Cma7, I suggest that you create a static Cmi7 vamp and try this to hear what that sounds like.

In both of these cases, you hear the dissonance of the avoid tone against the tonic chord—that is, the I chord. Avoid tones are a bit of a moving target. They're not a static phenomena in a scale. They are something to consider on a chord-to-chord basis. But don't despair, when you're thinking in terms of chord tones when you solo, you're already conscious of where the chord tones are in the scale, so being aware of notes one half step above them is not a stretch.

Experiment with avoid tones by playing the scale over the I chord and focus on how the 4th sounds over a Cma7 and how the ♭6th sounds over the Cmi7. That is a good way to understand their effect. But the reality of avoid tones is that you need to be aware of them on a chord-to-chord basis. In other words, the way you need to think about avoid tones is more about each chord than the scale played against the I chord.

FRETBOARD LOGIC

Avoid Tones

You learned about avoid tones in the Theory Module. Remember that this name is a bit of a misnomer, or perhaps better said, an incomplete description of notes that are labeled avoid tones. Avoid tones cause dissonance. Chord tones do not.

Avoid Tones in the Major Scale

Let's look at the Major and Minor Scales and find the avoid tones for each scale in each of the five octave shapes. You learned that the perfect 4th of the Major Scale is an avoid tone when the scale is played over the Ima7 chord because the perfect 4th is a half step above the major 3rd, which is a chord tone of the Ima7 chord.

Now, let's go through each of the five patterns of the Major Scale, and look at the highlighted avoid tones on the Ima7 chord.

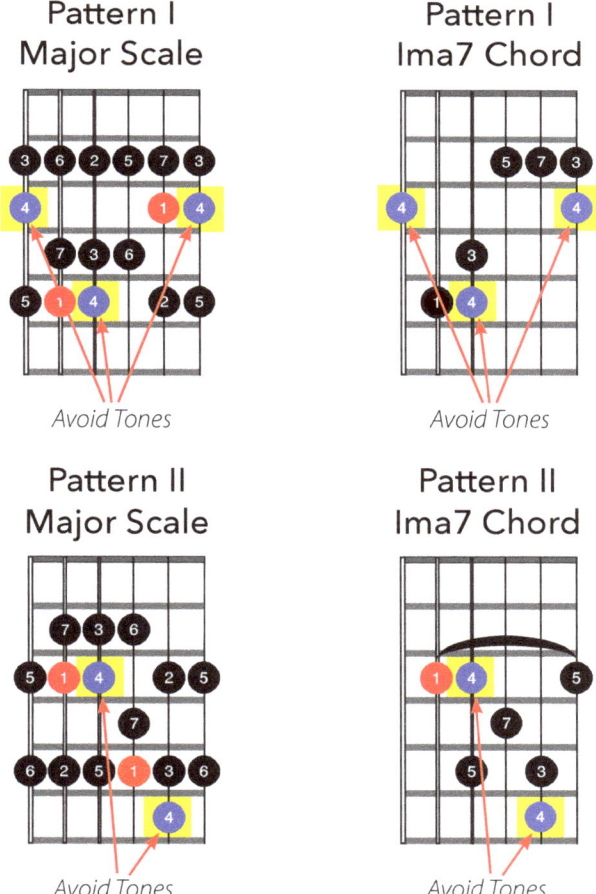

Pattern III Major Scale

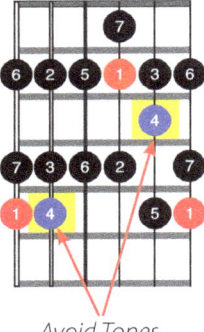

Avoid Tones

Pattern III Ima7 Chord

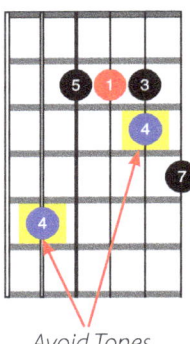

Avoid Tones

Pattern IV Major Scale

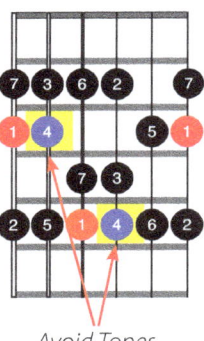

Avoid Tones

Pattern IV Ima7 Chord

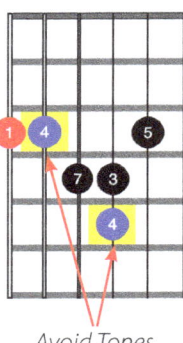

Avoid Tones

Pattern V Major Scale

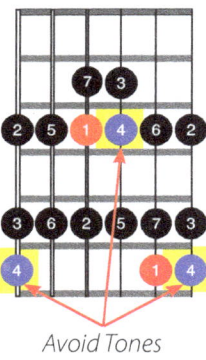

Avoid Tones

Pattern V Ima7 Chord

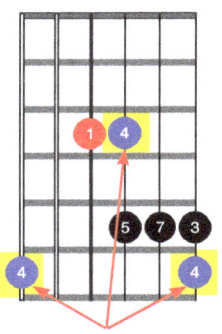

Avoid Tones

Avoid Tones in the Minor Scale

You learned that the minor 6th of the Natural Minor Scale is an avoid tone when the scale is played over the Imi7 chord. Let's go through the five patterns of the Natural Minor Scale, the Imi7 arpeggio/chord for each one and the avoid tones (♭6) for each scale highlighted. Make sure that you know where these avoid tones are relative to the I chord.

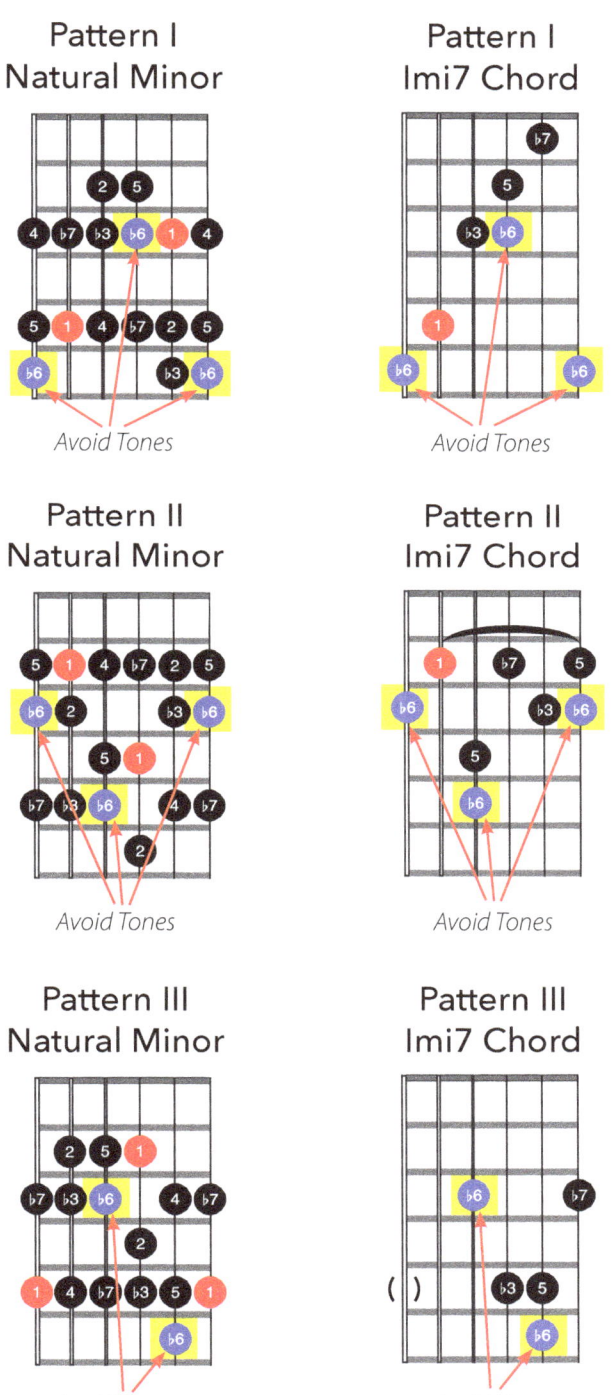

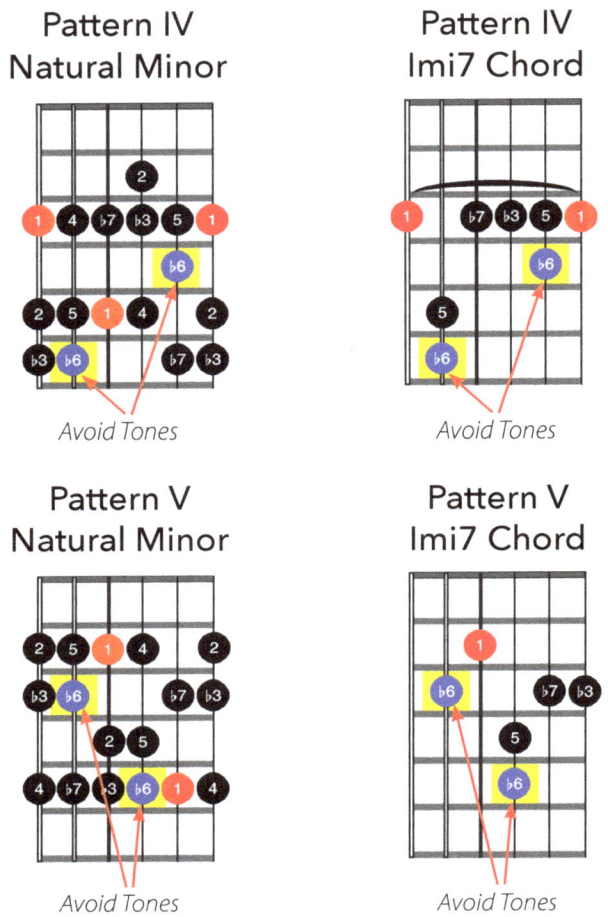

Avoid Tones in Harmonized Scales

While the 4th of the Major Scale is an avoid tone for the I chord, it's not an avoid tone for every chord in the key of the I chord. For example, take a look at the Pattern I Major Scale harmonized with arpeggios in-position. This pattern should be very familiar by now. Remember that arpeggios and chords are essentially the same thing because they are made up of the same notes. Notice that the II chord and the IV chord have no avoid tones.

Avoid Tones In the Pattern I Harmonized Major Scale

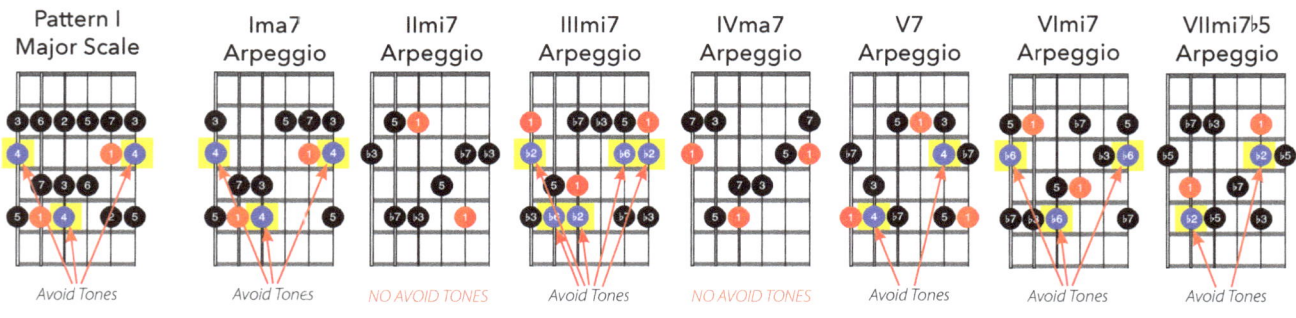

Now let's look at the harmonized Natural Minor Scale. Notice that the minor 6th of the Natural Minor Scale is not an avoid tone for every chord in the key of the I chord. Take a look at the Pattern IV Minor Scale harmonized with arpeggios in-position. This should be very familiar to you, and again, remember that arpeggios and chords are essentially the same. For each arpeggio/chord in the harmonized scale, the avoid tones for that specific chord are highlighted.

Avoid Tones In the Pattern IV Harmonized Minor Scale

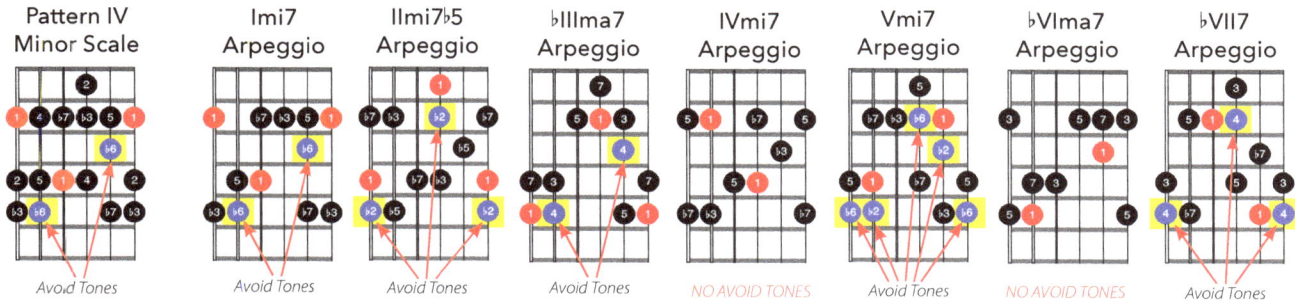

The important point here is to be conscious of the avoid tones for any chord or arpeggio, regardless of the scale pattern. Not all chords or arpeggios have avoid tones.

Don't feel like you need to memorize all of this right now. It takes time, so treat it as more of an ongoing and long-term effort. It's much more important for you to understand the principles rather than memorizing all the dots. Please relate all of this to the Family Tree. It's important that you keep that connection going!

RHYTHM GUITAR

In Level 5 you learned about reading charts. In the Level 6 Rhythm Guitar modules, you'll put those new skills together along with what you learned in all previous Rhythm Guitar modules. You'll read nine charts, one per unit in Units 2 through 10. Each chart will be a realistic version of what you might see on a gig, rehearsal, or recording session. Each unit will represent one of the genres covered in the Rhythm Guitar modules going back to Level I: Blues, Folk, Classic Rock, Reggae, Country, Funk, Classic R&B, Afro-Latin, and Odd Meter.

There won't be specific parts written for you. There will be mostly chord symbols and slash marks with a few rhythm figures written that are to be played by the whole band. The objective is for you to tap into the rhythm guitar vocabulary you acquired from the Rhythm Guitar modules coupled with your own personal experience to write some rhythm parts for a song you haven't seen before. The intent here is to simulate a real-life environment.

There are two objectives per module:

- Follow (or read) the chart
- Create rhythm guitar parts appropriate for the genre

Remember, this exercise is for you to create parts that are appropriate for the song and genre that would keep the producer, musical director, or band leader happy. This is an important exercise in helping you develop the rhythm guitar skills that would be expected of you in a professional environment where you are working for a client.

When writing your own music, you can get as creative and/or outlandish as you want. But when you are not the boss, it's important to know how to please the person who is. Approach this Module from that standpoint. You are a sideman, and need to do what is normally expected of you.

When approaching a chart for the first time, remember the quick pre-game Chart-Reading Checklist from Level 5:

The Chart-Reading Checklist

1. Look at the top left corner where all the preliminary information is: Key signature, Time signature, Style
2. Note the Tempo
3. Scan the form
4. Seek out any figures that need to be played
5. Scan the chords for the ones that are new or difficult for you
6. Seek out more detailed instructions like dynamics, accents, and expression markings

In addition to that information, there are some other really important things to consider, especially if there is no specific part written for you, such as when you get a basic chord chart that only shows the chord changes and slash marks.

The guiding mantra in creating a rhythm guitar part is to think like the producer. A producer's first thought when creating parts for a song is always, "what does this song need right here?" It's not about how interesting an individual part is for the musician to play. With that in mind, here's a list that should become your automatic approach:

- Make your part fit with the band. That means consider what the instrumentation is because that'll inform you of how busy or sparse your part should be. Sometimes it's OK to double another instrument and sometimes it's not. It'll also inform you about the density of your voicings and in what register you play.
- Make your part be supportive of the lead vocal or instruments. That's your job.
- Get the right guitar sound.
- Be as consistent as possible. Your band mates need to know where you are and what you're doing. You can't be all over the place. They are counting on you to be and stay in your lane.

Repeat the part-writing process two more times so you have three different parts that can either be used alone or layered to create a fuller texture. You will recall the multiple parts that were often presented in the Levels 1 through 5 Rhythm Guitar modules. Recording these parts using your preferred recording software program is encouraged. Then you can really hear how your parts work together (or not). It's always hard to predict what a band leader or producer may want so having prepared options is wise.

Creating rhythm guitar parts is one of the most rewarding and enjoyable parts of making music. The Level 6 Rhythm Guitar modules are most effective if you download the tracks and drop them into some recording software so you can record your part along with the backing track. In Unit 2 we begin with the charts, tracks, and parts but for this Module remember the two objectives:

1. Be able to read the chart
2. Come up with a part that's appropriate

CHART WRITING

Learning to write a chord chart is a valuable skill and with a little practice and focus on neatness, it's well within your reach with knowledge you have. As you learned in Level 5, a chord chart is a minimal representation of a song that usually fits on one or two pages. It usually has these components:

- Title
- Style
- Key signature
- Time signature
- The form of the song
- Chord changes
- Any rhythm figures played by the whole band
- Any signature bass, guitar, or keyboard riffs

Take a look at the sample chart on the opposite page. Can you find these components?

Writing Chord Charts

When writing a chord chart, the overarching goal is to create a short, simple, and accurate road map that is easy to navigate. Keep it lean. There are three things to keep in mind as you create a chord chart for yourself and your bandmates:

- Minimize clutter
- Charts should read themselves
- Music should look the way it sounds

As we delve into this subject, I will assume you have some ear-training skills. That means you have the ability to listen to a recording and identify and label chords, rhythms, and some short riff melodies by ear. Ear training is the skill of identifying what you hear and it's very important for all musicians. This series of modules, while not a transcription class, will only marginally touch on ear training, that is, the ways to identify what is heard on a recording and transfer it to paper. We'll assume you can decipher what you hear. This series of modules is about organizing the music you hear on the page.

A Good Chart Sets You Free

Rock ♩ = 116

Manny Roadit

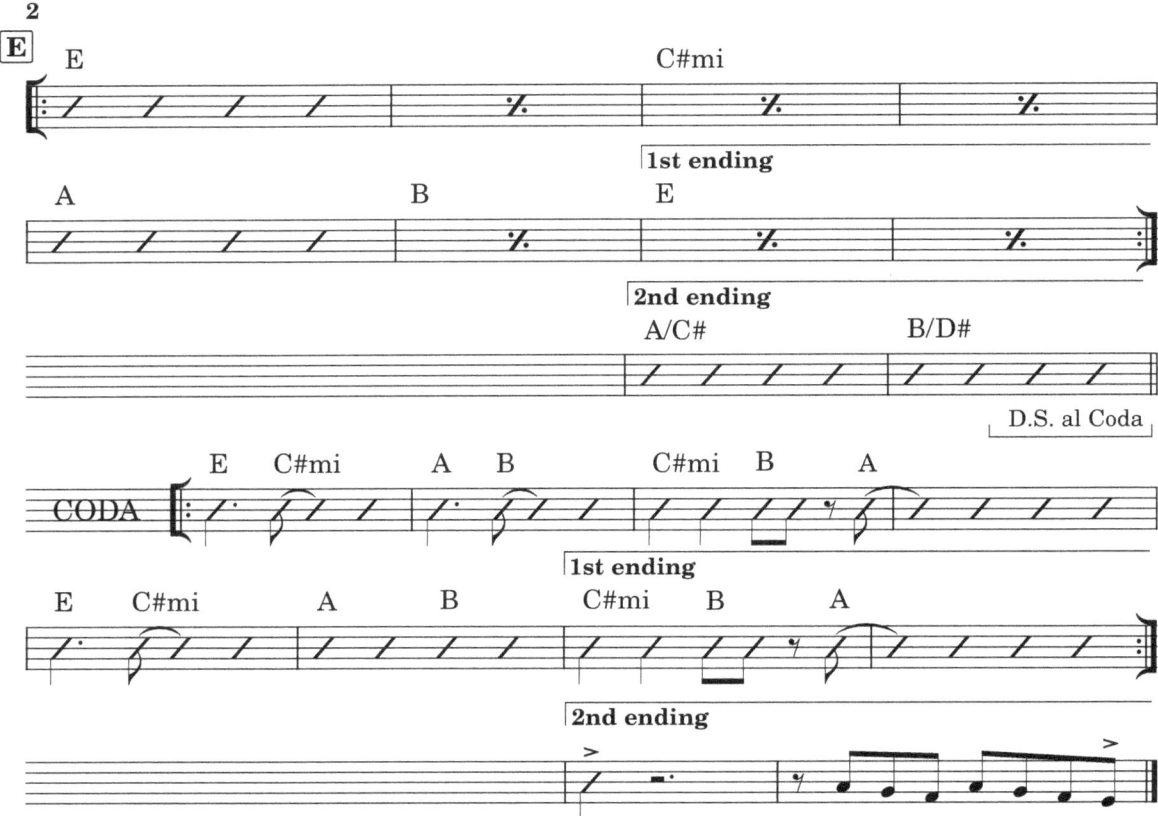

When writing a chord chart, there are many decisions to be made about how much detail to include. Your judgment about this will develop with experience. It's important to know where to start when writing a chord chart. There is no single way to approach the creation of a chart, so I'll offer a way that will work for everyone.

Again, the most important goal is to create a short, simple, and accurate road map that is easy to navigate. Because it's important to try to limit the number of pages, looking for places to use the various repeat devices you learned about in the Chart Reading modules is very important. The more sections you can write only once but then repeat, the less you have to write and the fewer pages you need. The less the reader has to read, the easier the song is to perform.

As a general rule, one-page chord charts are best. A two-page chart is OK, but when you get to three or more, you're drifting away from the goal of keeping it short. There may be times when keeping a chord chart short can create other problems. An example would be when a one or two-page chart requires a repeat scheme that's too complicated. If this happens by trying to make the chart too short, the goal of making the chart easy to navigate will suffer. With practice, you will develop ways to balance the options of how to best present a song in chart form. Every song is different with unique challenges and usually requires compromise.

You'll recall the phrase 'the chart reads itself' from the Chart Reading modules in the previous Level. That phrase could be applied to writing charts, too. There are some songs that chart easily; they almost write themselves. But usually every song has characteristics unique to it that require some decisions.

The process I use starts from the big picture and gradually works down to the detail. It's tempting to start with the detail and work up to the big picture, and you certainly can do that, but that sometimes results in having to rewrite the chart more times than is necessary, and that's inefficient. There is usually some tempting little riff or chord change that can distract you from the process of working big to small. That will happen, but don't worry, there are no "chart writing police" watching for violators.

Just to clarify: This is not a course in using music copying software. The information here is about gathering, organizing, and placing the essential information on the page. You can either create a handwritten chart or transfer your handwritten information to a music notation software program. How you make the music look on the page has a major impact on how the musician is able to perform what is written. You want a musician to use his or her brain power to perform the song musically and not for deciphering a poorly written chart. Put simply, you should write the chart from the perspective of the reader.

Before jumping into the process for writing a chart, let's define the names of sections a song may have:

Intro

This is the introduction to the song that comes before the body of the song, which is usually the vocal melody, or melody played by an instrument if it's an instrumental song. Sometimes intros have two or more parts. For example, the intro could start with guitar or piano playing alone, or maybe just a drum beat. Then after a few measures, the rest of the band comes in. Not all songs have intros.

Verse or 'A' Section

This is where the body of the song begins. Pop songs (by "pop" I mean almost any style that has some commercial audience) normally start with a vocal verse but there are many examples of songs that begin with the chorus. A verse is generally where the story of the song is told, and songs may have two or more verses. Second and third verses normally use the same general melody as the first verse, but the lyrics change as the story of the song is told. Sometimes the first-verse lyrics are sung or played again later in the song.

Prechorus

Many songs have a four- to eight-bar section that could be considered not part of the verse but also not quite yet the chorus. It serves as a transition between verse and chorus lyrically, melodically, harmonically, and dynamically. Sometimes the lyrics are the same in every prechorus. Not all songs have a prechorus, or in some cases, listeners hear it as the latter part of the verse. That's completely acceptable.

Chorus

A chorus is usually where the hook of the song is. The lyrics and melody of a chorus are usually the same every time so that the listener is repeatedly reminded of the song's most important message. It's usually more intense emotionally than the verses.

Bridge

A bridge is a section of a song that contrasts with the verses and chorus. Normally the lyrics, melody, and harmony are all different and that's what creates the contrast. Not all songs have a bridge.

Solo

A solo is generally an instrumental section that features a melodic instrument either improvising or playing a written melody that might be different than anything else in the song. A solo can be played over the verse or chorus chord changes but sometimes a solo has its own chord changes—almost like a second bridge. The solo IS the bridge in some songs.

Interlude

An interlude is a short section between more prominent sections. It's often the same content (or close to) as the intro. The interlude can be anywhere in a song but is most commonly found after a chorus, bridge, or solo as a palate-clearing device that allows the song to breathe before resuming a verse.

Ending

An ending is a way to bring the song to conclusion. Often recordings fade out but in live performances, that's hard to do. There are many ways to end a song. Sometimes an ending will borrow parts like riffs or rhythm figures from inside the song but sometimes it's brand new material. But the idea is to give the listener some sense of conclusion. Endings can be bold or understated.

Out Chorus

An out chorus is a repeating section at the end of the song. It could be the chorus of the song, a section that borrows from anything in the interior of the song, or even brand new material. Out choruses often fade out on studio recordings but they can also be capped off with a clearly defined ending.

These section names and definitions are not set in stone and you can get creative in how you decide to designate the sections. Just keep in mind that the purpose of thinking in sections is to understand the form of the song, and this helps you perform the song in ways that support its emotional arc.

Getting Started

Okay, let's get started writing a chord chart. For this part, go to the link on the introduction page for this Unit and download the track. You will need this audio track to complete this Module. Once you have done this, you are ready to proceed to step one.

Step One: The Big Picture

Start by listening to the song for the 'big picture'. It can sometimes be completed in just one pass listening through the song, but it could take two or more listenings if the song is complicated. The objective here is to jot down the sections of the song using very general terms like: Intro, Verse, Prechorus, Chorus, Bridge, Solo, Interlude, Ending. You're listening for the structure of the song, that is, the order of the sections. Jot these down on a blank piece of paper, like creating a list. For this first step, it doesn't even have to be staff paper, but it can be.

Take your piece of paper, start the tune, and jot down what you hear. The result should look something like the example on the next page.

There are different ways to label the sections, but one thing is always true: Making the structure of the song clear is important to the musician who is reading the chart, and also to you as you organize it on paper. Again, the goal is to create a short, simple, and accurate road map that is easy to navigate. Don't lose sight of that.

The Form Chart for the song, "A Good Chart Sets You Free"

Intro
Verse
Verse
Prechorus
Chorus
Verse
Prechorus
Chorus
Guitar Solo
Prechorus
Chorus
Out Chorus
Out Chorus

Now you see the big picture or structure of the song. You can already see which sections happen just once and which happen more than once. Let's call this first rough draft the Form Chart. It's simply the list of the sections as they occur in the song. In other words, the Form Chart illustrates the structure of the song. We'll spend more time with this a little later, but pay attention as you create the list and order of sections, and look for the opportunities to reduce how much you have to write by repeating sections using the devices you learned like DS and DC, repeat signs, or two-bar repeat signs.

Also keep on the lookout for slight variations in sections as they reoccur. The little variations can create major headaches and rob you of opportunities to repeat sections. Say, for example, in the first verse there are four bars of Ami, followed by two bars of Dmi and then two bars of Ami. But on the second verse the second bar goes to Dmi for one bar and then back to Ami. You may need to write the whole section again to show this tiny little variation. There are tricks for avoiding that which you will learn in this Level. The main point is that once you've done this first mapping of the song structure, you'll have an idea of how to organize the sections on the page. I recommend doing step one before you count measures, figure out the chords, or transcribe any riffs or rhythm figures, as tempting as that is.

IMPROVISATION

This first Improvisation Module in Level 6 will be short and simple. We're going test the effect of avoid tones using one-chord vamps. The idea is simple: If you want to know how it feels to do something, you can't just read about it, you have to experience it for yourself.

Avoid Tone in Major

Let's review what you have learned about the avoid tone in the Major Scale:

- An avoid tone is a half step above a chord tone.
- The Major Scale, when played over a ma7 chord built on its tonic, has one avoid tone and that's the perfect 4th of the scale. It is a half step above the major 3rd of the scale.
- The sound of the perfect 4th of the scale played against the major 3rd of the chord is dissonant.
- If you want to avoid dissonance, don't dwell on the avoid tone.
- If you want dissonance, dwell on the avoid tone.

Avoid Tone on a Cma7

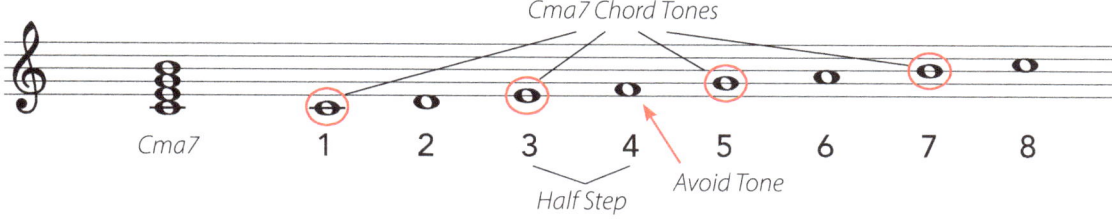

Let's hear what playing the avoid tone sounds like over a Cma7 vamp. To get started, go to the track for this Module. Experiment improvising with the C major scale over the Cma7 vamp. Try playing the 4th in passing only, and pay attention to its effect on you. Then try the opposite. Try pausing or dwelling on the 4th and pay attention to the effect. Are there situations where the tension of the avoid tone should be avoided? Are there situations where the tension of the avoid tone could be used for effect?

Avoid Tone in Minor

Let's review what you have learned about the avoid tone in the Natural Minor Scale:

- The Natural Minor Scale, when played over a mi7 chord built on its tonic, has one avoid tone and that's the minor 6th of the scale. It's a half step above the perfect 5th of the scale.
- The sound of the minor 6th of the scale played against the perfect 5th of the chord is dissonant.
- If you want to avoid dissonance, don't dwell on the avoid tone.
- If you want dissonance, dwell on the avoid tone.

Avoid Tone on a Cmi7

Let's hear what playing the avoid tone sounds like over a Cmi7 vamp. Listen to the track and experiment improvising with the C natural minor scale over a Cmi7 vamp. Try playing the minor 6th in passing only and pay attention to its effect on you. Then try the opposite. Try pausing or dwelling on the minor 6th and pay attention to its effect. Like with the avoid tones in major, are there situations where the tension of the avoid tone should be avoided? Are there situations where the tension of the avoid tone could be used for effect?

Much of the Level 6 Improvisation module series focuses on modes and their use as chord scales. Understanding where the avoid tones are in each mode is important. Whenever working on a new scale application, always look for the avoid tones.

PRACTICE

Theory

- ☐ Understand what an avoid tone is.
- ☐ Quiz yourself about what the avoid tones are for every chord.
- ☐ Memorize the avoid tone in the Major Scale over the Ima7 chord.
- ☐ Memorize the avoid tone in Natural Minor scale over the Imi7 chord.

Fretboard Logic

- ☐ Explore where the avoid tones in the scale are for each chord in the harmonized major scale for each major scale pattern.
- ☐ Explore where the avoid tones are in the scale for each chord in the harmonized natural minor scale for each minor scale pattern.

Rhythm Guitar

- ☐ Learn to scan the top left corner where all the preliminary information is: Key signature, Time signature, Style, Tempo.
- ☐ Learn to scan the form and seek out any figures that need to be played.
- ☐ Learn to scan the chords for the ones that are new or difficult for you.
- ☐ Learn to scan for more instructions like instructions like dynamics, accents, and expression markings.

Chart Writing

- ☐ Learn the defintions of section names.
- ☐ Learn to make a Form Chart.

Improvisation

- ☐ Explore where the avoid tone is in the Major Scale over the Ima7 chord.
- ☐ Explore where the avoid tone is in the Minor Scale over the Imi7 chord.

UNIT 2

Learning Modules

> **Theory** - Methods of Viewing the Seven Modes, Mode Qualities, Mode Key Signatures

> **Fretboard Logic** - Reassign the Numbers of Scale Degrees to Learn Modes

> **Rhythm Guitar** - Creating a Rhythm Guitar part for a Blues Song

> **Chart Writing** - Creating a Crude Chord Chart

> **Improvisation** - Learing the Sound of the Lydian, Mixolydian, Dorian, and Phrygian Modes

> **Practice** - Continue Practice Routine Development

The tracks for this Unit can be found at the following link:

https://fretboardbiology.com/book6/#u2

THEORY

Modes

Now that we have discussed avoid tones, let's turn our attention back to learning the modes. These were developed in the Middle Ages in Greece, and so the term 'Greek Modes' is often used. Because they were used for sacred compositions in the Middle Ages, they are sometimes referred to as 'church modes'. In modern times, they were rediscovered by Jazz musicians and hence the term 'Jazz modes' is sometimes used. Musicians from a variety of genres use modes as tools for improvising as well as a basis for composition.

Here are five facts about modes:
1. There are seven modes related to the Major Scale.
2. Modes are seven-note scales, like the Major Scale and the Natural Minor Scale.
3. Each mode has its own interval formula, just like the Major Scale and the Natural Minor Scale.
4. The Major Scale and the Natural Minor Scale are two of the seven modes, so you already have a good understanding of two modes. The Major Scale is called the Ionian Mode and the Natural Minor Scale is called the Aeolian Mode.
5. The interval formulas for each of the seven modes are already known to you.

There are three ways to think about modes:
1. As whole- and half-step interval formulas derived from the Major Scale formula
2. As derivatives of Major and Natural Minor Scales
3. As derivatives of Major and Minor Pentatonic Scales

I suggest you strive to understand all approaches equally well. We will begin with understanding modes as derivatives of the Major Scale formula.

The Major Scale Formula

All whole- and half-step interval formulas for the modes are derived from the Major Scale interval formula. You will recall this formula for the Major Scale from all the way back in Level 1: W W H W W W H

Major Scale

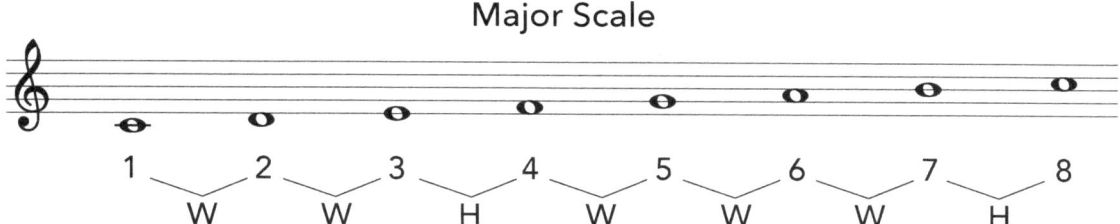

In Level 2, we discussed that the Major Scale formula was a set of seven intervals:

Major Scale Intervals

ma2 ma3 P4 P5 ma6 ma7 P8

Now, let's expand the pattern of intervals into more octaves, both above and below. This is an infinite pattern that extends up and down. Here is the Major Scale interval pattern repeated several times. Notice each segment is separated with a dash so you can see that it's just the same seven-interval pattern repeated in an endless continuum.

Major Scale Pattern

W W H W W W H – W W H W W W H – W W H W W W H – W W H W W W H

Here is the same pattern written without separation between the seven-interval segments. It just looks like one infinite stream of the interval pattern.

Major Scale Pattern

W W H W W W H W W H W W W H W W H W W W H W W H W W W H

Here is how the first approach to understanding modes works. We will use this repeating whole- and half-step interval pattern of the C major scale as a basis for explanation, since the Major Scale is one of the modes. It is the first mode, and it is called the Ionian Mode.

Ionian Mode

The first mode, Ionian, is easy because we already know it: It's the Major Scale. Examine this expanded interval pattern and select the seven-interval segment that we know is the Major Scale (or Ionian Mode).

Ionian Mode (Major Scale)

Next, examine the Major (or Ionian) Scale from two perspectives:

1. The interval pattern between scale degrees

Ionian Mode (Major Scale)

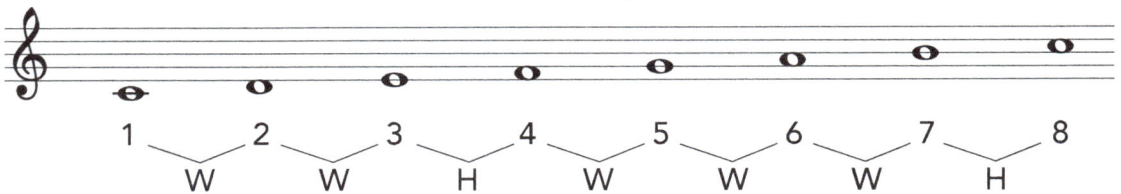

2. The interval pattern from the 1 to the other notes in the scale:

1, ma2, ma3, P4, P5, ma6, ma7

Ionian Mode Interval Pattern

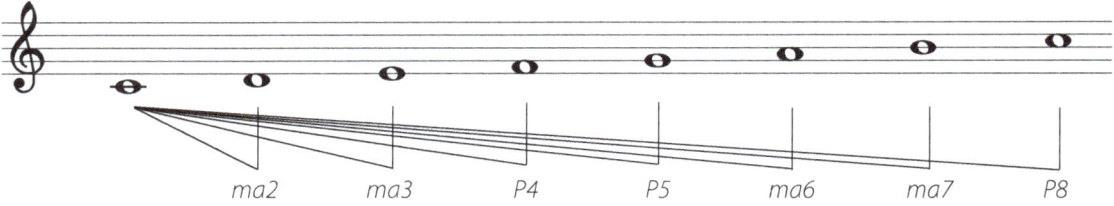

Notice that this scale has a major 3rd. The quality of the 3rd in each mode is significant and we'll come back to that shortly.

Notice the 7th chord contained within the Ionian Mode: 1, ma3, P5, ma7

Recognize that? It's a ma7 chord.

Ionian I Chord (ma7)

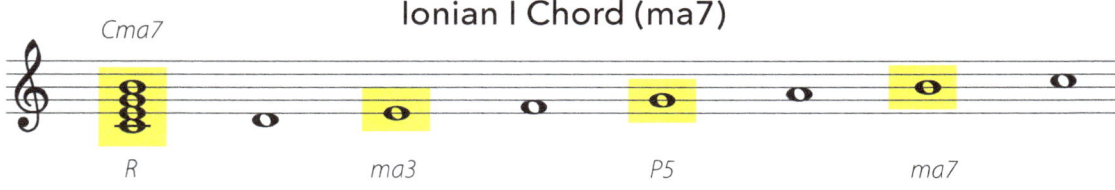

Dorian Mode

The second mode is called Dorian and it's very popular in all kinds of music. Let's look at the same expanded interval pattern and then select the next seven-interval segment. If we select this specific set-of-seven segment, we have the interval pattern for the Dorian Mode.

Dorian Mode

W W H W W W H W W H W W W H W W H W W W H W W H W W W H

Dorian Mode

Next, examine the Dorian Scale or Mode from two perspectives:

1. The interval pattern between scale degrees

2. The interval pattern from the 1 to the other notes in the scale:

1, ma2, mi3, P4, P5, ma6, mi7

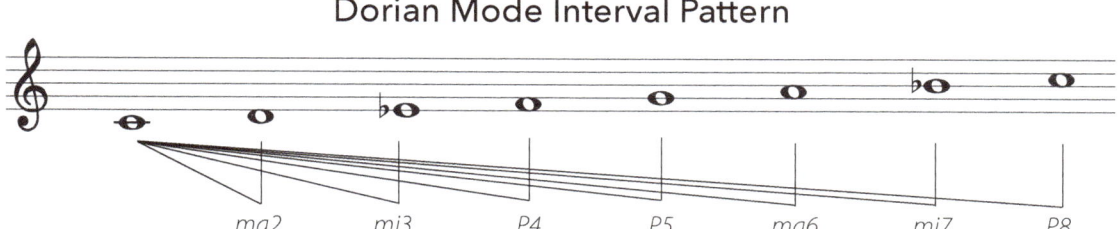

Notice that this scale has a minor 3rd. The quality of the 3rd in each mode is significant and we'll discuss that further shortly.

Notice the 7th chord within the Dorian Mode: 1, mi3, P5, mi7

Recognize that? It's a mi7 chord.

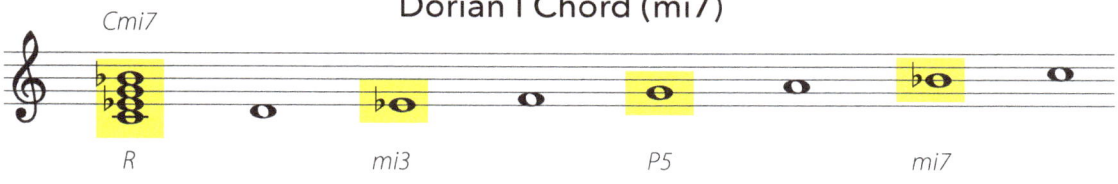

Phrygian Mode

The third mode is called Phrygian and it's used less in popular music than some of the other modes. Let's look at the same expanded interval pattern again and then select the next seven-interval segment. If we select this specific set-of-seven segment, we have the interval pattern for the Phrygian Mode.

Phrygian Mode

Next, examine the Phrygian Scale or Mode from two perspectives:

1.   The interval pattern between scale degrees

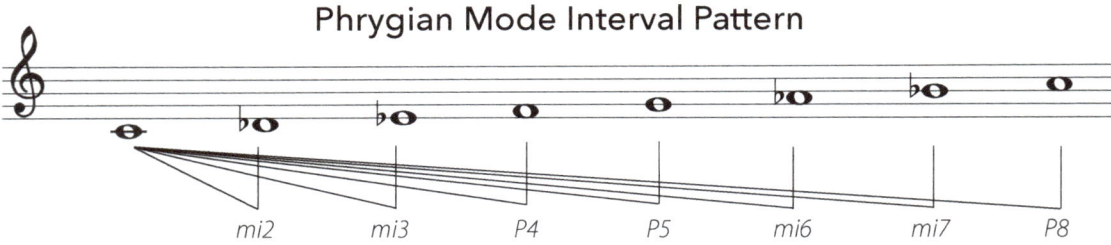

2.   The interval pattern from the 1 to the other notes in the scale:

1, mi2, mi3, P4, P5, mi6, mi7

Notice that this scale has a minor 3rd. That is significant and we'll come back to that.

Notice the 7th chord within the Phrygian Mode: 1, mi3, P5, mi7

Recognize that? It's a mi7 chord.

Lydian Mode

The fourth mode is called Lydian and it's not used a lot in popular music. Let's look at the same expanded interval pattern again and then select the next seven-interval segment. If we select this specific set-of-seven segment, we have the interval pattern for the Lydian Mode.

Lydian Mode

W W H W W W H W W H W W W H W W H W W W H W W H W W W H

Lydian Mode

Next, examine the Lydian Scale or Mode from two perspectives:

1. The interval pattern between scale degrees

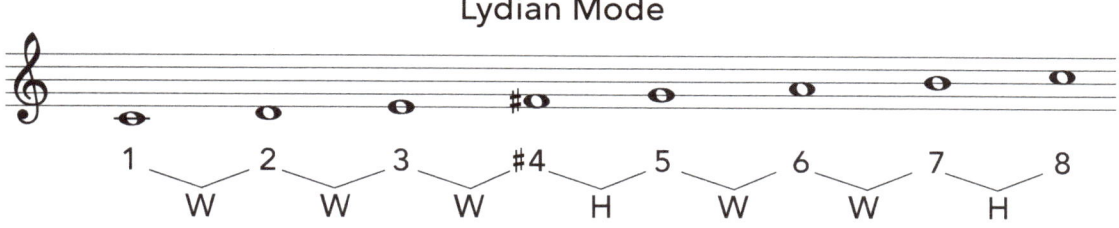

2. The interval pattern from the 1 to the other notes in the scale:
   1, ma2, ma3, A4, P5, ma6, ma7

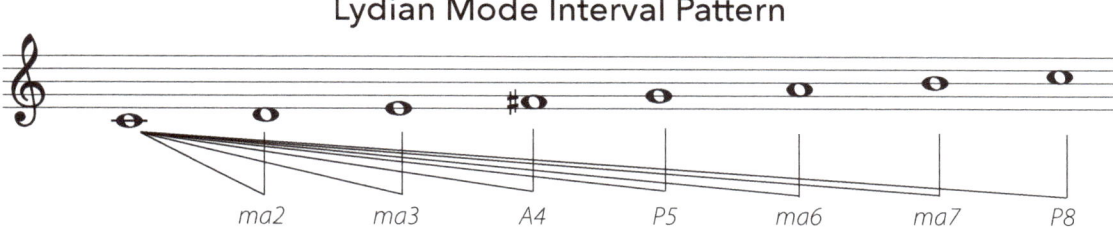

Notice that this scale has a major 3rd. We'll come back to that shortly.

Notice the 7th chord within the Lydian Mode: 1, ma3, P5, ma7

Recognize that? It's a ma7 chord.

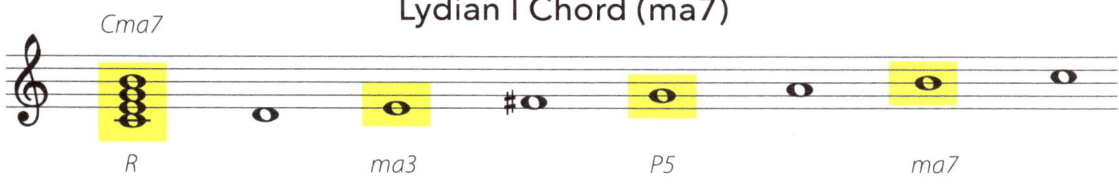

Mixolydian Mode

The fifth mode is Mixolydian. This is a popular sound because it works over a dom7 chord. Let's look at the expanded interval pattern again and then select the next seven-interval segment. If we select this specific set-of-seven segment, we have the interval pattern for the Mixolydian Mode.

Mixolydian Mode

Mixolydian Mode

Next, examine the Mixolydian Scale or Mode from two perspectives:

1.　　The interval pattern between scale degrees

Mixolydian Mode

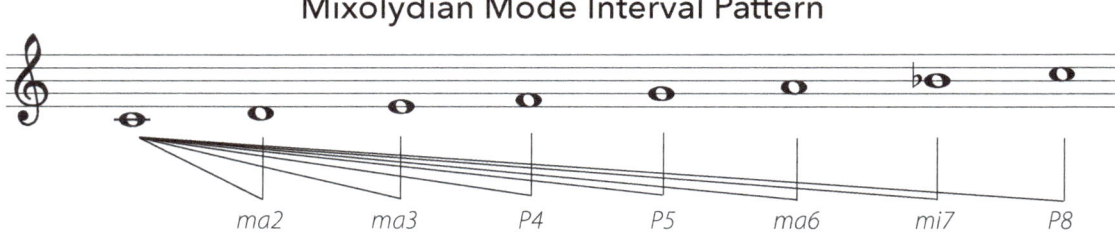

2.　　The interval pattern from the 1 to the other notes in the scale:
1, ma2, ma3, P4, P5, ma6, mi7

Mixolydian Mode Interval Pattern

Notice that this scale also has a major 3rd. We will talk about the significance of this.
Notice the 7th chord within the Mixolydian Mode: 1, ma3, P5, mi7
Recognize that? It's a dom7 chord.

Mixolydian I Chord (7)

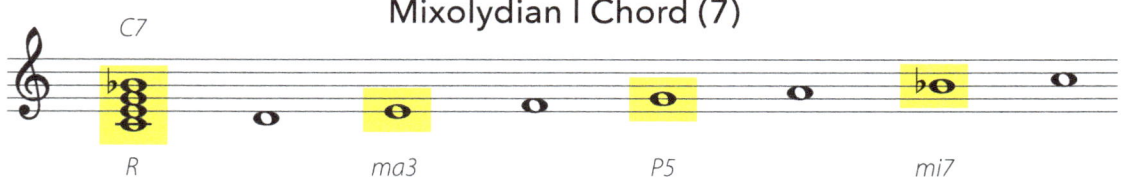

Aeolian Mode (Natural Minor)

The sixth mode is Aeolian, which is also called the Natural Minor Scale, so its formula will look very familiar. If we select this specific set-of-seven segment, we have the interval pattern for the Aeolian Mode. Let's look at the same expanded interval pattern again and then select the next seven-interval segment.

Aeolian Mode

Next, examine the Aeolian Scale or Mode from two perspectives:

1. The interval pattern between scale degrees

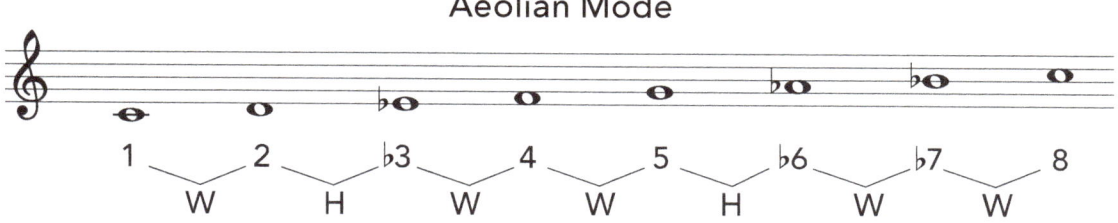

2. The interval pattern from the 1 to the other notes in the scale:

   1, ma2, mi3, P4, P5, mi6, mi7

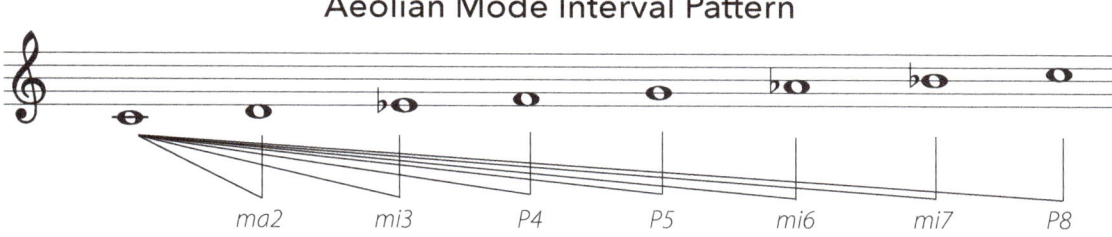

Notice that this scale has a minor 3rd. Again, we'll talk about that shortly.

Notice the 7th chord within the Aeolian Mode: 1, mi3, P5, mi7

Recognize that? It's a mi7 chord.

Locrian Mode

The seventh mode is Locrian. The Locrian Mode is usually not used as a basis for composition due to its dissonance. Let's look at the same expanded interval pattern one more time and then select the next seven-interval segment. If we select this set-of-seven segment, we have the interval pattern for the Locrian Mode.

Locrian Mode

W W H W W W H W W H W W W H W W H W W W H W W H W W W H
⎣_____⎦
Locrian Mode

Next, examine the Locrian Mode from two perspectives:

1. The interval pattern between scale degrees

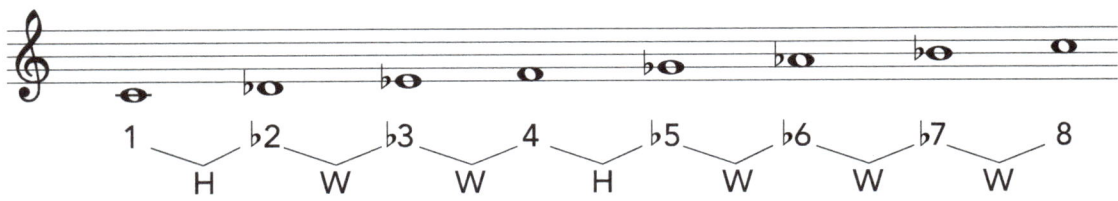

2. The interval pattern from the 1 to the other notes in the scale:

1, mi2, mi3, P4, D5, mi6, mi7

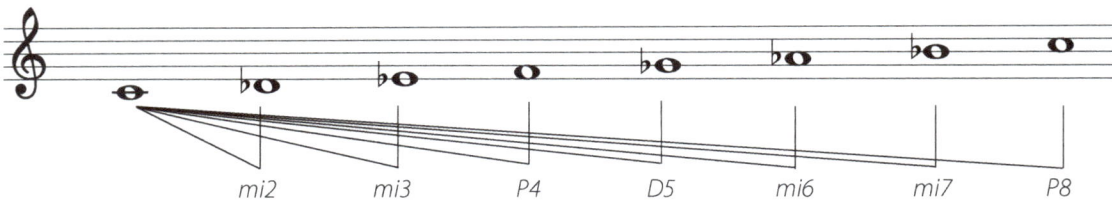

Notice that this scale has a minor 3rd, which we'll talk about shortly.

Notice the 7th chord within the Locrian Mode: 1, mi3, D5, mi7

Recognize that? It's a mi7(♭5) chord.

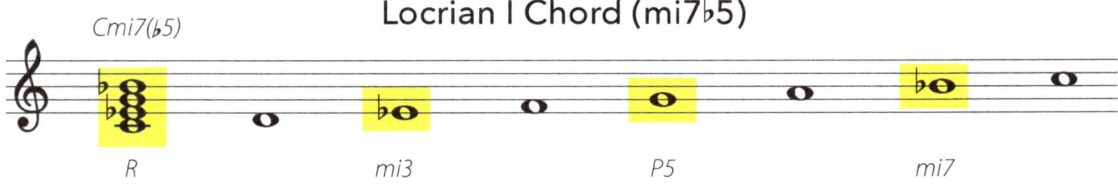

Let's review. To understand each mode, we took the "infinite pattern of intervals" and extracted seven different seven-interval sets. Each of these seven sets represents a different mode: Ionian, Dorian, Phrygian, Lydian, Mixolydian, Aolean, and Locrian.

The Seven Modes

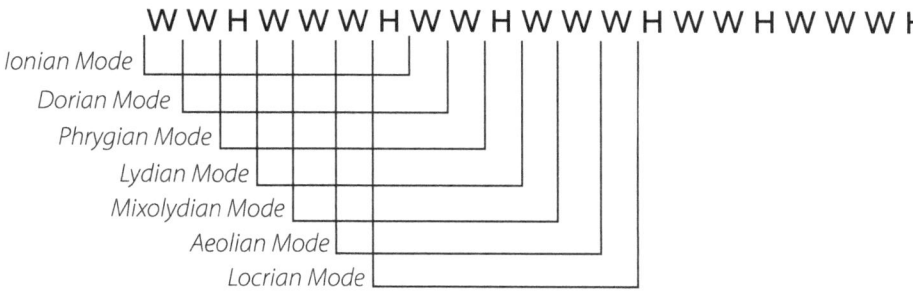

Mode Qualities

Now let's talk about mode qualities. There are modes with a major quality and modes with a minor quality. The quality of the mode, major or minor, is determined by the quality of the 3rd in the mode. So, if a mode has a major 3rd, it's considered to be a major-sounding mode. If a mode has a minor 3rd, it's considered to be a minor-sounding mode.

We made a special note of the qualities of the 3rds as we were going through each interval formula of the seven modes:

- The Ionian (Major Scale), Lydian, and Mixolydian Modes all have a major 3rd. So they are considered "major modes".

- Dorian, Phrygian, Aeolian (Natural Minor Scale), and Locrian Modes all have a minor 3rd, so they are considered "minor modes".

To carry this one step further, modes reflect the quality of the 7th chord built on the same number scale degree of the Major Scale. In other words:

- The Ionian Mode is the first mode and is built from the first note of the Major Scale. The I chord in the Major Scale is major 7. Therefore, the Ionian Mode has a major 7 sound.

- The Dorian Mode is the second mode and is built from the second note of the Major Scale. The II chord in the Major Scale is minor 7. Therefore, the Dorian Mode has a minor 7 sound.

- The Phrygian Mode is the third mode and is built from the third note of the Major Scale. The III chord in the Major Scale is minor 7. Therefore, the Phrygian Mode has a minor 7 sound.

- The Lydian Mode is the fourth mode and is built from the fourth note of the Major Scale. The IV chord in the Major Scale is major 7. Therefore, the Lydian Mode has a major 7 sound.

- The Mixolydian Mode is the fifth mode and is built from the fifth note of the Major Scale. The V chord in the Major Scale is dominant 7. Therefore, the Mixolydian Mode has a dominant 7 sound.

- The Aeolian Mode is the sixth mode and is built from the sixth note of the Major Scale. The VI chord in the Major Scale is minor 7. Therefore, the Aeolian Mode has a minor 7 sound.

- The Locrian Mode is the seventh mode and is built from the seventh note of the Major Scale. The VII chord in the Major Scale is minor 7(♭5). Therefore, the Locrian Mode has a minor 7(♭5) sound.

This is a great place to take a break and make sure you're in control of the information we've discussed so far in this Unit. So far, we have looked at the modes as whole-step/half-step interval formulas derived from the Major Scale formula. Now let's take a closer look at the second approach to understanding modes: as derivatives of the Major and Natural Minor Scales.

Modes as Derivatives of Major and Natural Minor Scales

Let's look at understanding modes as derivatives of the Major and Natural Minor Scales. This is similar, with a little different approach, to looking at modes as with the process we just went through. You already have some experience with this approach.

You'll recall from Level 5 that the Harmonic Minor Scale is a derivative of the Natural Minor Scale. The 7th scale degree was adjusted to create the Harmonic Minor Scale. The same can be done to create the minor-sounding modes. Those are the modes with a minor 3rd. Adjustments can be made to the Natural Minor Scale to create other variants. The same can also be done to the create the major-sounding modes. Those are the modes with a major 3rd. Adjustments can be made to the Major Scale to create other variants.

Major Modes

We'll start with the major modes. Based on the formulas you learned earlier in this Module, compare the three major modes. Those are: Ionian, Lydian, and Mixolydian. Using Ionian, which we know as the Major Scale, as the starting point, with an adjustment to one note, you can arrive at the Lydian and Mixolydian Modes.

Deriving the major-sounding modes from the Ionian (Major) Scale:

- The Lydian Scale is like a Major Scale with a raised 4th scale degree (augmented 4th).

- The Mixolydian Scale is like a Major Scale with a lowered 7th scale degree (minor 7th).

Modes as Derivatives of the Major Scale

Ionian Mode	1	ma2	ma3	P4	P5	ma6	ma7
Lydian Mode	1	ma2	ma3	A4	P5	ma6	ma7
Mixolydian Mode	1	ma2	ma3	P4	P5	ma6	mi7

Minor Modes

Next, let's look at the minor modes. Using Aeolian, which we know as the Natural Minor Scale, as the starting point, with an adjustment of one or two notes you can derive the Dorian, Phrygian, and Locrian Modes.

Deriving the minor-sounding modes from the Aeolian (Natural Minor) Scale:

- The Dorian Scale is like Natural Minor Scale with a raised 6th scale degree (major 6th).
- The Phrygian Scale is like Natural Minor Scale with a lowered 2nd scale degree (minor 2nd).
- The Locrian Scale is like Natural Minor Scale with a lowered 2nd scale degree (minor 2nd) and a lowered 5th scale degree (or diminished 5th).

Modes as Derivatives of the Minor Scale

Aeolian Mode	1	ma2	mi3	P4	P5	mi6	mi7
Dorian Mode	1	ma2	mi3	P4	P5	ma6	mi7
Phrygian Mode	1	mi2	mi3	P4	P5	mi6	mi7
Locrian Mode	1	mi2	mi3	P4	D5	mi6	mi7

The bottom line for this second approach to the modes is that they can be viewed as derivatives of the Major and Natural Minor Scales.

Modes as Derivatives of Major and Minor Pentatonic Scales

Next, let's look at the third approach to understanding modes: as derivatives of Major and Minor Pentatonic Scales. You already have a lot of experience with this approach going all the way back to Level 1. You'll recall that you learned the physical Major and Minor Pentatonic shapes on the fretboard and filled in notes to create the Major, Minor, and Blues Scales.

The Major Scale was presented as a derivative of the Major Pentatonic Scale. Two notes were added to create Major Scale. The same can be done to create the other major-sounding modes, and those are the modes with a major 3rd. Notes can be added to the Major Pentatonic Scale to create other variants.

The Natural Minor Scale and Blues Scale were presented as derivatives of the Minor Pentatonic Scale. Notes were added to create Natural Minor Scale and Blues Scale variants. The same can be done to create the other minor-sounding modes—that is, the modes with a minor 3rd. Notes can be added to the Minor Pentatonic Scale to create other variants.

Let's begin with the major modes.

Modes as Derivatives of the Major Pentatonic Scale

Major Pentatonic	1	ma2	ma3		P5	ma6	
Ionian Mode	1	ma2	ma3	P4	P5	ma6	ma7
Lydian Mode	1	ma2	ma3	A4	P5	ma6	ma7
Mixolydian Mode	1	ma2	ma3	P4	P5	ma6	mi7

Notice that the only difference between the modes and the Major Pentatonic Scale is the quality of the 4th and 7th scale degrees.

Modes as Derivatives of the Minor Pentatonic Scale

Minor Pentatonic	1		mi3	P4	P5		mi7
Aeolian Mode	1	ma2	mi3	P4	P5	mi6	mi7
Dorian Mode	1	ma2	mi3	P4	P5	ma6	mi7
Phrygian Mode	1	mi2	mi3	P4	P5	mi6	mi7
Locrian Mode	1	mi2	mi3	P4	D5	mi6	mi7

Notice that the only difference between the modes and the Minor Pentatonic Scale is the quality of the 2nd and 6th scale degrees. The only exception being Locrian, which also has a diminished 5th.

The bottom line for this third approach to the modes is that the modes can be viewed as derivatives of the Major and Minor Pentatonic Scales. This is a particularly good way think about them on the fretboard. You're going to see this again.

The Modes and Key Signatures

Let's talk about key signatures and modes. You first learned key signatures for major keys. Soon after, you learned key signatures for minor keys. The reality is that each key signature can represent two relative keys: the major key and its relative minor. You also learned how to determine whether the key signature represents major or its relative minor by looking at the final chord. This works in most cases, and in other instances you can tell by the way the chords move within the progression.

There are two schools of thought regarding how to write a key signature for a mode. The first is to write the key signature for the Major Scale for all major modes like Lydian and Mixolydian and then use accidentals throughout the piece to adjust the scale to fit the specific major mode. Likewise, for the minor modes like Dorian, Phrygian, or Locrian, you would write the key signature for the Natural Minor Scale and then use accidentals throughout the piece to adjust the scale to fit the minor mode.

For example, if a song is in D Mixolydian, D major's key signature (two sharps) would be written at the beginning and then each time the note C appears, a natural sign would be used to cancel the C# in the key signature so the scale will have a mi7 (♭7).

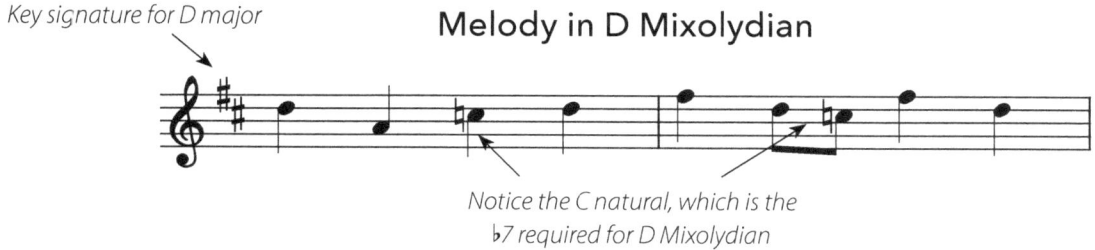

Key signature for D major

Melody in D Mixolydian

Notice the C natural, which is the ♭7 required for D Mixolydian

If a song is in F Lydian, F major's key signature (one flat) would be written at the beginning and then each time the note B appears, a natural sign would be used to cancel the B♭ in the key signature so the scale will have an augmented 4th (#4).

Key signature for F major

Melody in F Lydian

Notice the B natural, which is the aug 4 required for F Lydian

If a song is in B Dorian, B minor's key signature (two sharps) would be written at the beginning and then each time the note G appears, a sharp sign would be used to raise the G to G#, the major 6th.

Key signature for B minor

Melody in D Dorian

Notice the G#, which is the ma6 (raised 6th) required for D Dorian

The upside of this way is that at a glance, a key signature will inform the musician whether it's generally a major or minor sound. The downside of this way is that the music can get very messy with natural signs or sharps and flats, depending on which is required to adjust the major or minor scale for the desired mode.

The second school of thought is to write the key signature that has exactly the sharps or flats needed to represent the mode.

For example, B Dorian would have three sharps. Why? B is the second mode of A major. A major's key signature has three sharps: B Dorian is spelled B, C#, D, E, F#, G#, and A.

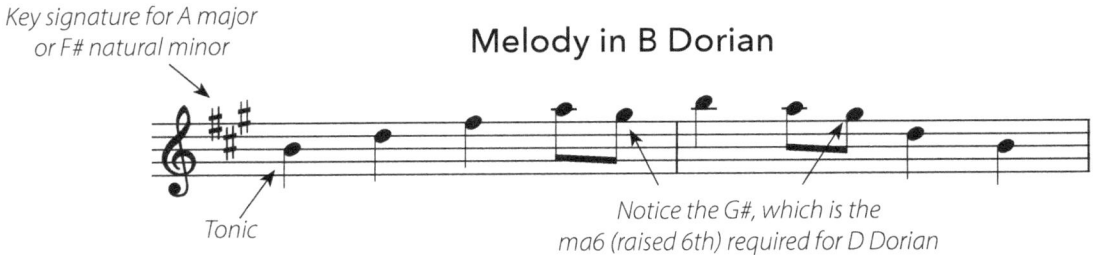

Key signature for A major or F# natural minor

Melody in B Dorian

Tonic

Notice the G#, which is the ma6 (raised 6th) required for D Dorian

Here's another example: F Mixolydian would have two flats. Why? F is the 5th mode of B♭. The key of B♭ has two flats: F Mixolydian is spelled F, G, A, B♭, C, D, and E♭.

Key signature for B♭ major

Melody in F Mixolydian

Tonic

Notice the E♭, which is the ♭7 required for F Mixolydian

The upside of this way is that there's no need for a lot of accidentals throughout the music. It keeps the page neat and tidy.

The downside is that each key signature could represent seven different scales. For example, one flat would represent all of these modes: F major (Ionian), G Dorian, A Phrygian, B♭ Lydian, C Mixolydian, D Aeolian, and E Locrian. So some examination of the progression and last chord is required to know what note is considered the tonic.

It's perfectly fine to write the name of the mode above the key signature. That's not a formally accepted way to do it, but it sure works. It's clear and removes any doubt right away. For example, if the creator of the chart is writing for E♭ Lydian and writes two flats, they can write E♭ Lydian above the clef sign and key signature to ensure the musician sees the mode as E♭ Lydian and not B♭ major or G minor.

I personally prefer to not clutter the page with accidentals and I write in the mode name at the beginning of the chart.

FRETBOARD LOGIC

As you know from the Theory Module, Level 6 focuses on modes. You learned a few ways to go about constructing the modes. If you don't have a strong grasp of the information in the Theory Module, go back and study it more.

You learned these three ways to think about modes:

- As whole-step/half-step interval formulas derived from the Major Scale interval formula
- As derivatives of Major and Natural Minor Scales
- As derivatives of Major and Minor Pentatonic Scales

Over the course of this Logic Module and the next, you'll learn the fingering patterns for the modes in these three ways, too. In this Module you'll learn them as derivatives of the Major Scale. Remember that the Major Scale's interval formula is W W H W W W H and it can be repeated in multiple octaves. You also learned that this seven-interval sequence can be segmented seven different ways to create seven different, but related, interval formulas, and each one represents one of the modes. The goal of this Module is to take the Major Scale fingering patterns you already know and adapt them as the seven modes.

Ionian Mode

Let's use the Pattern I Octave Shape and Major Scale pattern to illustrate this idea. Here is Ionian Mode (Major Scale) on the fretboard with the scale degrees numbered and the interval formula highlighted.

Ionian Mode (Major Scale)

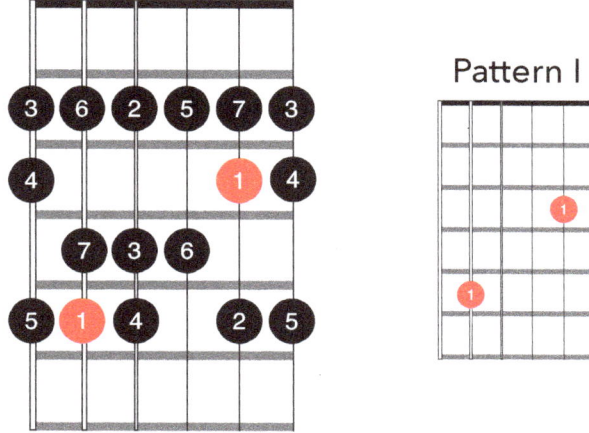

Interval Formula: W W H W W W H W W H W W W H

Ionian Mode

Dorian Mode

Let's move on to the six other modes that can be derived from this scale pattern starting with the Dorian Mode. To do this, assign the number 1 to the note that is 2 in the Major Scale. Then shift the remaining numbers in order.

- Assign the number 2 to the note that is 3 in the Major Scale.
- Assign the number ♭3 to the note that is 4 in the Major Scale.
- Assign the number 4 to the note that is 5 in the Major Scale.
- Assign the number 5 to the note that is 6 in the Major Scale.
- Assign the number 6 to the note that is 7 in the Major Scale.
- Assign the number ♭7 to the note that is 1 in the Major Scale.

Notice that the interval pattern starting with the 'new 1' is W H W W W H W. That is the Dorian Mode or Scale. It begins on 2 of the Major Scale so therefore it is the second mode. The conclusion is that the Dorian Scale fingering pattern is the same as the Major Scale fingering pattern starting on 2. Then of course the scale degree numbers need to be adjusted accordingly. And what is the octave shape of the 'new 1'? Pattern V.

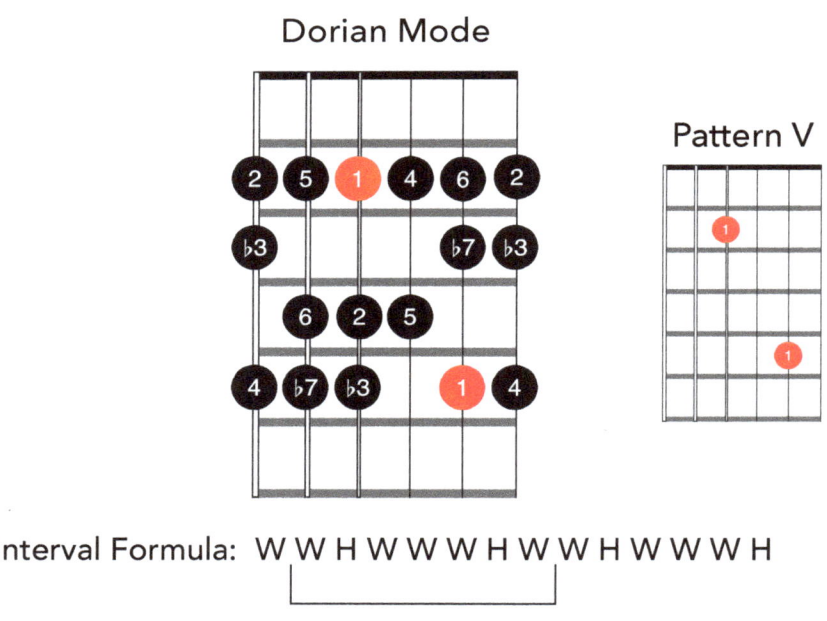

Interval Formula: W W H W W W H W W H W W W H

Dorian Mode

Phrygian Mode

Next, assign the number 1 to the note that is 3 in the Major Scale. Then shift the remaining numbers in order. Assign the number 2 to the note that is 4 in the Major Scale, assign the number b3 to the note that is 5 in the Major Scale, and so forth. This continues on into the next octave.

Now the interval pattern starting with the 'new 1' is H W W W H W W. That is the Phrygian Mode or Scale. It begins on 3 of the Major Scale so therefore it is the third mode.

The conclusion is that the Phrygian Scale fingering pattern is the same as the Major Scale fingering pattern starting on 3. Then of course the scale degree numbers need to be adjusted accordingly. And what is the octave shape of the 'new 1'? Pattern IV.

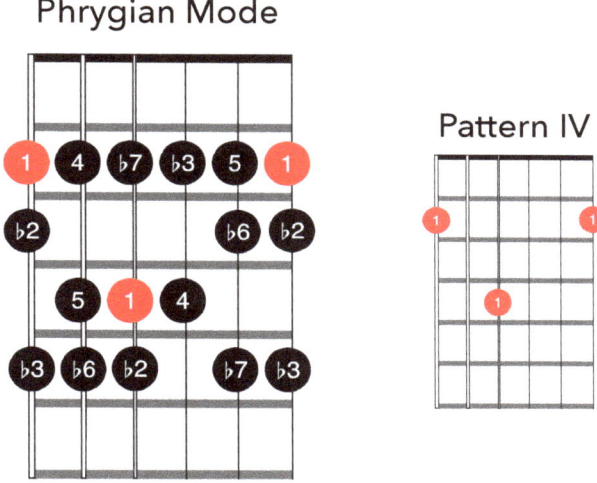

Interval Formula: W W H W W W H W W H W W W H

Phrygian Mode

Lydian Mode

Next, assign the number 1 to the note that is 4 in the Major Scale. Then shift the remaining numbers in order. Assign the number 2 to the note that is 5 in the Major Scale, assign the number 3 to the note that is 6 in the Major Scale, and so on. This continues on into the next octave.

Now the interval pattern starting with the 'new 1' is W W W H W W H. That is the Lydian Mode or Scale. It begins on 4 of the Major Scale so therefore it is the fourth mode.

The conclusion is that the Lydian Scale fingering pattern is the same as the Major Scale fingering pattern starting on 4. Then of course the scale degree numbers need to be adjusted accordingly. And what is the octave shape of the 'new 1'? Pattern IV.

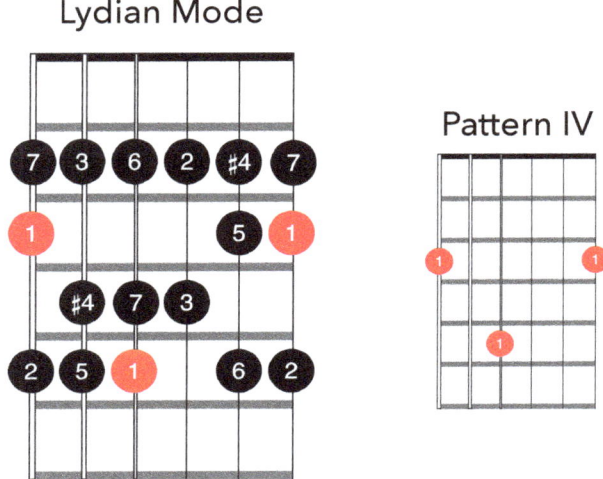

Interval Formula: W W H W W W H W W H W W W H

Lydian Mode

Mixolydian Mode

Next, assign the number 1 to the note that is 5 in the Major Scale. Then shift the remaining numbers in order. Assign the number 2 to the note that is 6 in the Major Scale, assign the number 3 to the note that is 7 in the Major Scale, and so on. This continues on into the next octave.

Now the interval pattern starting with the 'new 1' is W W H W W H W. That is the Mixolydian Mode or Scale. It begins on 5 of the Major Scale so therefore it is the fifth mode.

The conclusion is that the Mixolydian Scale fingering pattern is the same as the Major Scale fingering pattern starting on 5. Then of course the scale degree numbers need to be adjusted accordingly. And what is the octave shape of the 'new 1'? Pattern III.

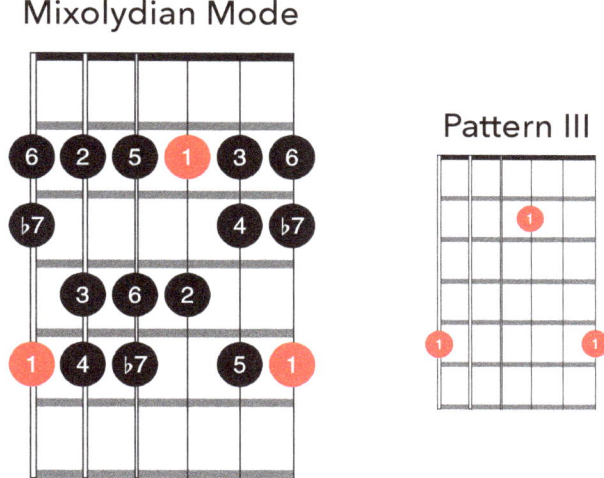

Interval Formula: W W H W W W H W W H W W W H

Mixolydian Mode

Aeolian Mode (Natural Minor)

Next reassign the number 1 to the note that is 6 in the Major Scale. Then shift the remaining numbers in order. Assign the number 2 to the note that is 7 in the Major Scale, assign the number b3 to the note that is 1 in the Major Scale, and so on. This continues on into the next octave.

Now the interval pattern starting with the 'new 1' is W H W W H W W. That is the Aeolian Mode and we also know it as the Natural Minor Scale. It begins on 6 of the Major Scale so therefore it is the sixth mode.

The conclusion is that the Aeolian Scale fingering pattern is the same as the Major Scale fingering pattern starting on 6. Then of course the scale degree numbers need to be adjusted accordingly. And what is the octave shape of the 'new 1'? Pattern II.

Aeolian Mode (Natural Minor)

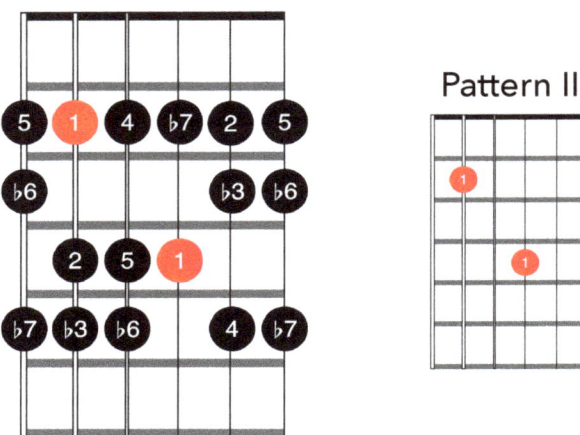

Interval Formula: W W H W W W H W W H W W W H

Aeolian Mode

Fretboard Biology Level 6 • Unit 2: Fretboard Logic 47

Locrian Mode

Next, reassign the number 1 to the note that is 7 in the Major Scale. Then shift the remaining numbers in order. Assign the number ♭2 to the note that is 1 in the Major Scale, assign the number ♭3 to the note that is 2 in the Major Scale, and so on. This continues on into the next octave.

Now the interval pattern starting with the 'new 1' is H W W H W W W. That is the Locrian Mode or Scale. It begins on 7 of the Major Scale so therefore it is the seventh mode.

The conclusion is that the Locrian Scale fingering pattern is the same as the Major Scale fingering pattern starting on 7. Then of course the scale degree numbers need to be adjusted accordingly. And what is the octave shape of the 'new 1'? Pattern I.

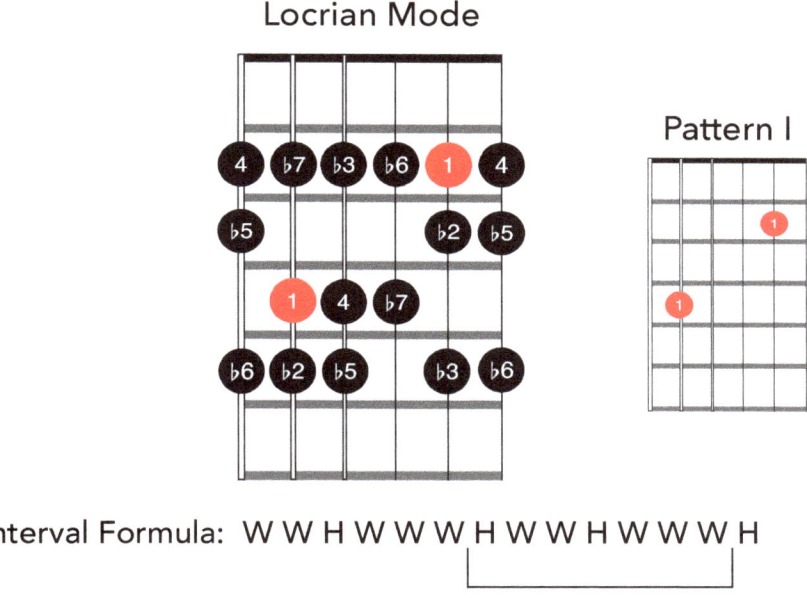

Interval Formula: W W H W W W H W W H W W W H
                                    └─────────────┘
                                      Locrian Mode

This process can be applied to each of the other major scale patterns. Before you look too far and get worried about the scope of the task of learning this, understand that this is a mountain of information and it's completely unrealistic to expect to learn all of it quickly. This method of playing the modes is included here for mainly your reference and to help you understand how the process of using major scale patterns can be applied.

You can repeat this process on your own with each of the other major scale patterns. There's no need for us to go through each of them here. You understand the process of how the modes can be derived from each major scale pattern moving the assignment of 1 to each of the scale degrees to play each of the modes.

As an exercise, I suggest you spend some time and repeat this process with the Patterns II, III, IV, and V Major Scales. Download some diagram paper and convert each of the other major scale patterns to Dorian, Phrygian, Lydian, Mixolydian, Aolean, and Locrian. Reassign the number 1 to each scale degree for each mode and continue numbering the rest accordingly.

I will also mention that in the next Module, you will learn how to derive the modes from Major and Minor Pentatonic shells. The result will be the exact same patterns found here. I believe this next method is much easier on the brain. Some guitar players prefer that way because of their familiarity with pentatonic shells. It also helps eliminate the muscle memory issue when converting major scales to modes and thinking of 1 in a new place that I mentioned earlier.

A Note of Caution

Converting a Major Scale pattern to any of the modes works really well in the initial stages. Because you already know all five Major Scale patterns so well, you can instantly have all seven modes under your fingers. But there is a serious issue I've seen trip up many guitarists when they first learn this method. After months or years of playing the physical shapes of the five Major Scale patterns, muscle memory takes root in a very strong way. Fingers become trained to travel through the scale with a strong orientation to where 1 is when the physical pattern is used as the Major Scale. When the same physical pattern is now re-purposed to be used as another mode, like Dorian or any of the others, it sounds strange and often you feel a little disoriented because muscle memory has not adjusted to the new number 1, the new number 2, the new number 3 and so on. This is a real problem, but it can be overcome. We'll address this in Unit 3 by associating the major modes to the Major Pentatonic Scale and the minor modes to the Minor Pentatonic Scale.

This is a lot of raw information and it's useless unless you put it to work. You certainly know by now that the Fretboard Logic modules are about the matrix of the fretboard and how scales, arpeggios, and chords are laid out. This information needs to be exercised in the Improvisation modules. You'll get many opportunities to work through the modes in the Units 2 through 10 Improvisation Modules.

RHYTHM GUITAR

Creating Parts for the Blues

Blues was the first style you studied in the Rhythm Guitar modules back in Level 1. There are two objectives in this Module:

- Follow the chart
- Create a rhythm guitar part appropriate for the track

There are no exactly right or wrong parts, but there are definitely parts that fit a genre and others that don't. The goal of the Level 6 Rhythm Guitar modules is to create parts that are typical and appropriate for the style and that would make the producer, musical director, or band leader in a professional environment happy. These Rhythm Guitar modules are all an exercise in helping you develop parts appropriate for the song. You recall that in every Rhythm Guitar module you worked through, and in all the styles, I urged you to log away the material you learned as vocabulary to be used later. Where we are right now is the 'later' I was talking about. So pull out that vocabulary and let's get it to work.

You learned comping parts for a normal 12-Bar Blues in the Rhythm Guitar modules back in Level 1. If you haven't been actively using the comping vocabulary you learned back then, it might be a good idea to go back and review that material. Don't assume all those parts will work in every song. Some may work, some may need some modification, and some may not work at all. And there may be room for two parts, so keep that in mind.

First, let's look at the road map on the following page and use your Chart-Reading Checklist from Level 5.

Chart-Reading Checklist

1. Look at the top left corner where all the preliminary information is: Key signature, Time signature, Style
2. Note the Tempo
3. Scan the form
4. Seek out any figures that need to be played
5. Scan the chords for the ones that are new or difficult for you
6. Seek out more detailed instructions like dynamics, accents, and expression markings

Blues Song Chart

Next, listen to the track for this Module and think like a producer. Listen from the perspective of what the song needs from a rhythm guitar player, who happens to be you. What kind of a rhythm guitar part would add to the song?

Always keep in mind:

- You are listening for a part that fits with the band; consider the instrumentation so you know how busy or sparse you should be and also the kind of voicings you should use and in what register they are.
- Make your part be supportive of the lead vocal or instruments. That's your job.
- Get the right guitar sound.
- Be as consistent as possible. Your band mates are counting on you to be and stay in your lane.

Your job now is to create a part, record it, and listen back. Ask yourself, "would I want to hear this part on a recording?" Also ask yourself, "is there room for a second or even third rhythm guitar part?" If you can, share the part with other musicians you trust and see what they have to say. Once you have a part that sounds good to you, create another, then a third. Try layering parts. One of the most enjoyable parts of producing and recording music is building a track by layering parts.

The point is to get experience creating parts, not to produce the "perfect part". There are no right or wrong parts, but you should be thinking in terms of what would a producer or band leader expect of you. That is the goal of all Level 6 Rhythm Guitar modules.

This should be fun. You can revisit this chart and track as many times as you want. If you think of something new you want to try, record it and see how it sounds in the context of the rest of the band. Listening to new music will give you new ideas; let that creativity happen. It's important. Inspiration for parts can come from a lot of different places, maybe even from a commercial.

The Level 6 Rhythm Guitar modules are most effective if you download the minus-one tracks and drop them into some recording software so you can record your parts and judge them from the perspective of a listener.

CHART WRITING

The last Module began explaining an approach to writing a chord chart that starts with figuring out the big picture and then gradually working down to the detail. You learned to listen to the overall structure of the song and jot down the major sections of the song in order. We're calling this first draft a Form Chart.

Remember: The goal in writing a chord chart is to create a short, simple, and accurate road map that is easy to navigate. Fitting it all on one page is optimal, two pages is OK, but three or more makes it hard to fit on a music stand if you're using paper.

Please understand the logic behind this methodical approach. If you don't have a clear idea of the bigger structure of the song before you start writing, chances are the chart will be messy and hard to read.

Step One

Step one was pretty simple. It was creating the Form Chart. Now it's time for step two, where you'll learn to count measures within each section of the Form Chart. At the same time, you can listen for sections or parts of sections that repeat. These are opportunities to save space by using repeat devices.

The Form Chart for the song "A Good Chart Sets You Free"

Intro
Verse
Verse
Prechorus
Chorus
Verse
Prechorus
Chorus
Guitar Solo
Prechorus
Chorus
Out Chorus
Out Chorus

Step Two

Using the Form Chart as a reference, start a new draft on a piece of blank paper and lay it over the Form Chart to the right of the list of sections. It doesn't need to be staff paper. In fact, I'd suggest it not be staff paper. Count and write out blank measures for each section. I suggest you organize the page in groups of four or eight measures per line if possible. Four- and eight-bar phrases are by far the most common length. For the sake of organization, start new sections on the left margin. It helps you to see the form at a glance. This is important.

Writing out all of the blank measures might seem like an unnecessary step but I've found having this crude layout is really helpful before writing anything on staff paper. You usually find you won't need to notate as much as you might think.

Listen to the track for this Module again while looking at this example of what your paper should look like.

The Form Chart for the song "A Good Chart Sets You Free"

Section	Measures
Intro	| | | | | | | | |
Verse	| | | | | | | | |
Verse	| | | | | | | | |
Prechorus	| | | | | | | | |
Chorus	| | | | | | | | | |
Verse	| | | | | | | | |
Prechorus	| | | | | | | | |
Chorus	| | | | | | | | |
Guitar Solo	| | | | | | | | | | | | | | | |
Prechorus	| | | | | | | | |
Chorus	| | | | | | | | | |
Out Chorus	| | | | | | | | |
Out Chorus	| | | | | | | | |

You haven't figured out any repeats, chords, or rhythm figures yet, but you can already see a very crude representation of how the chart will be organized and where repeat devices can be used.

After completing steps one and two, it's time to figure out the chords. I suggest you do this before you start looking for opportunities to use repeat devices. This is because sometimes sections are repeated and identical until the last measure or two. In other words, the chords of the verse two might be identical to the chords in verse one up until the last measure. In these cases, you may want to use first and second endings or other similar tools.

IMPROVISATION

In the Fretboard Logic Module you learned to adapt the Major Scale fingering patterns as the seven modes. You worked with the Pattern I Octave Shape and Major Scale pattern to illustrate the idea.

In this Module you'll get a feel for each of the four commonly used modes, other than Ionian (Major) and Aeolian (Natural Minor). This will not be an in-depth study of each mode. That will come in subsequent modules. The purpose of this Module is to experience playing each mode in a very surface-level way, much the same way you did in the early levels with key-center soloing in major and minor keys. Approach this and the next Module with that mindset.

Lydian Mode

First let's look at Lydian. You were introduced to the Lydian Mode in the Theory and Fretboard Logic Modules. Start by looking at the Pattern I Major Scale in the key of G. Next assign the number 1 to the note that is 4 in the Major Scale. Then shift the remaining numbers in order.

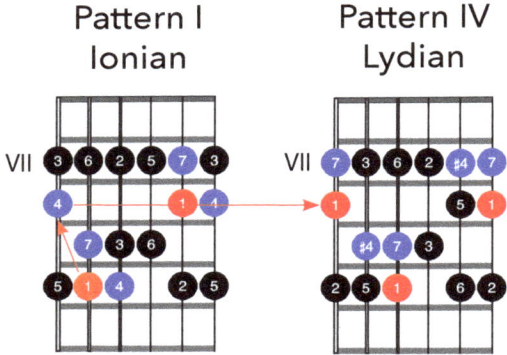

This is the Lydian Mode or Scale. It begins on 4 of the Major Scale so therefore it is the fourth mode. And because we started with G major, and G major's 4th scale degree is C, this is C Lydian. What octave shape is this? Pattern IV.

Next, experiment with the C Lydian Scale over a static Cma7(#11) chord using the track provided for this Module There is no special agenda or goal other than to wander around to get a feel for the sound. A more detailed Lydian Scale improvisation study will happen in Unit 8. You can see some of the Lydian phrases I used in the chart on the next page.

Cma7(#11) Vamp

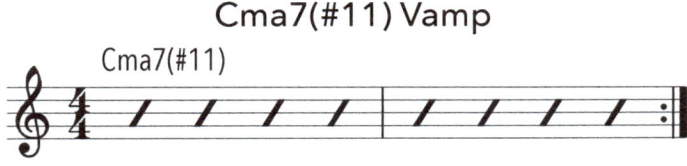

Level 6 Unit 2 • Lydian Demo

Mixolydian

Next, let's look at Mixolydian. You were introduced to the Mixolydian Mode in the Theory and Fretboard Logic Modules. Start by looking at the Pattern I Major Scale in the key of G. Next assign the number 1 to the note that is 5 in the Major Scale. Then shift the remaining numbers in order.

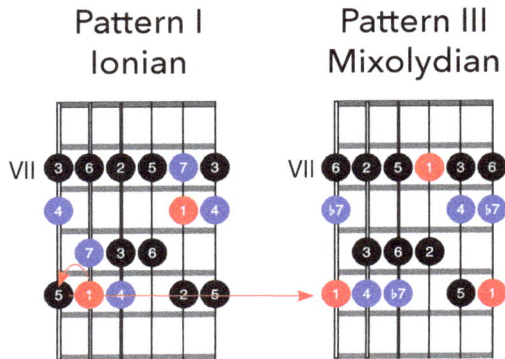

This is the Mixolydian Mode or Scale. It begins on 5 of the Major Scale so therefore it is the fifth mode. And because we started with G major, and G major's 5th scale degree is D, this is D Mixolydian. What octave shape is this? Pattern III.

Experiment with the D Mixolydian Scale over a static D7 chord using the track provided for this Module. There is no special agenda or goal other than to wander around to get a feel for the sound. A more detailed Mixolydian Scale improvisation study will happen in Unit 7.

You can see some of the Mixolydian phrases I used in the chart on the next page.

* Please make note of the author's gaff with regard to the explanation of the Pattern III D Mixolydian as a derivative of the Pattern I G major scale. The gaff is that during the recording of the example, which is transcribed on the following page, the key in the text, which was D Mixolydian, was overlooked and the example was performed in C Mixolydian. So note that it is performed and notated one whole step below where the diagrams illustrate the relationships are. After over a thousand pages of complicated text, please understand that mistakes happen and forgive the error.

Level 6 Unit 2 • Mixolydian Demo

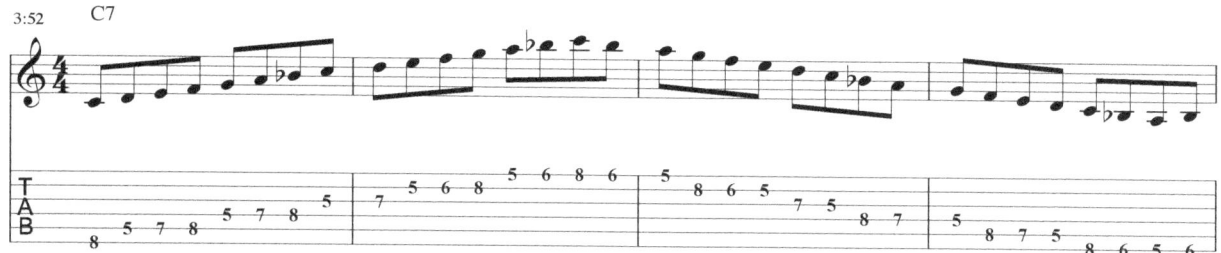

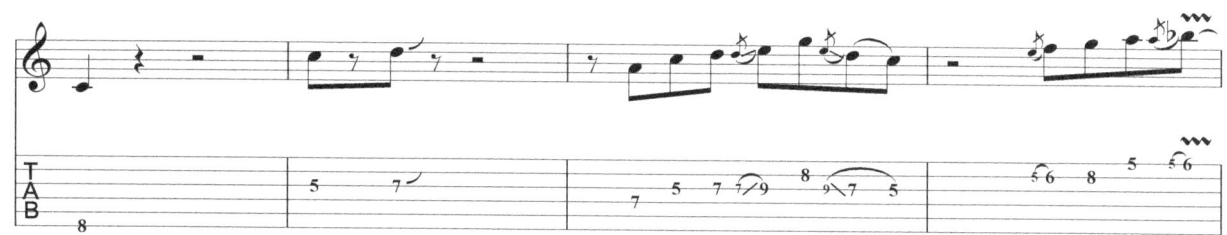

Dorian

Next look at Dorian. Start by looking at the Pattern I Major Scale in the key of G. Next assign the number 1 to the note that is 2 in the Major Scale. Then shift the remaining numbers in order.

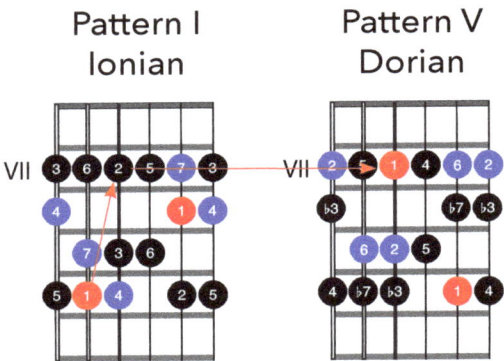

This is the Dorian Mode or Scale. It begins on 2 of the Major Scale so therefore it is the second mode. And because we started with G major, and G major's 2nd scale degree is A, this is A Dorian. What octave shape is this? Pattern V.

Experiment with the A Dorian Scale over a static Ami7 chord using the track provided for this Module. There is no special agenda or goal other than to wander around to get a feel for the sound. A more detailed Lydian Scale improvisation study will happen in Unit 4.

Ami7 Vamp

You can see some of the Dorian phrases I used in the chart on the next page.

Level 6 Unit 2 • Dorian Demo

Phrygian

Next look at Phrygian. Start by looking at the Pattern I Major Scale in the key of G. Next assign the number 1 to the note that is 3 in the Major Scale. Then shift the remaining numbers in order.

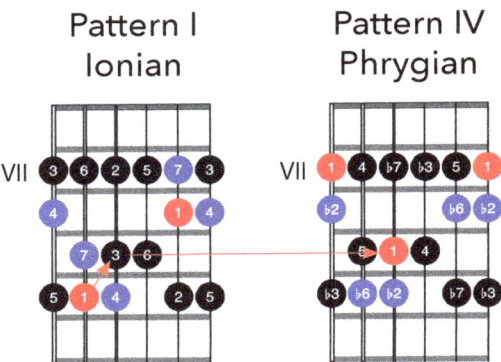

This is the Phrygian Mode or Scale. It begins on 3 of the Major Scale so therefore it is the third mode. And because we started with G major, and G major's 3rd scale degree is B, this is B Phrygian. What octave shape is this? Pattern IV.

While it was Octave Shape I when we started with Pattern I G major, when adapted as B Phrygian, it's Octave Shape IV.

Experiment with the B Phrygian Scale over a static Bmi7 chord using the track provided for this Module. There is no special agenda or goal other than to wander around to get a feel for the sound. A more detailed Phrygian Scale improvisation study will happen in Unit 9.

You can see some of the Phrygian phrases I used in the chart on the next page. Again, the goal of this Module wasn't to go very deep into playing on the modes but rather get a key-center feel for the scale when applied to static chord.

Level 6 Unit 2 • Phrygian Demo

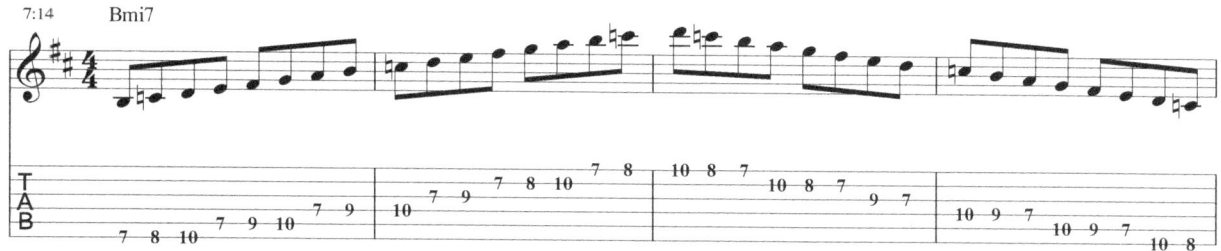

PRACTICE

Theory

- ❏ Study the three ways to think of the modes: as derivatives of the interval formula for the Major Scale, by making adjustments to the Major and Minor scales and by adding notes to Major and Minor Pentatonic scales.
- ❏ Memorize the quality of each mode (i.e. ma7, dom7, mi7, mi7(♭5)).
- ❏ Study the two ways to use key signatures with modes.
- ❏ Memorize the quality of the chord reflected in each mode (i.e. ma7, dom7, mi7, mi7(♭5)).

Fretboard Logic

- ❏ Learn to see the modes on the fretboard by reassigning numbers for each of the major scale patterns.

Rhythm Guitar

- ❏ Follow the chart and create and record one or more rhythm guitar parts.

Chart Writing

- ❏ Learn step two of building a chord chart by counting and writing down the measures of the sections for your step one Form Chart you created in Unit 1. Now you're creating a Crude Chord Chart.

Improvisation

- ❏ Sample and get a feel for the Lydian, Mixolydian, Dorian, and Phrygian Modes using the tracks.

UNIT 3

Learning Modules

> **Theory** - Harmonized Modes

> **Fretboard Logic** - Major Modes and the Major Pentatonic Scale, Minor Modes and the Minor Pentatonic Scale

> **Rhythm Guitar** - Creating a Rhythm Guitar Part for a Folk Song

> **Chart Writing** - Figuring out the Chords of a Song for the Crude Chart

> **Improvisation** - Sounds of the Major and Minor Pentatonic Scales in Modal Contexts

> **Practice** - Continue Practice Routine Development

The tracks for this Unit can be found at the following link:

https://fretboardbiology.com/book6/#u3

THEORY

Harmonizing the Modes

Modes can be harmonized just like the Major, Natural Minor, and Harmonic Minor Scales. There are several reasons for knowing the harmonized modes:

- Whole songs can be written in modes. In other words, the mode is used as the basis for a composition, so the chords of the scale are what support the melody and make up the harmony of the song.

- Knowing the harmonized modes helps us understand more ways that modal interchange can occur. There are many instances where songs borrow chords from parallel modes. We already covered examples of this idea with parallel minor scales.

- It helps us with harmonic analysis in modes other than major (Ionian) and minor (Aeolian).

It's a good idea to write each harmonized mode out on the staff and I suggest you do that as an exercise. But a convenient shortcut is available if you relate the modes back to the pattern established with the harmonized Major Scale.

The Harmonized C Major Scale with 7th Chords

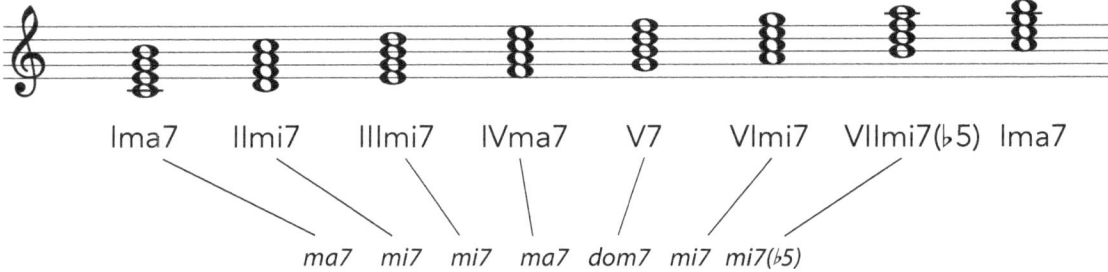

Ima7   IImi7   IIImi7   IVma7   V7   VImi7   VIImi7(♭5)   Ima7

ma7   mi7   mi7   ma7   dom7   mi7   mi7(♭5)

Consider this: The following order of chord qualities remains consistent through all modes. In this case, the sequence is specifically that of the harmonized Major Scale:

Order of Chord Qualities - Major Scale

ma7   mi7   mi7   ma7   dom7   mi7   mi7(♭5)

This should look really familiar. Let's review and break it down. You know that in all major scales, no matter the key, I is ma7, II is mi7, III is mi7, IV is ma7, V is dom7, VI is mi7, and VII is mi7(♭5).

Now, let's expand this chord-quality pattern like we did earlier in this Level with the W W H W W W H interval pattern. This shows the sequence of chord qualities repeating in subsequent octaves.

Order of Chord Qualities

ma7   mi7   mi7   ma7   dom7   mi7   mi7(b5)   ma7   mi7   mi7   ma7   dom7   mi7   mi7(b5)   ma7

Let's take seven chord segments that represent the chords of each of the harmonized modes:

Ionian Mode Order of Chord Qualities

ma7   mi7   mi7   ma7   dom7   mi7   mi7(b5)   ma7   mi7   mi7   ma7   dom7   mi7   mi7(b5)   ma7

Ionian Mode

Dorian Mode Order of Chord Qualities

ma7   mi7   mi7   ma7   dom7   mi7   mi7(b5)   ma7   mi7   mi7   ma7   dom7   mi7   mi7(b5)   ma7

Dorian Mode

Phrygian Mode Order of Chord Qualities

ma7   mi7   mi7   ma7   dom7   mi7   mi7(b5)   ma7   mi7   mi7   ma7   dom7   mi7   mi7(b5)   ma7

Phrygian Mode

Lydian Mode Order of Chord Qualities

ma7   mi7   mi7   ma7   dom7   mi7   mi7(b5)   ma7   mi7   mi7   ma7   dom7   mi7   mi7(b5)   ma7

Lydian Mode

Mixolydian Mode Order of Chord Qualities

ma7   mi7   mi7   ma7   dom7   mi7   mi7(b5)   ma7   mi7   mi7   ma7   dom7   mi7   mi7(b5)   ma7

Mixolydian Mode

Aeolian Mode Order of Chord Qualities

ma7   mi7   mi7   ma7   dom7   mi7   mi7(b5)   ma7   mi7   mi7   ma7   dom7   mi7   mi7(b5)   ma7

Aeolian Mode

Locrian Mode Order of Chord Qualities

ma7   mi7   mi7   ma7   dom7   mi7   mi7(b5)   ma7   mi7   mi7   ma7   dom7   mi7   mi7(b5)   ma7

Locrian Mode

You will learn to solo using the modes. But before that, it's important for you to have a solid grasp of the material we've presented in this Unit.

Drill yourself on the chords that result from harmonizing each mode. You know two modes already very well: Ionian and Aeolian. Locrian is not one to spend any time on as a practical matter. That leaves four new ones: Dorian, Phrygian, Lydian, and Mixolydian.

Let's take a quick preview of each of these four modes harmonized with 7th chords. This Level will focus on using these four modes and devote a unit to each one. Let's go through each one.

Order of Chord Qualities for the Modes

Ionian:	Ima7	IImi7	IIImi7	IVma7	V7	VImi7	VIImi7(b5)
Dorian:	Imi7	IImi7	bIIIma7	IV7	Vmi7	VImi7(b5)	bVIIma7
Phrygian:	Imi7	bIIma7	bIII7	IVmi7	Vmi7(b5)	bVIma7	bVIImi7
Lydian:	Ima7	II7	IIImi7	#IVmi7(b5)	Vma7	VImi7	VIImi7
Mixolydian:	I7	IImi7	IIImi7(b5)	IVma7	Vmi7	VImi7	bVIIma7
Aeolian:	Imi7	IImi7(b5)	bIIIma7	IVmi7	Vmi7	bVIma7	bVII7
Locrian:	Imi7(b5)	bIIma7	bIIImi7	bIVmi7	bVma7	bVI7	bVIImi7

FRETBOARD LOGIC

In the last Fretboard Logic Module you learned to adapt the five Major Scale patterns to play the other six modes; Dorian, Phrygian, Lydian, Mixolydian, Aeolian, and Locrian.

I brought up a serious issue that trips up many guitarists when they learn modes if they convert the Major Scale: After months or years of playing the physical shapes of the five Major Scale patterns, muscle memory takes hold and fingers become trained to travel through the scale with a strong orientation to where 1 is when the pattern is used for the Major Scale. When the same physical pattern is now re-purposed to be used as another mode, it sounds a little unclear and undefined because muscle memory has not adjusted. This is a real problem not to be taken lightly. It can be overcome by associating the major modes to the Major Pentatonic Scale and the minor modes to the Minor Pentatonic Scale. This works wonders and usually has guitarists making sense out of the modes much quicker.

Modes from Pentatonic Shells

The primary goals of this Module are to learn the major modes by adding notes to the Major Pentatonic shells, and to learn the minor modes by adding notes to the Minor Pentatonic shells. Recall that:

- The major modes are those with major 3rds. They are Ionian (which we know as the Major Scale), Lydian, and Mixolydian.
- The minor modes are those with minor 3rds. They are Dorian, Phrygian, Aeolian (which we know as the Natural Minor Scale), and Locrian.

Way back in Level 1, you learned about the pentatonic shells and that by adding two additional notes to the five-note scales, new derivative scales could be created. You learned the Major Scale fingering patterns by adding a perfect 4th and Major 7th to the Major Pentatonic patterns or shells. You learned the Natural Minor Scale fingering patterns by adding a major 2nd and minor 6th to the Minor Pentatonic patterns or shells.

Because most guitarists learn the pentatonic scales first, adding two notes to them can be the smoothest transition into effectively using the modes. The muscle memory for each pentatonic shape is already developed and the addition of the two notes that define the derivative mode doesn't change that.

You're free to learn the modes whichever way you prefer; by adapting the seven-note major scales or by adding to the pentatonic shells, but it's been my experience that guitarists learn more quickly using the pentatonic shell approach. With that, let's begin.

The Major Modes

We'll start with the major modes: Ionian, Lydian, and Mixolydian. Study what scale degrees are added to the Major Pentatonic shell to create each mode.

Modes as Derivatives of the Major Pentatonic Scale

Major Pentatonic	*1*	*ma2*	*ma3*		*P5*	*ma6*	
Ionian Mode	*1*	*ma2*	*ma3*	*P4*	*P5*	*ma6*	*ma7*
Lydian Mode	*1*	*ma2*	*ma3*	*A4*	*P5*	*ma6*	*ma7*
Mixolydian Mode	*1*	*ma2*	*ma3*	*P4*	*P5*	*ma6*	*mi7*

Pattern I

The diagram on the left is the Pattern I Major Pentatonic shell. To its right is the same shell with a perfect 4th and major 7th added. This is the Ionian Mode or Major Scale. To its right is the same shell with an augmented 4th and major 7th added. This is the Lydian Mode. On the far right is the same shell with a perfect 4th and minor 7th added. This is the Mixolydian Mode.

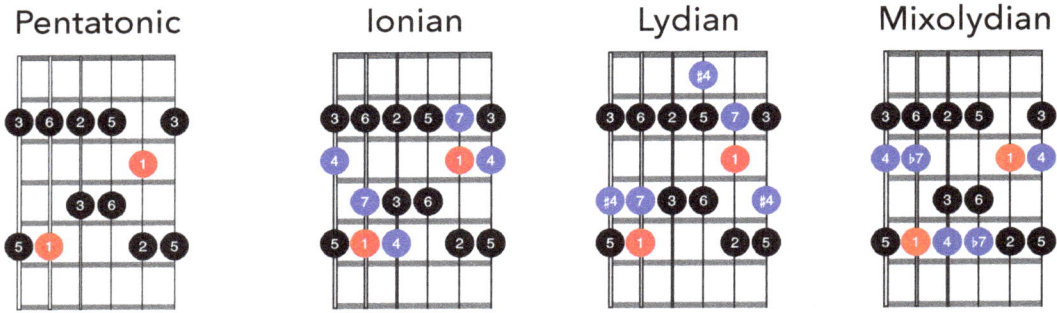

Pattern II

Let's take a look at Pattern II. The diagram on the left is the Pattern II Major Pentatonic shell. To its right is the same shell with a perfect 4th and major 7th added. This is the Ionian Mode or Major Scale. To its right is the same shell with an augmented 4th and major 7th added. This is the Lydian Mode. On the far right is the same shell with a perfect 4th and minor 7th added. This is the Mixolydian Mode.

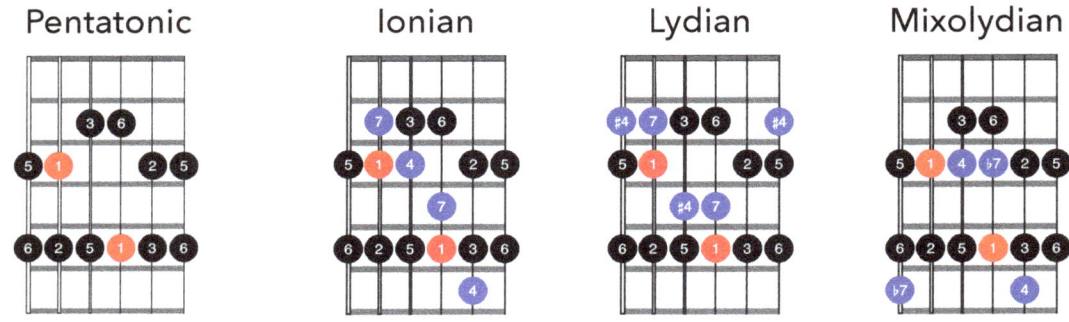

Pattern III

Let's take a look at Pattern III. Follow the same process of adding a 4th and a 7th to the pentatonic shell to create the Ionian, Lydian, and Mixolydian Modes.

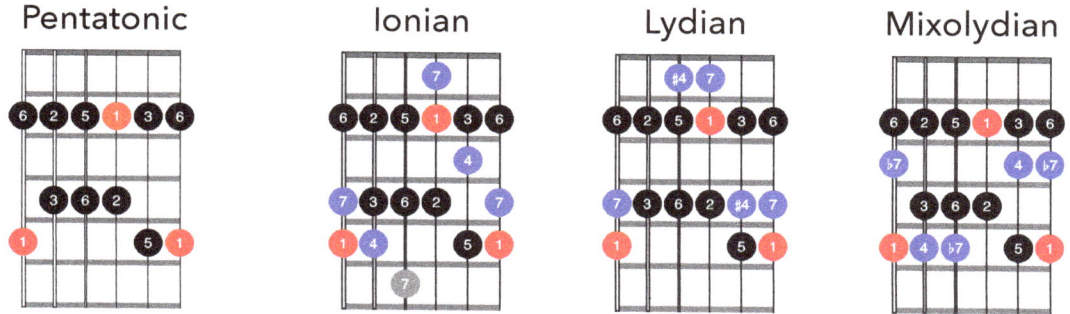

Pattern IV

Let's take a look at Pattern IV. Again, follow the same process of adding a 4th and a 7th to the pentatonic shell to create the Ionian, Lydian, and Mixolydian Modes.

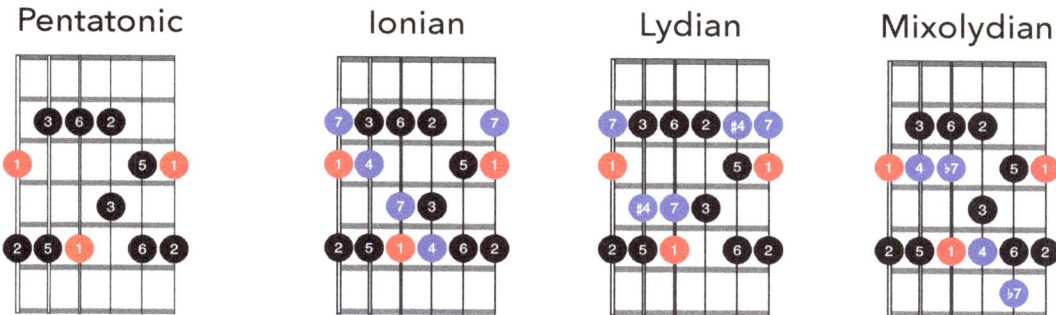

Pattern V

Let's take a look at Pattern V. Once again, follow the same process of adding a 4th and a 7th to the pentatonic shell to create the Ionian, Lydian, and Mixolydian Modes.

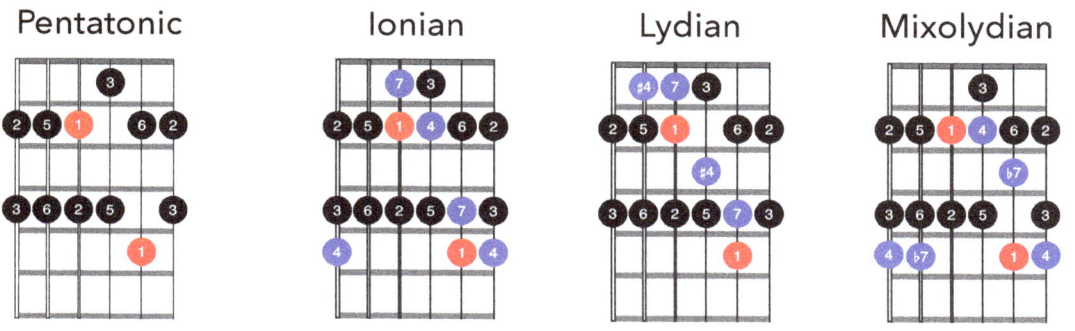

The Minor Modes

Next look at the minor modes: Dorian, Phrygian, Aeolian, and Locrian. Study what scale degrees are added to the Minor Pentatonic shell to create each mode.

Modes as Derivatives of the Minor Pentatonic Scale

Minor Pentatonic	*1*		*mi3*	*P4*	*P5*		*mi7*
Aeolian Mode	*1*	*ma2*	*mi3*	*P4*	*P5*	*mi6*	*mi7*
Dorian Mode	*1*	*ma2*	*mi3*	*P4*	*P5*	*ma6*	*mi7*
Phrygian Mode	*1*	*mi2*	*mi3*	*P4*	*P5*	*mi6*	*mi7*
Locrian Mode	*1*	*mi2*	*mi3*	*P4*	*D5*	*mi6*	*mi7*

Pattern I

Let's take a look at the Pattern I Minor Pentatonic shell. The diagram on the left is the Pattern I Minor Pentatonic shell. To its right is the same shell with a major 2nd and a major 6th added. This is the Dorian Mode. Next, the same shell with a minor 2nd and a minor 6th added is Phrygian Mode. Then the same shell with a major 2nd and a minor 6th added is Aeolian Mode or Natural Minor Scale. On the far right is the same shell with a minor 2nd, a minor 6th added and a diminished 5th replacing the perfect 5th. This is the Locrian Mode.

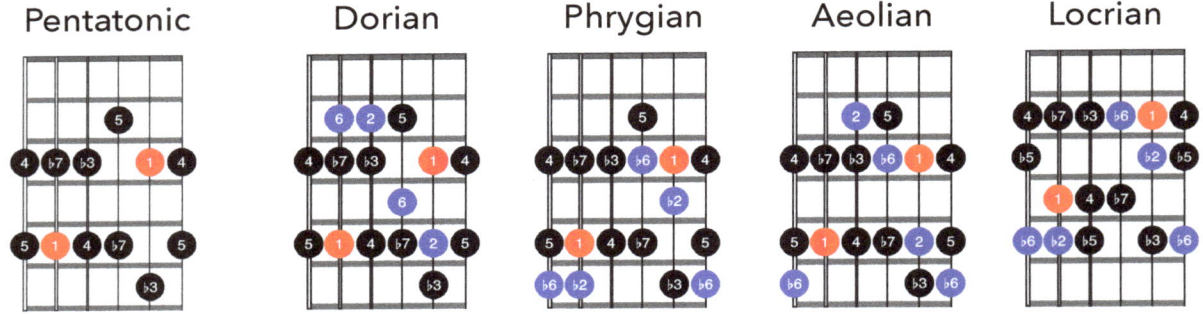

Pattern II

Let's do the same with Pattern II. Add a 2nd and a 6th to the Minor Pentatonic shell to create the Aeolian, Dorian, Phrygian, and Locrian Modes. Remember the diminished 5th in the Locrian Mode.

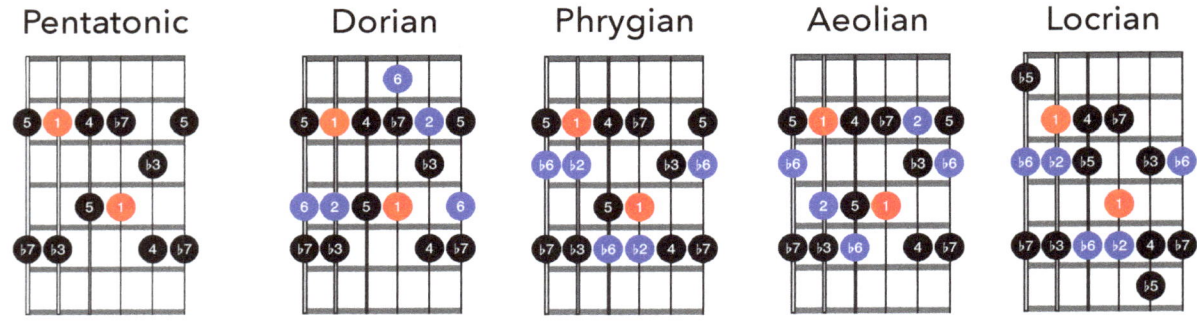

Fretboard Biology — Level 6 • Unit 3: Fretboard Logic

Pattern III

Let's do the same with Pattern III. Like the previous modes, add a 2nd and a 6th to the Minor Pentatonic shell to create the Aeolian, Dorian, Phrygian, and Locrian Modes. Remember the diminished 5th in the Locrian Mode.

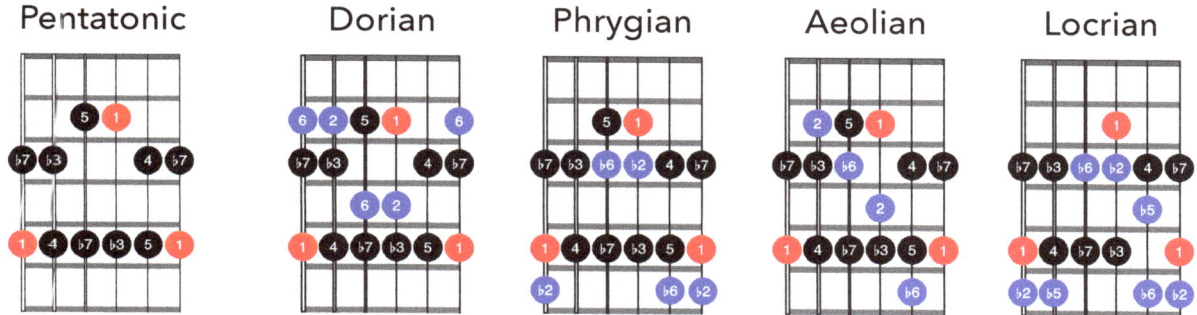

Pattern IV

Next is Pattern IV. Add a 2nd and a 6th to the Minor Pentatonic shell to create the Aeolian, Dorian, Phrygian, and Locrian Modes. Remember the diminished 5th in the Locrian Mode.

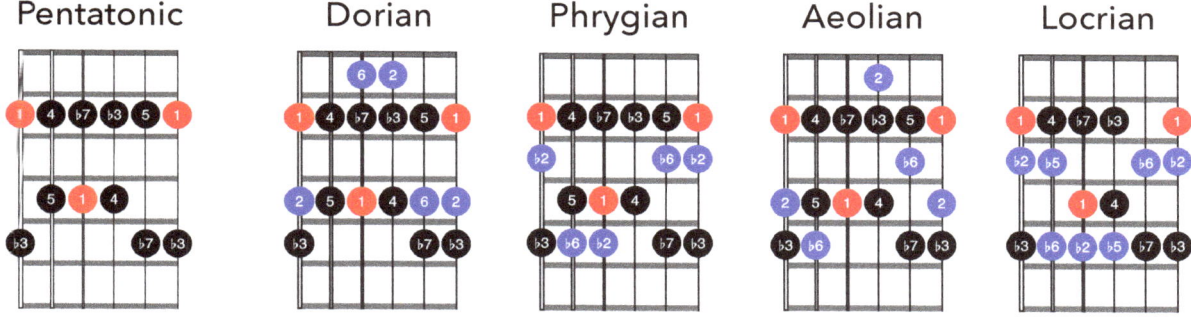

Pattern V

Finally, let's look at Pattern V. Again, add a 2nd and a 6th to the Minor Pentatonic shell to create the Aeolian, Dorian, Phrygian, and Locrian Modes. Remember the diminished 5th in the Locrian Mode.

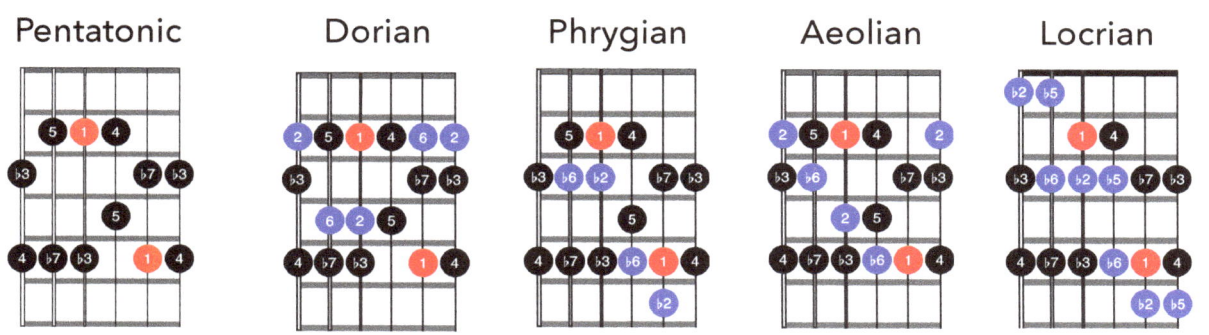

The association of the modes to the familiar pentatonic shells can be a great help to you. And remember this as a survival technique: If you are in the heat of a solo using a particular mode and can't quite remember the additional notes needed to fill out the pentatonic shell, there's no harm. The five pentatonic notes are still part of the mode you are struggling to play.

As I've said before, don't feel like you need to memorize all of this right now. It takes time, so treat it as more of an ongoing and long-term effort. It's much more important for you to understand the principles rather than memorizing all the dots.

Please relate all of this to the Family Tree. It's important that you keep that connection going!

RHYTHM GUITAR

Creating Parts for Folk Songs

You studied Folk rhythm guitar parts back in an earlier Rhythm Guitar module.

There are two objectives in this and all the Level 6 Rhythm Guitar modules:

- Follow the chart
- Create a rhythm guitar part appropriate for the track

Like we did when creating parts for the Blues, let's approach this like we want to make a producer, musical director, or band leader happy. There are no exactly right or wrong parts but strive for having your part be one that fits. You may find it helpful to refer back to the Folk rhythm guitar parts you created back in Level 2.

First, let's take a look at the road map in the following page and use your Chart-Reading Checklist.

Chart-Reading Checklist

1. Look at the top left corner where all the preliminary information is: Key signature, Time signature, Style
2. Note the Tempo
3. Scan the form
4. Seek out any figures that need to be played
5. Scan the chords for the ones that are new or difficult for you
6. Seek out more detailed instructions like dynamics, accents, and expression markings

Folk Song Chart

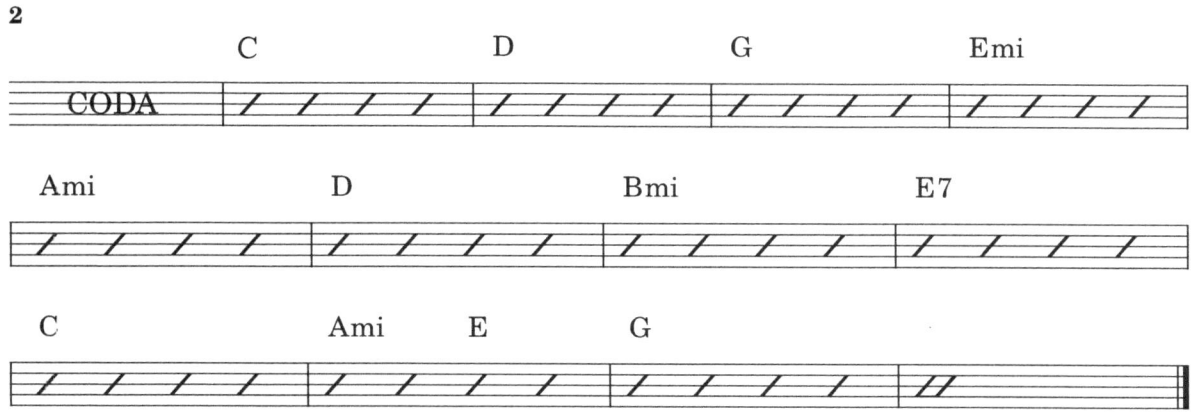

Next, listen to the track for this Module and think like a producer. Listen from the perspective of what the song needs from a rhythm guitar player, who happens to be you. What kind of a rhythm guitar part would add to the song?

Always keep in mind:

- You are listening for a part that fits with the band, so consider the instrumentation so you know how busy or sparse you should be and also the kind of voicings you should use and in what register they are.
- Make your part be supportive of the lead vocal or instruments. That's your job.
- Get the right guitar sound.
- Be as consistent as possible. Your band mates are counting on you to be and stay in your lane.

Your job now is to create a part, record it, and listen back. Ask yourself, "would I want to hear this part on a recording?" Also ask yourself, "is there room for a second or even third rhythm guitar part?" If you can, share the part with other musicians you trust and see what they have to say. Once you have a part that sounds good to you, create another, then a third. Try layering parts. One of the most enjoyable parts of producing and recording music is building a track by layering parts. The point is to get experience creating parts, not to produce the "perfect part". There are no right or wrong parts, but you should be thinking in terms of what would a producer or band leader expect of you. That is the goal of all Level 6 Rhythm Guitar modules.

You can revisit this chart and track as many times as you want. If you think of something new you want to try, record it and see how it sounds in the context of the rest of the band. Listen to new music give you news ideas and let that creativity happen.

CHART WRITING

So far you have taken the first two steps in writing chord charts. Step one was the form chart. Step two was counting measures and creating the crude first draft. After completing steps one and two, it's time for step three, where you figure out the chords. It's good to do this before you start looking for opportunities to use repeat devices. This is because often times sections are nearly identical up until the last measure or two. In these cases, you may need to use first and second endings or other similar tools. This affects how you will lay out the page.

Step Three

In step three, you will be adding the chords to your chart. At this point in the process, you will need to identify the key by ear. If it doesn't jump out at you, think about a technique you learned to do harmonic analysis: Focus on the last chord, which is often the tonic chord. Knowing the key can sometimes provide clues about the roots and qualities of the chords based on what you know about harmonic analysis.

Use the crude first draft (remember it's only blank measures at this point) and begin writing the chord symbols above the blank measures as you identify each chord. The chords may be in root position or inverted, in which case you'll use slash chords.

Keep in mind what you learned from the Chart Reading modules, and place the chord symbols roughly above the place in the measure where they occur. For example, a chord that is played on beat one should be written above the beginning of the measure. A chord that is played on beat three of a 4/4 measure should be placed roughly above the midway point. This second draft of the chart is rough at this point, and for your eyes only.

I usually listen for the bass note to start figuring out the chords. As you know, chords are usually, but not always, in root position. Focus on the notes the bass player plays, especially the first note they play when the chords change.

Using the track provided for this Module, begin transcribing the chords and place them above the measures where they occur on your crude first draft. An example of what your paper should look like is on the next page.

The Form Chart for "A Good Chart Sets You Free"

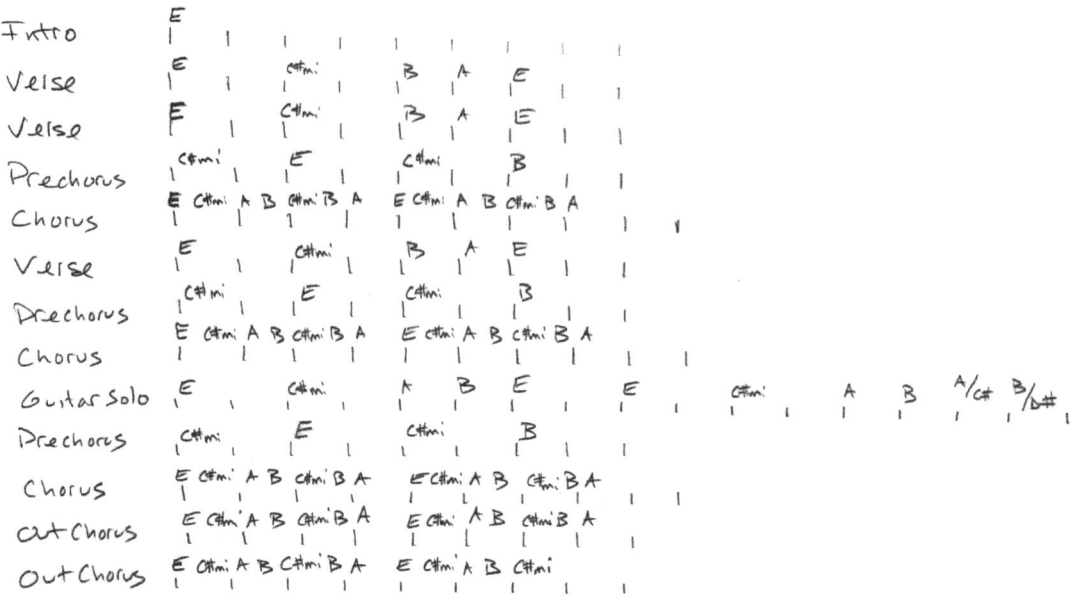

As you gain more experience transcribing, chords become easier to identify. If you utilize your understanding of harmony, groups of chords can often be identified together because they may follow familiar and common root paths. The root movement might follow the scale as in Ima, IImi, IIImi, and IVma. Or often the root movement is up in 4ths or down in 5ths. You know from harmonic analysis that the same short series of chords in the same progression may be used again and again in song after song. Pay attention to these reoccurring harmonic situations. Take note of the ones you encounter repeatedly.

There are characteristics and components of the chord that need to be determined:

- The bass note: Is the bass note the root of the chord? If so, it's in root position. If not, it's an inversion.
- The quality: Is it a major, minor, diminished, or augmented triad? Is a sus chord? Is it a 7th chord? Is it a power chord?

So many musicians who never formally study ear training develop 'really good ears' by recognizing chord sequences or short melodies that were part of other songs. It's a really important habit to develop. As you analyze and learn new songs, store the progression analysis and how it sounds away for future reference. This is a huge point.

After you identify the chords, there are still a couple of steps before you transfer the information to staff paper. You need to locate rhythm figures and riffs played by the whole band that need to be notated. This is important because measures with a lot of information in them, like rhythm figures and riffs, require more physical space on the page than measures with less complexity.

IMPROVISATION

The goal of the last Improvisation Module was to get a key-center feel for the Lydian, Mixolydian, Dorian, and Phrygian Modes when played over a static chord. The idea was to not dig too deep, but to get a sense of each scale's personality.

Looking ahead in Level 6, you'll spend time learning more detail about each mode:

- Unit 4 will focus on the detail of Dorian
- Unit 7 will focus on the detail of Mixolydian
- Unit 8 will focus on the detail of Lydian
- Unit 9 will focus on the detail of Phrygian

In the Fretboard Logic Module, you learned the process of adding two notes to Major and Minor Pentatonic shells to create the modes. The focus of this Module is to get a feel for the sound of the pentatonic shells we will build from to create these four modes.

This will be simple, but understand this point: The pentatonic shells contain five of the seven notes needed for each of these modes: Lydian, Mixolydian, Dorian, and Phrygian. If you can make melodic sense playing the pentatonic shells over common harmonic situations that use these modes, you will certainly be in a better position to make sense with the mode itself once the two additional notes are added. But it's smart to work with the comfortable pentatonic shells first where your muscle memory is strong.

Lydian

Let's work with Lydian first. The track is a static Dma7(#11). You have not learned a ma7(#11) chord yet but you know that the #11 in the chord is a good match for the Lydian Scale which has a #4. #4 is the same as #11.

D Lydian will be the scale of choice but for this exercise, we'll just use the Major Pentatonic shell. Experiment playing over the track provided for this Module using the Pattern III D Major Pentatonic shell.

Dma7(#11) Vamp

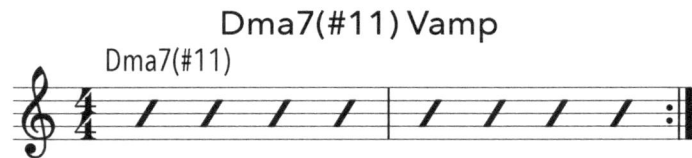

You can see some of the Lydian phrases I used in the chart on the next page.

Level 6 Unit 3 • Lydian Demo

Mixolydian

Let's work with Mixolydian next. The progression for this is in E. E7 to Bmi7. I7 to Vmi7. E Mixolydian will be the scale of choice, but for this exercise, we'll just use the Pattern III Major Pentatonic shell. Experiment playing over the track provided for this Module using the Pattern III E Major Pentatonic shell.

Progression in E Mixolydian

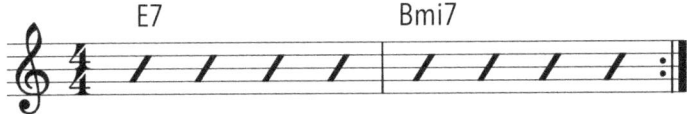

You can see some of the Mixolydian phrases I used in the chart below

Level 6 Unit 3 • Mixolydian Demo

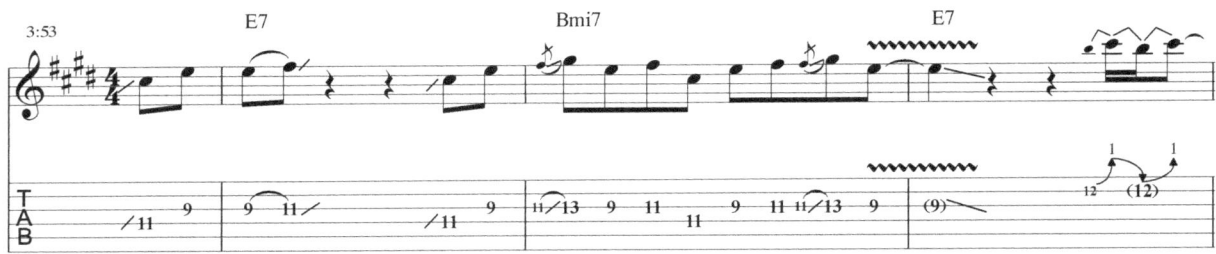

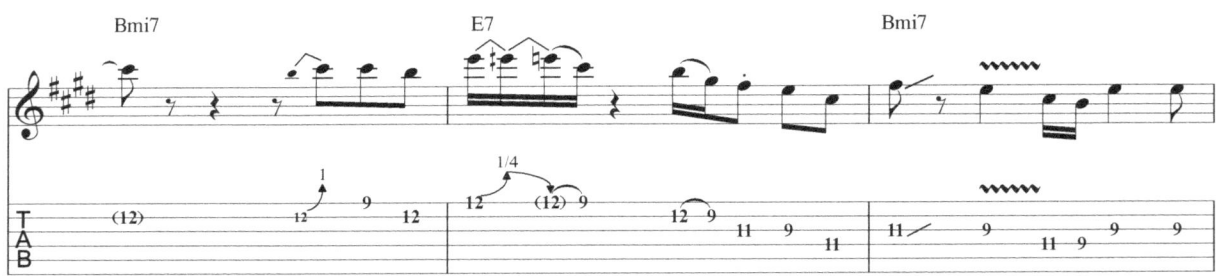

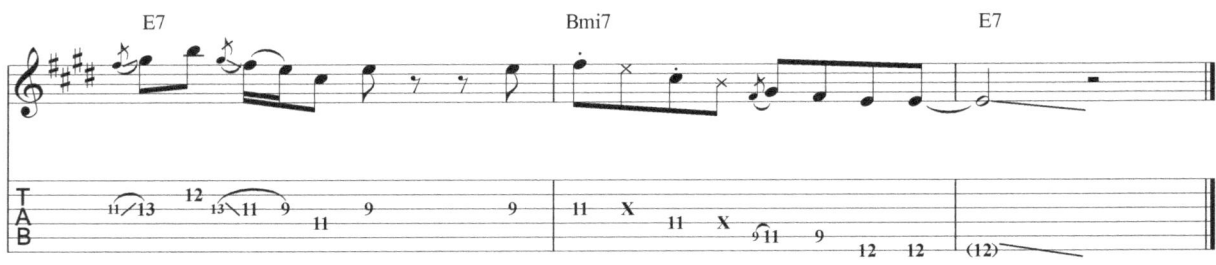

Fretboard Biology — Level 6 • Unit 3: Improvisation

Dorian

Let's work with Dorian next. Here's a progression in A Dorian. Ami7 to D7. Imi7 to IV7. A Dorian will be the scale of choice, but for this exercise, we'll just use the Minor Pentatonic shell. Experiment playing over the track provided for this Module using the Pattern IV A Minor Pentatonic shell.

Progression in A Dorian

You can see some of the Dorian phrases I used in the chart below

Level 6 Unit 3 • Dorian Demo

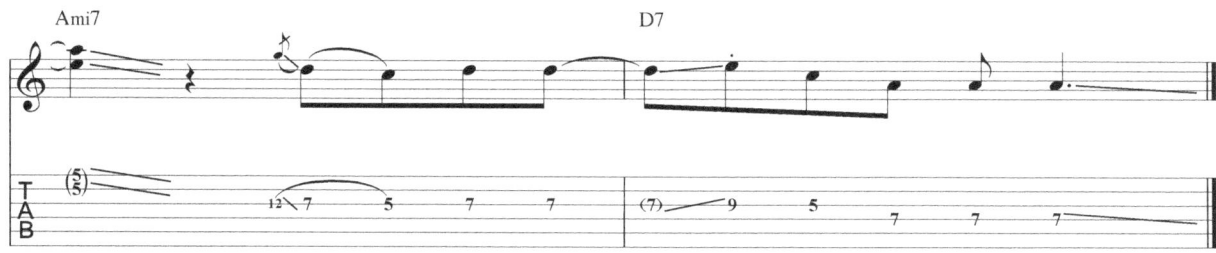

Phrygian

Let's work with Phrygian next. Here's a track in G Phrygian. Gmi to A♭. Imi to ♭IIma. G Phrygian will be the scale of choice, but for this exercise, we'll just use the Minor Pentatonic shell. Experiment playing over the track provided for this Module using the Pattern IV G Minor Pentatonic shell.

Progression in G Prygian

You can see some of the Phrygian phrases I used in the chart below

Level 6 Unit 3 • Phrygian Demo

That exercise was simple, but again, please understand this point: The pentatonic shells have five of the seven notes in these modes. If you can make melodic sense playing the pentatonic shells over common harmonic situations that use these modes, you will certainly be in a better position to drop in the two additional notes that the mode formulas require. But it's important to work with the comfortable pentatonic shells where your muscle memory is strong.

PRACTICE

Theory

- ☐ Know each of the modes harmonized with 7th chords. Use the repeating pattern of ma7, mi7, dom7, and mi7(♭5) chords to ease the required effort.

Fretboard Logic

- ☐ Know how to add two notes to the major pentatonic shell to create the Ionian, Lydian, and Mixolydian Modes.
- ☐ Know how to add two notes to the minor pentatonic shell to create the Dorian, Phrygian, and Aeolian Modes, and additionally, add two notes and change one note to create the Locrian Mode.

Rhythm Guitar

- ☐ Follow the chart and create a rhythm guitar part for a Folk song.

Chart Writing

- ☐ Know how to decipher the chords of a song and place them on the Crude Chord Chart correctly.

Improvisation

- ☐ Know how to use pentatonic scales in harmonic situations where you will soon learn to use seven-note modes.

UNIT 4

Learning Modules

> **Theory** - Dorian Scale Construction and Progressions

> **Fretboard Logic** - Five Patterns of the Dorian Scale, Adding a Major 2nd and Major 6th to the Minor Pentatonic Scale Patterns

> **Rhythm Guitar** - Creating a Rhythm Guitar Part for a Classic Rock Song

> **Chart Writing** - Figuring Out the Rhythm Figures and Riffs of a Song for the Crude Chord Chart

> **Improvisation** - Soloing Over the Most Common Dorian Progressions

> **Practice** - Continue Practice Routine Development

The tracks for this Unit can be found at the following link:

https://fretboardbiology.com/book6/#u4

THEORY

In the last Module you learned that Modes can be harmonized just like the Major, Natural Minor, and Harmonic Minor scales. One of the reasons for knowing the harmonized modes is that entire songs are written in modes other than Ionian (Major Scale) and Aeolian (Natural Minor Scale). If a mode can be used as the basis for a composition, the chords of the harmonized mode support the melody and make up the harmony of the song.

The Dorian Scale

In this Module, we'll work with the Dorian Scale. You may hear musicians use the terms Dorian Scale, Dorian Mode, and Dorian Minor. They all mean the same thing.

Let's review the construction of the Dorian Scale. Tonic, major 2nd, minor 3rd, perfect 4th, perfect 5th, major 6th, and minor 7th. Because it has a minor 3rd, it is a minor-sounding mode.

Dorian Mode Interval Pattern

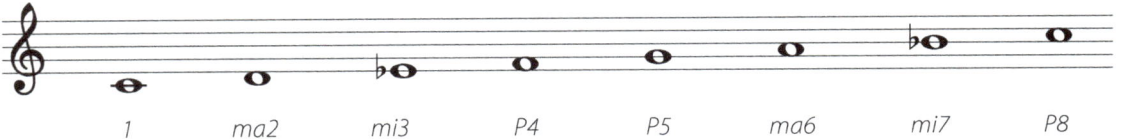

1   ma2   mi3   P4   P5   ma6   mi7   P8

Now, let's look at the comparison of the Minor Pentatonic, Natural Minor, Blues, and Dorian Scales.

Minor Scale Comparison

Minor Pentatonic	1		mi3	P4		P5		mi7
Natural Minor	1	ma2	mi3	P4		P5	mi6	mi7
Blues	1		mi3	P4	D5	P5		mi7
Dorian	1	ma2	mi3	P4		P5	ma6	mi7

Notice that the scale degree that distinguishes the Dorian Scale from the other minor scales is the major 6th. It's a very distinct sound in the scale and stands in contrast to the ♭6 of the Natural Minor Scale. The major 6th affects the chords that result from harmonizing the Dorian Scale, too.

Chords

In a previous Module, you learned the chords of the harmonized Dorian Scale. They are:

Dorian Mode Chord Qualities

Imi7   IImi7   ♭IIIma7   IV7   Vmi7   VImi7(♭5)   ♭VIIma7

Progressions

The discussion about each mode will focus on the common harmonic situations where they are used. So in this Module we'll focus on harmonic situations where the Dorian Scale is used. Sometimes Dorian is the scale of choice for a mi7 chord where the harmony is inactive, meaning that the chord doesn't change, or at least not very often. This situation is often referred to as 'static', as in a 'static Cmi7', for example. When there's a static mi7 chord for any length of time in a song, most musicians hear the Dorian Scale as the most desirable sound. One reason Dorian is a popular sound for static mi7 chords is because there are no avoid tones.

Take a look at the A Dorian Scale below. The chord tones of an Ami7 are highlighted. Note that the scale degree above each note of Ami7 is a whole step higher and therefore not an avoid tone.

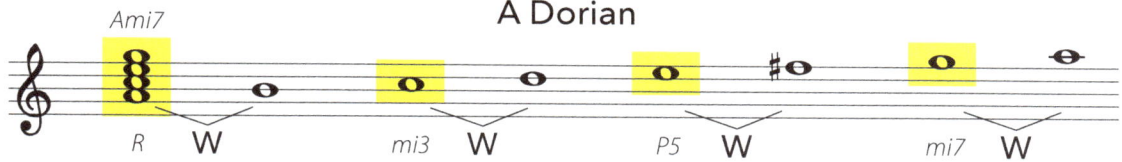

Now, play each note of the A Dorian scale but play an Ami7 chord between playing each scale degree. Notice what that sounds like.

Let's look at the most common short progressions from the harmonized Dorian Scale. The following progressions are signature Dorian progression fragments.

This first two-chord Dorian progression fragment is the most classic and commonly used. It's been the basis for countless songs and is easily recognizable when you hear it. It appears in music from nearly all genres: Latin, Jazz, Rock, R&B, Funk, Soul, Fusion, and Country. In fact, there are songs where this two-chord combination makes up the entire song. In other cases, this fragment may be just a section of the song. It is Imi7 to IV7.

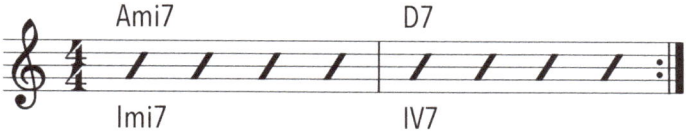

Listen to the track for this Module to hear the A Dorian Scale played over this progression.

The signature sound in this progression is the voice that moves from the minor 7th of the Imi7 to the major 3rd of the IV7. In A Dorian, the minor 7th of the Ami7, that's G, moves down a half step to the major 3rd of the D7. That's F#. That half-step move is one of the most exploited little ditties in popular music.

Try playing this short progression and pay attention to that movement.

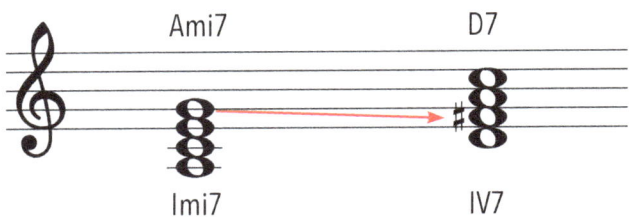

This next Dorian progression fragment is common, too. It's been the basis for many songs as well. This one is Imi7 to IImi7.

Listen to the track for this Module to hear the A Dorian Scale played over this progression.

There are songs where this two-chord combination makes up the entire song. The signature sound in this progression is the voice that moves from the minor 7th of the Imi7 to the 5th of the IImi7. In A Dorian, the minor 7th of the Ami7, that's G, moves down a half step to the perfect 5th of the Bmi7. That's F#. The half-step movement between these two scale degrees is the same as the first progression we looked at, Ami7 to D7.

Try playing this short progression and pay attention to that movement.

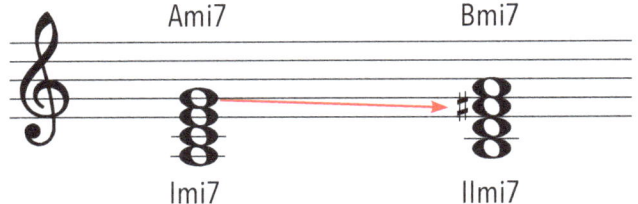

This next Dorian progression fragment is common, too. It's been the basis for many songs as well. This is Imi7 to Vmi7. The progression can also be found in Natural Minor.

Progression in A Dorian

Listen to the track for this Module to hear the A Dorian Scale played over this progression.

Like the others, there are songs where this two-chord combination makes up the entire song. The signature sound in this progression is the voice that moves from the 5th of the Imi7 to the minor 7th of the Vmi7. In A Dorian, the perfect 5th of the Ami7, that's E, moves down a whole step to the minor 7th of the Emi7. That's D.

Try playing this short progression and pay attention to that movement.

The Perfect 5th Moves to the ♭7

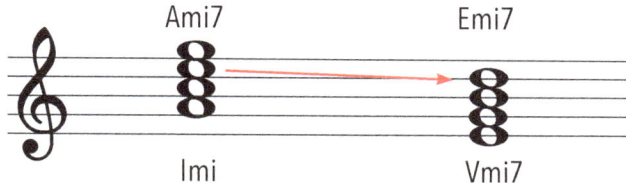

All of these progression scenarios will be addressed from a performance standpoint in the Improvisation Module.

Imi7, IImi7, IV7, and Vmi7 chords are the most commonly-used chords from the harmonized Dorian Scale.

FRETBOARD LOGIC

In the last Fretboard Logic Module you learned how to create the modes by adding notes to the pentatonic shells. This Module will focus on Dorian.

The goal in this Module is to learn all five patterns of Dorian by adding two notes to each of the five Minor Pentatonic shells. By deriving the Dorian Scale from the Minor Pentatonic Scale, the muscle memory you developed there will make Dorian feel and sound much more natural, and sooner.

Let's take another look at the side-by-side comparison of the Minor Pentatonic and Dorian Scales. Recall from the Theory Module that to create the Dorian Scale from a Minor Pentatonic Scale, you add a major 2nd and major 6th. That's it.

Dorian as a Derivative of the Minor Pentatonic Scale

Minor Pentatonic	*1*		*mi3*	*P4*	*P5*		*mi7*
Dorian	*1*	*ma2*	*mi3*	*P4*	*P5*	*ma6*	*mi7*

It's important to have a clear understanding of the correlation between the following shapes: the Minor Pentatonic and Dorian Scales and the chord and arpeggio built on the 1st scale degree.

Pattern I

The diagram on the left is the Pattern I Minor Pentatonic shell. To its right is the same shell with a major 2nd and a major 6th added. This is the Pattern I Dorian Mode. To its right is the mi7 chord voicing built on the 1st scale degree and on the far right is the mi7 arpeggio built on the 1st scale degree.

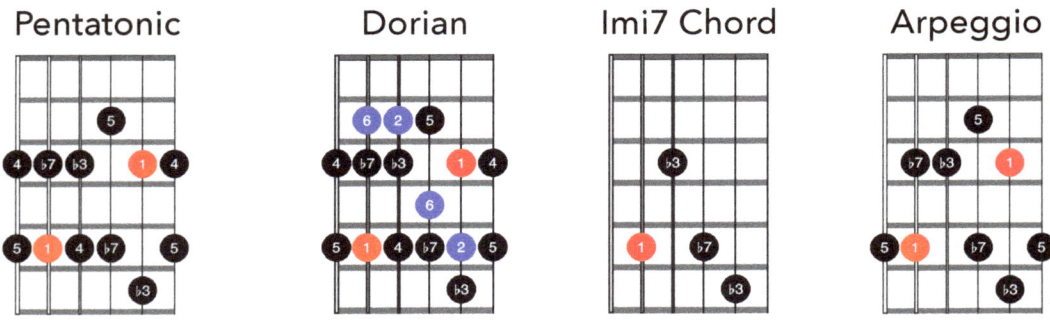

Pattern II

Let's take a look at Pattern II. The diagram on the left is the Pattern II Minor Pentatonic shell. To its right is the same shell with a major 2nd and a major 6th added. This is the Pattern II Dorian Mode. To its right is the mi7 chord voicing built on the 1st scale degree and on the far right is the mi7 arpeggio built on the 1st scale degree.

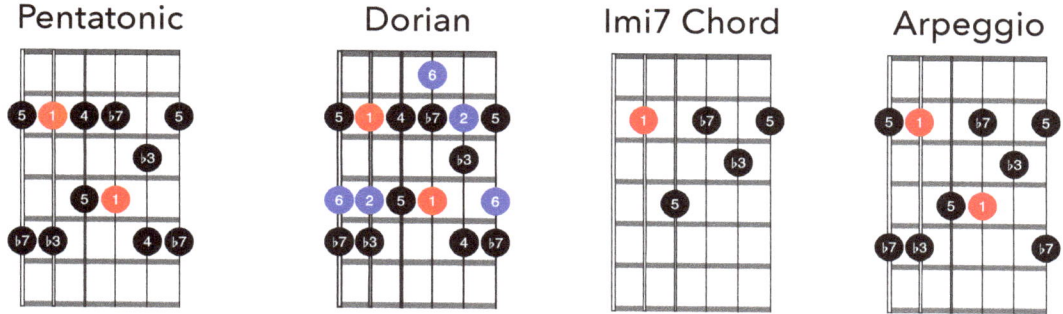

Pattern III

Let's do the same with Pattern III. Add a major 2nd and a major 6th to the Pentatonic to create the Pattern III Dorian Mode. Again, build the Imi7 chord voicing built on the 1st scale degree, and the mi7 arpeggio built on the 1st scale degree.

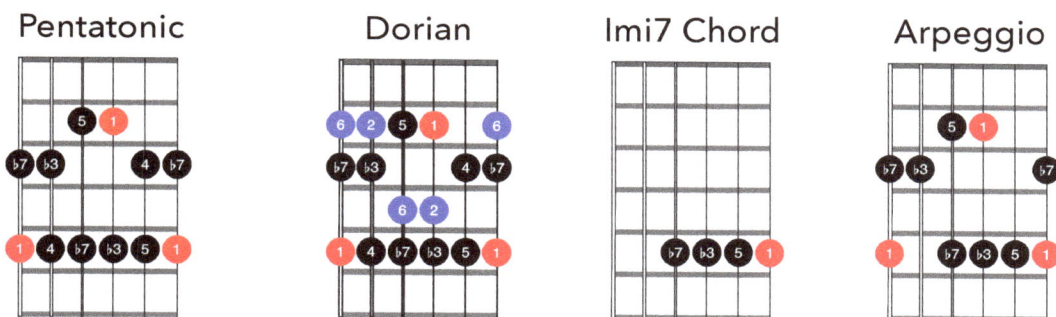

Pattern IV

It's the same process with Pattern IV. Add a major 2nd and a major 6th to the Pentatonic to create the Dorian Mode. The chord voicing and arpeggio are both built from the tonic.

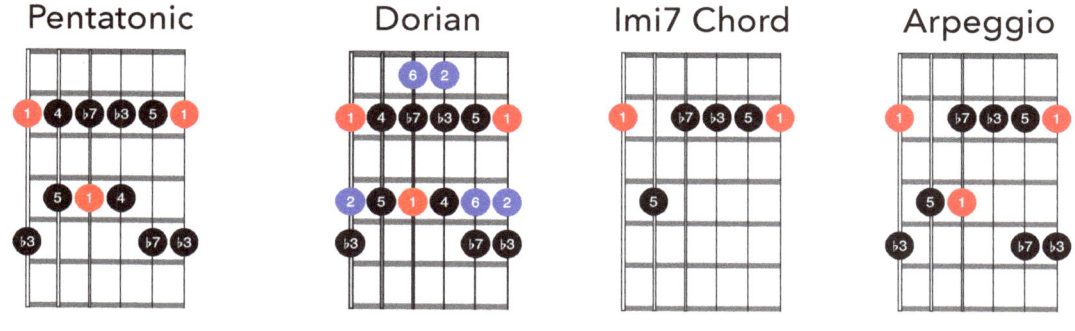

Pattern V

Finally, let's take a look at Pattern V. You should have figured out the process now for creating the Dorian Scale from the Pentatonic and deriving the Imi7 chord and arpeggio. It's all about the major 2nd and a major 6th.

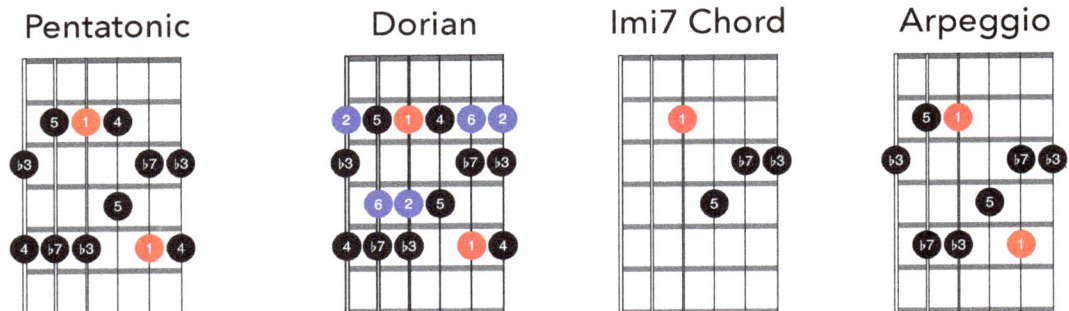

Don't feel like you need to memorize all these dots. Understanding the process is far more important. Truth be told, most guitarists find a couple patterns that become their go-to places on the fretboard. Over time you will add other patterns to your arsenal.

Dorian Harmony

Let's move on to Dorian harmony. It's important to get a feel for the progressions that clearly present the sound of Dorian. Here are two of the progression fragments that were presented in Theory that will also be used in the Improvisation Module.

Practice playing chords in a few ways with whatever groove you like or play along with the Improv tracks. You can use barre chords, shell voicings, and in some cases, open chords. The point here is to familiarize yourself with the sound.

Progressions in A Dorian

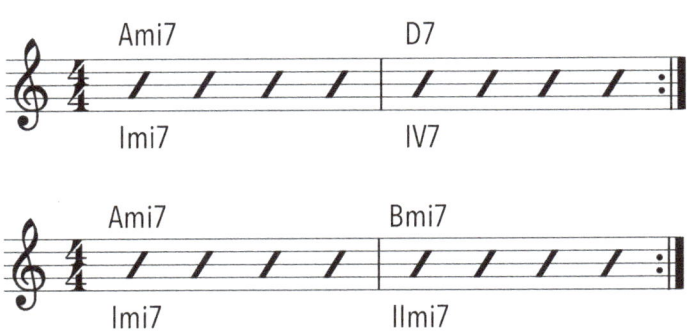

Keep in mind, the Imi7, IImi7, IV7, and Vmi7 chords are the most commonly-used chords from the harmonized Dorian Scale. Please relate all of this to the Family Tree. It's important that you keep that connection going!

RHYTHM GUITAR

Creating Parts for Classic Rock

Classic Rock was one of the first styles you studied in the Rhythm Guitar modules. Again, there are two objectives in these modules:

- Follow the chart
- Create a rhythm guitar part appropriate for the track

Like we did when creating parts for the Blues and Folk, let's approach this like we want to make a producer, musical director, or band leader happy. There are no exactly right or wrong parts but strive for having your part be one that fits. You may find it helpful to refer back to the Classic Rock rhythm guitar parts you created back in Level 2.

First, let's take a look at the road map in the following page and use your Chart-Reading Checklist.

Chart-Reading Checklist

1. Look at the top left corner where all the preliminary information is: Key signature, Time signature, Style
2. Note the Tempo
3. Scan the form
4. Seek out any figures that need to be played
5. Scan the chords for the ones that are new or difficult for you
6. Seek out more detailed instructions like dynamics, accents, and expression markings

As before, we will listen to the track from the perspective of what the song needs from you, the rhythm guitar player. You recall that in the Rock Rhythm Guitar modules you learned parts with power chords, super-shape triads, power chord-like inversions, and riffs. Let's put all that to work; let's put on our producer hat and listen to what this track needs.

In the Rock Rhythm Guitar modules in Level 2, I gave you a few suggestions as if I was the producer and wrote parts for you. But another producer might want something else. What if you were the producer, what parts do you think would sound good?

Classic Rock Song Chart

Again, your job is to create a part, record it, and listen back. Ask yourself, "would I want to hear this part on a recording?" Also ask yourself, "is there room for a second or even third rhythm guitar part?" If you can, share the part with other musicians you trust and see what they have to say. Once you have a part that sounds good to you, create another, then a third. Try layering parts. One of the most enjoyable parts of producing and recording music is building a track by layering parts. The point is to get experience creating parts, not to produce the "perfect part". There are no right or wrong parts, but you should be thinking in terms of what would a producer or band leader expect of you.

Revisit this chart and track as many times as you want. If you think of something new you want to try, record it and see how it sounds in the context of the rest of the band. Listen to new music give you news ideas and let that creativity happen.

CHART WRITING

So far you have taken the first three steps in writing chord charts. Step one was the Form Chart. Step two was counting measures and creating the crude first draft. Step three was writing down the chords.

Now that you have completed steps one, two, and three, it's time for step four where you locate the rhythm figures and riffs played by the whole band. These measures may be more complex and have a lot of information, so they may require more physical space on the page than measures with less complexity. The amount of information in each measure will be a factor in how you lay out the measures when we finally transfer this crude chart to staff paper.

Step Four

Here are the tasks for step four:

- Identify and mark every measure on the crude chord chart where there is a rhythm figure or riff.
- Transcribe and notate the rhythm figures and riffs on a separate piece of scrap staff paper.

Let's start by locating where there's a rhythm figure or riff by listening to the track provided for this Module. When you are done, your Form Chart should look something like this.

The Form Chart for "A Good Chart Sets You Free"

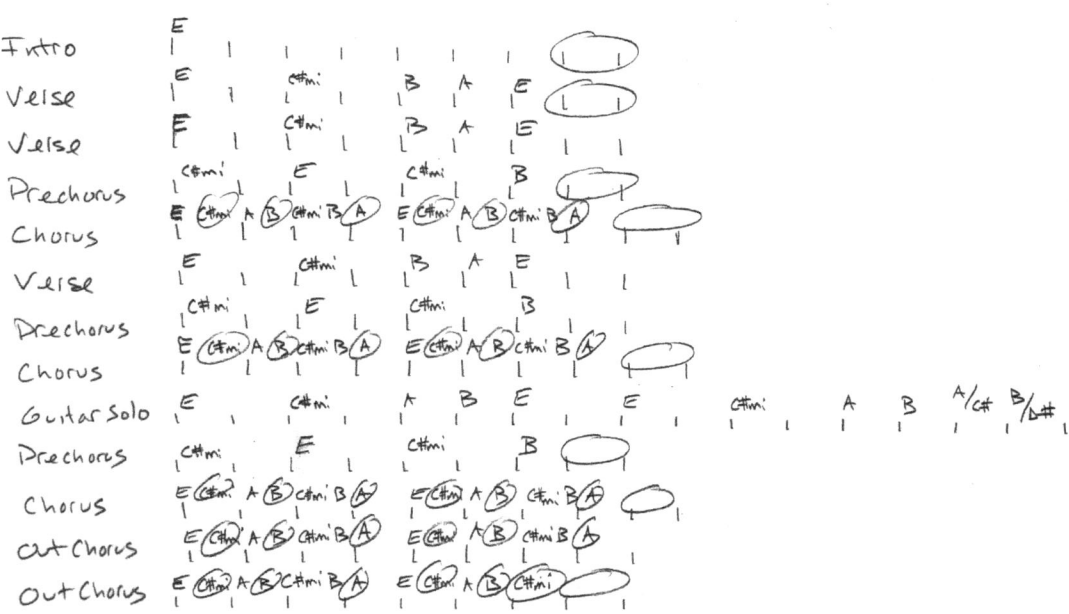

Fretboard Biology   Level 6 • Unit 4: Chart Writing   97

Now that we've located where the figures are, let's go back and figure out each one and notate them on a separate piece of staff paper. We'll use the same process as when we identified the chords. We'll listen to the sections and transcribe the melodic and rhythm figures. Go back to the track and transcribe rhythm figures and riffs. When you are done, those rhythm figures and riffs should look something like the ones below.

#1 Riff

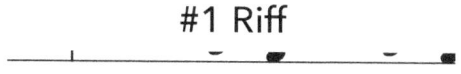

To be used: • *8th bar of Intro*
• *8th bar of 1st verse*
• *last bar of song*

#2 Rythm Figure

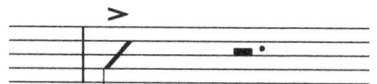

To be used: • *8th bar of Prechorus*
• *9th bar of Chorus*
• *2nd to last bar of song*

#3 Rythm Figure

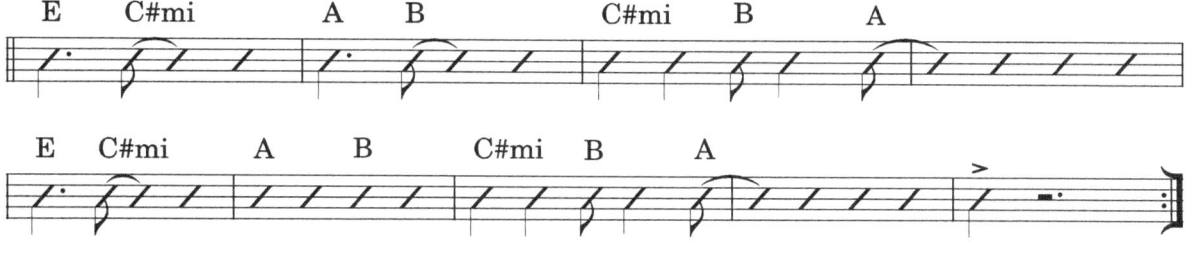

To be used: • *1st Chorus*
• *2nd Chorus*
• *3rd Chorus*

#4 Rythm Figure

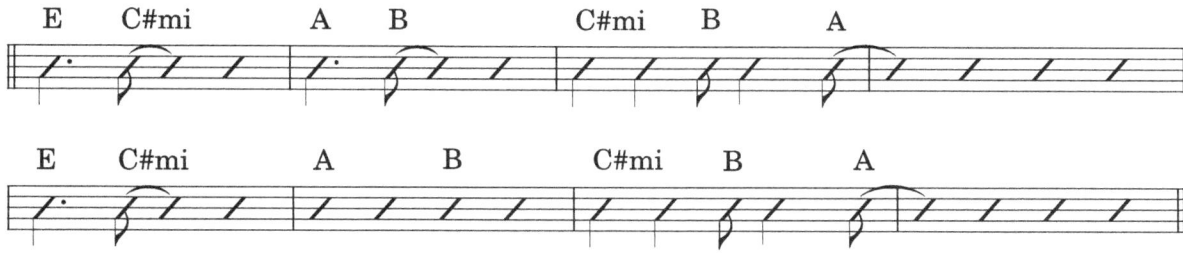

To be used: • *1st Outchorus*

#5 Rythm Figure and Riff

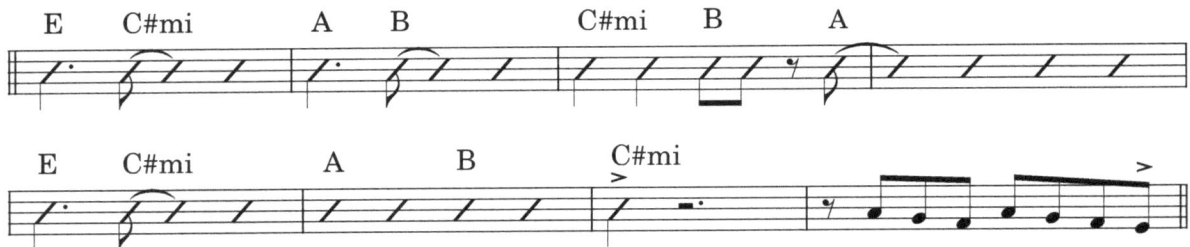

To be used: • 2nd Outchorus

When you actually start putting measures on staff paper, you'll strive to do several things:

- Start new sections on the left margin
- Start new four- or eight-bar phrases on the left margin when possible
- Limit the number of measures per line to even numbers when possible
- Limit the number of measures per line to four or eight bars when possible
- Not have measures look crowded with information

I'll repeat all of that again when we are to that stage, but be aware that everything just listed helps simplify how the reader's eyes travel across the page.

Use Four to Eight Bars Per Line

Here's the relationship between having four to eight bars per line to identifying the rhythm figures and riffs we just notated. You can place four measures (or more) on one line, but they don't all need to occupy an equal amount of physical space. For example, if measures one, two, and three of a four-bar phrase each have one chord, but measure four has a chord on each beat, the chart will look neater if the fourth measure is given more space. That way the chord symbols aren't all crammed into a small space.

The same goes for a rhythm figure or riff that might require a little more space to look neat. It's best to plan where these 'bigger' measures are going to be before you transfer all of this information from the crude chord chart to staff paper or a software program.

IMPROVISATION

Dorian Mode

You had a taste of playing the Dorian Scale over a static mi7 chord in the second Improvisation Module. The idea was to just get a feel for the sound. In this Module we'll get into some finer detail about the Dorian Scale. Remember that all of the scales and arpeggios you learn are tools and it's important to know how they work. Each note in every scale or arpeggio has a personality and will effect the listener in some way. At the very least, get to know how each note makes you feel against the chord.

First, I urge you to think of Dorian, and all the modes for that matter, as a pentatonic shell with two notes added. I'll remind you of the reason: Relating the modes to the Major Scale patterns comes with some troublesome muscle memory issues that result in the modes sounding vague. That's because your fingers want to travel through the physical pattern as if it was the Major Scale and not the desired mode. But by relating modes to pentatonic shells, you benefit from the muscle memory you've already developed playing the pentatonic scales. Your fingers travel through the pattern as if it's the Pentatonic Scale you already know so well, but with two additional notes. You had some experience with this in the last Improvisation Module. It may not seem like a big deal, but it is. After teaching this subject for many years, I've seen what a difference this pentatonic approach makes.

We'll be working in the Pattern IV Dorian Scale in this Module because it's derived from the Pattern IV Minor Pentatonic Scale, which is a pattern most guitarists are very comfortable with. But everything we discuss in this Module can be applied to any of the five patterns of the Dorian Scale.

Hearing the Dorian Sound

Let's start by playing the Pattern IV Minor Pentatonic Scale over the static Ami7 vamp provided in the link for this Module. Then play the Pattern IV Dorian Scale. Experiment playing the Minor Pentatonic for a moment and then Dorian Scale over the same Ami7 vamp.

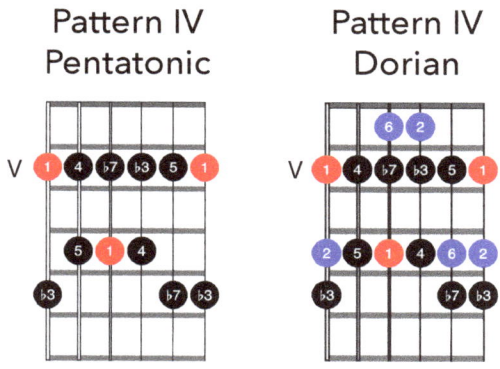

Both the Pentatonic and Dorian Scales sound minor, they both fit nicely, and they both have the five notes of the Minor Pentatonic Scale in common. As we discussed earlier, the Dorian Scale has the added major 2nd and major 6th. These two notes are the notes that distinguish Dorian from Minor Pentatonic. The major 6th is the note that distinguishes Dorian from the Natural Minor Scale.

You recall that there are four chord tones within the scale and seven notes in the scale. The notes that are not the chord tones are the major 2nd, perfect 4th, and major 6th. And it's important to see how the four chord tones and the other three notes combine to create the scale.

Notes of the Dorian Scale

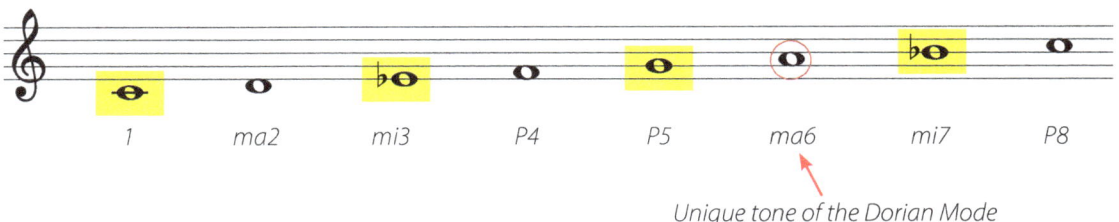

Unique tone of the Dorian Mode

Remember the Dorian Scale has no avoid tones. That's why it's such a great option to use over a static mi7 chord. The major 2nd, perfect 4th, and major 6th are each a whole step above chord tones. I encourage you to play both the minor pentatonic scale and the Dorian scale over a static Imi7 chord to so you get a feel for the Dorian sound.

Each note in every scale or arpeggio has a personality and an effect on the listener. Play each note of the scale against the static chord vamp provided on the track. The exercise is to dwell on every note of the scale and experience how each one makes you feel when played over the chord. Come up with your own adjectives to describe how you hear each note of the scale against the chord and work at remembering them. If you know the 'personality' of a note, you can use it to set a mood to start a phrase with or perhaps find a note to dwell on in a solo.

Spend some time soloing on a static mi7 chord sampling the unique effect of each scale tone. Experiment with combinations, too.

Progressions in Dorian

Next, let's look at some progressions. In the Theory Module you learned some of the standard progression fragments that highlight the most commonly used chords from the harmonized Dorian Scale. Let's review the chords of the harmonized Dorian Scale.

Dorian Mode Chord Qualities

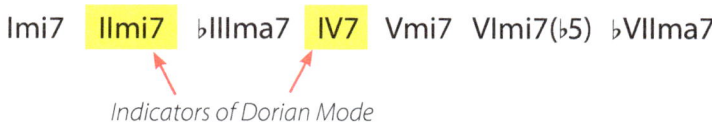

Indicators of Dorian Mode

Of these, IV7 and IImi7 are the most common chords from Dorian other than Imi7. In fact, when you are first scanning a progression for analysis clues, IV7 and IImi7 are strong indicators that the progression is in the Dorian world, at least momentarily. Why is that? IV7 and IImi7 aren't part of any of the other modes. They are unique to Dorian.

It's important to practice soloing on the most common short progressions from the harmonized Dorian Scale. This first two-chord progression is a classic and probably the most recognizable as Dorian. It is 'signature' Dorian. And remember, in the world of modes, IV7 is unique to Dorian. It is Imi7 to IV7.

Progression in A Dorian

Listen to the track for this Module and practice soloing over the progression using the Dorian Scale. A demo of my soloing is in the transcription below.

Level 6 Unit 4 • Dorian Demo 1

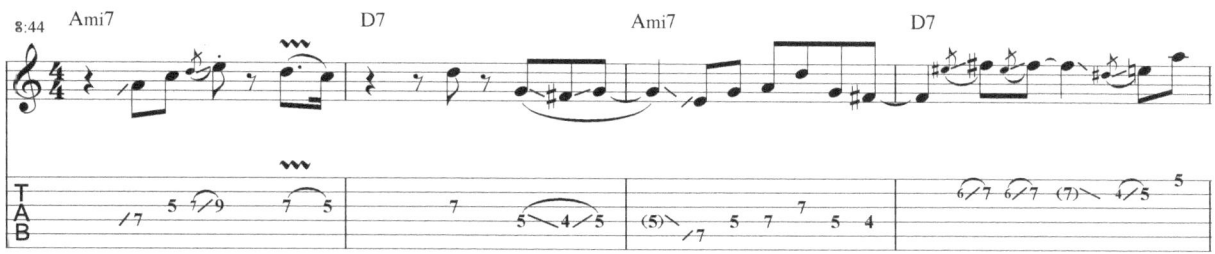

The signature sound in this progression is the voice that moves from the minor 7th of the Imi7 to the major 3rd of the IV7. In A Dorian, the minor 7th of the Ami7, that's G, moves down a half step to the major 3rd of the D7. That's F#. This half-step move is one of the most exploited little moves in popular music.

The ♭7 Moves to the Major 3rd

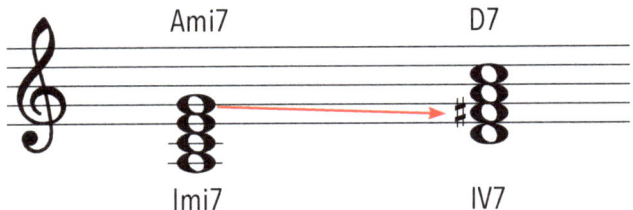

Let's work that a little. Go back to the track and play around with the movement between the G and F#. Pay attention to how that sounds. You're playing chord tones when you exploit the G to F#. The transcription below is a demo of this. You can use this as inspiration to develop your own vocabulary.

Level 6 Unit 4 • Dorian Demo 2

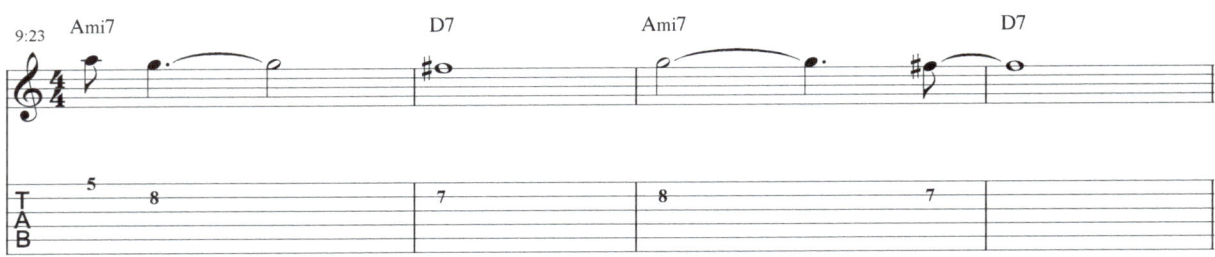

Fretboard Biology — Level 6 • Unit 4: Improvisation

What other chord tones can you take advantage of? It's helpful to see both arpeggios together in-position. Here is the Pattern IV A Dorian Scale with the Ami7 (Imi7) arpeggio and the D7 (IV7) arpeggio all in-position.

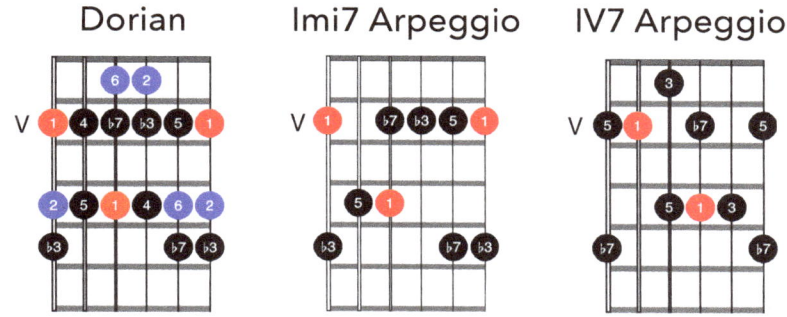

Practice soloing over this vamp blending the Dorian Scale and the arpeggio of each chord.

Level 6 Unit 4 • Dorian Demo 3

What notes are common between the two chords? A and C. That means they can be used on either chord or held for some time.

What notes are not in both chords? E and G from the Ami7, and D and F# from the D7. Those notes can mark the chord change, but don't feel like you need to avoid any scale tone on either chord.

This next Dorian progression fragment is common, too. It is Imi7 to IImi7.

Progression in A Dorian

Listen to the track and practice playing the A Dorian Scale over it.

Level 6 Unit 4 • Dorian Demo 4

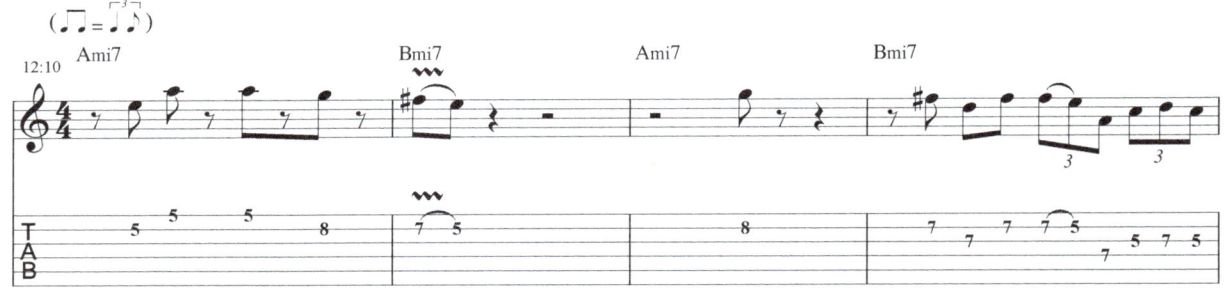

The signature sound in this progression is the voice that moves from the minor 7th of the Imi7 to the 5th of the IImi7. In A Dorian, the minor 7th of the Ami7, that's G, moves down a half step to the perfect 5th of the Bmi7. That's F#. That half-step move is the same as the first progression we looked at. Let's work that a little.

The ♭7 Moves to the Major 3rd

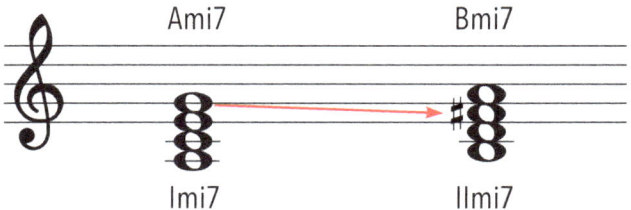

Fretboard Biology Level 6 • Unit 4: Improvisation

The transcription below is a demo of this. You can use this as inspiration to develop your own vocabulary.

Level 6 Unit 4 • Dorian Demo 5

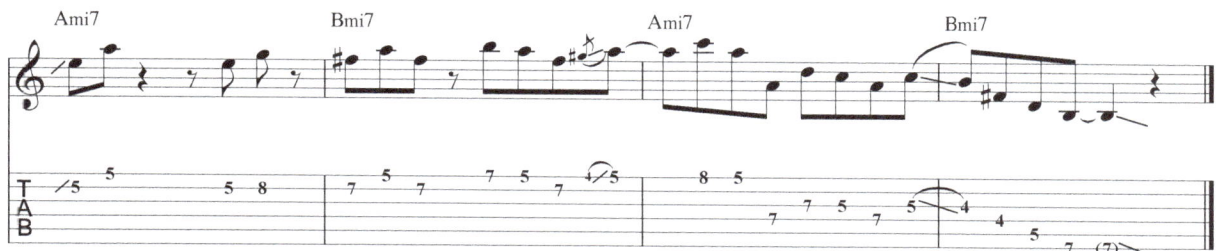

What other chord tones can you take advantage of? It's helpful to see both arpeggios together in-position. Here is the Pattern IV A Dorian Scale with the Ami7 (Imi7) arpeggio and the Bmi7 (IImi7) arpeggio all in-position.

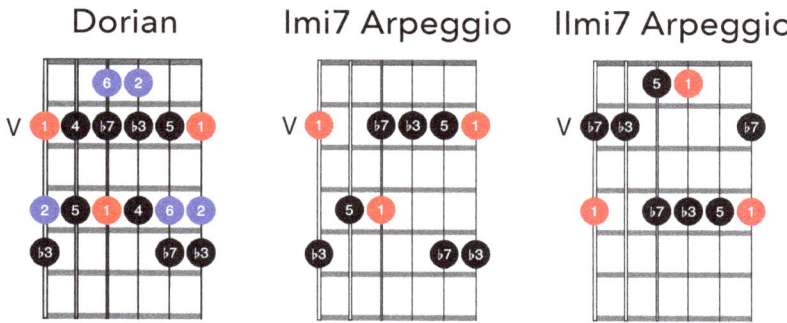

Practice soloing over this vamp blending the Dorian Scale and the arpeggio of each chord. What notes are common between the two chords? Only A. That means it can be used on either chord or held for some time.

What notes are not in both chords? C, E, and G from the Ami7 and B, D, and F#. Those notes can mark the changes, but don't feel like you need to avoid any scale tone on either chord.

PRACTICE

Theory

- ❏ Know the construction of the Dorian Scale.
- ❏ Know the most common Dorian progression fragments.

Fretboard Logic

- ❏ Learn the five patterns of the Dorian Scale.
- ❏ Know how to add a major 2nd and major 6th to a minor pentatonic scale to create the Dorian scale.

Rhythm Guitar

- ❏ Follow the chart and create and record one or more rhythm guitar parts.

Chart Writing

- ❏ Know how add rhythm figures and riffs to the Crude Chord Chart.

Improvisation

- ❏ Practice playing solos over the most common Dorian progression fragments.

UNIT 5

Learning Modules

> **Theory** - Composite Minor

> **Fretboard Logic** - Visualizing Parallel Minor Scales within the Same Octave Shape

> **Rhythm Guitar** - Creating a Rhythm Guitar Part for a Reggae Song

> **Chart Writing** - Using One-Bar, Two-Bar, and Four-Bar Repeats on a Chart

> **Improvisation** - Improvising over Progressions with Chords from Parallel Minor Scales

> **Practice** - Continue Practice Routine Development

The tracks for this Unit can be found at the following link:

https://fretboardbiology.com/book6/#u5

THEORY

Your knowledge of harmonic analysis has grown by leaps and bounds. You know how to analyze chord progressions that are all diatonic as well as progressions with modal interchange. You learned how to analyze inversions, too. In Level 5 you learned harmonic analysis for minor modal interchange. That's where a chord progression based in Natural Minor borrows chords and melody notes from the parallel Harmonic Minor Scale. You have also learned harmonic analysis for secondary dominants. You've come a long way.

In the last Module you learned more about the Dorian Mode and progressions that consist of chords that are all from the harmonized Dorian Scale. Before getting into the detail of the other modes, let's shift our focus for a couple of units to a different but related topic. Now that you have some experience with the Dorian sound, let's expand the concept of minor modal interchange.

Let's review what that means. It's common for progressions in a minor key to draw upon one or more parallel minor scales for both chords and melody, and more than just the Natural Minor Scale and Harmonic Minor Scale as you learned in Level 5. We're going to add Dorian Minor to the list of scales used in a minor modal interchange way. We've been using the term minor modal interchange to describe the mix of parallel minor scales.

Composite Minor

There's a another descriptive term I like to use: Composite Minor.

- Composite means to combine different elements.
- Composite Minor means a combination of several minor scales.

For now let's consider minor modal interchange, that is, Composite Minor, to be the combined use of these three parallel minor scales:

- Natural Minor
- Harmonic Minor
- Dorian Minor

Knowing that, consider a song written in the key of C minor. It's common for the primary harmonic and melodic orientation and the key signature to be that of C Natural Minor and for single or small groups of chords and melody notes to be from the parallel Harmonic Minor and/or Dorian Minor Scales.

Here is a progression that's a good example of this. Let's listen to the track provided for this Module, analyze it, and determine from what scale or scales each chord could have originated.

Progression in C Minor

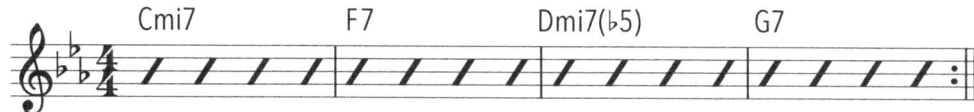

If we look at this progression, we can see that:

- Cmi7 is the I chord in both C Natural Minor and Dorian Minor.
- F7 is the IV7 in C Dorian Minor. It does not belong to C Natural Minor or C Harmonic Minor.
- Dmi7(♭5) is the IImi7(♭5) in both C Natural Minor and C Harmonic Minor.
- G7 is the V7 in C Harmonic Minor.

After this analysis, it's clear that there is no single minor scale that fits all of the chords. Some of the chords belong to Natural Minor, others to either Harmonic Minor or Dorian Minor, and some chords belong to two of the parallel minor scales.

Clearly the key is C minor, but it's C minor in a broader sense. To play the 'right' sound or what we call 'inside sound' for each chord, we need to make slight adjustments to accommodate the sound and chord tones of each chord. We need to make subtle shifts to play different C minor scales for different chords.

For a better understanding of the world of parallel minor scales, or Composite Minor, examine the following table, which compares some of the parallel minor scales.

Minor Scale Comparison

Minor Pentatonic	1		mi3	P4		P5		mi7
Natural Minor	1	ma2	mi3	P4		P5	mi6	mi7
Dorian	1	ma2	mi3	P4		P5	ma6	mi7
Harmonic Minor	1	ma2	mi3	P4		P5	mi6	ma7
Blues	1		mi3	P4	D5	P5		mi7

What do all these minor scales have in common?

The tonic, minor 3rd, perfect 4th, and perfect 5th. What's significant is that they all have a minor 3rd, and that's what makes them minor scales. It's also interesting that the tonic, minor 3rd, and perfect 5th spell a minor triad.

For our purposes, let's choose a smaller group of these parallel minor scales to examine more closely. We'll take the Minor Pentatonic and Blues Scales out of the equation.

Composite Minor Scales

Natural Minor	*1*	*ma2*	*mi3*	*P4*	*P5*	*mi6*	*mi7*
Dorian	*1*	*ma2*	*mi3*	*P4*	*P5*	*ma6*	*mi7*
Harmonic Minor	*1*	*ma2*	*mi3*	*P4*	*P5*	*mi6*	*ma7*

What do the Natural Minor, Harmonic Minor, and Dorian Minor Scales all have in common? They're the identical from 1st to the 5th scale degree. The difference between them is only in the 6th and 7th scale degrees. Are these really different scales or just slight variations? That's a good argument topic for a long road trip.

I want to stress this point: The whole idea of a minor tonality is centered around the minor 3rd of the scale. It's the minor 3rd that defines the sound as minor. After that, the various flavors of minor are defined by which other scale tones are present.

I urge you to think of the 'world of minor' as a tonal environment with these constants: the tonic and the minor 3rd (and usually a perfect 5th). Beyond that, each scale in the family of minor scales has a different combination of the other possible scale degrees: 2nds, 4ths, 6ths, and 7ths.

I believe the most pragmatic way to approach the world of minor is to think of the minor triad at the core and then what other scale degrees are added. The other scale degrees that can be added will color the minor environment, each in a unique way. Focus on the three-note triad first (and usually the 4th is perfect), then the quality of the 7th next. After that, the 2nd and 6th.

The three scales we are including in Composite Minor so far can all be harmonized, as you know. The use of the chords from these harmonized scales is at the heart of this discussion.

For a better understanding of the chords of the harmonized parallel minor scales, examine the following table, which shows the three most commonly mixed harmonized parallel minor scales: Natural Minor, Harmonic Minor, and Dorian Minor.

Composite Minor Harmonized 7th Chords

NAT MINOR:	Imi7	IImi7(b5)	bIIIma7	IVmi7	Vmi7	bVIma7	bVII7
	Cmi7	Dmi7(b5)	Ebma7	Fmi7	Gmi7	Abma7	Bb7
DORIAN:	Imi7	IImi7	bIIIma7	IV7	Vmi7	VImi7(b5)	bVIIma7
	Cmi7	Dmi7	Ebma7	F7	Gmi7	Ami7(b5)	Bbma7
HARMONIC:	Imi(ma7)	IImi7(b5)	bIIIma7(#5)	IVmi7	V7	bVIma7	VII°7
	Cmi(ma7)	Dmi7(b5)	Ebma7(#5)	Fmi7	G7	Abma7	B°7

Think of all of these chords as normal components of the minor tonal environment. But know the most common chords from Dorian used in Composite Minor are IIm7 and IV7. This is important; memorize it.

And also know the most common chords from Harmonic Minor used in Composite Minor are V7 and VIIdim7. This is important; memorize it.

This is very important information and should be front and center in your mind as the most important takeaways from this Module.

FRETBOARD LOGIC

In the Theory Module you learned about minor modal interchange and another more descriptive term, Composite Minor. In the next two Modules, we'll compare and contrast scale patterns of the parallel scales most commonly used in Composite Minor situations. Remember that Natural Minor, Dorian, and Harmonic Minor are identical to the 5th scale degree. It's only the 6th and 7th scale degree that vary.

Let's take a look at the Minor Pentatonic shell again, to see how the scales of Composite Minor relate:

Scales of Composite Minor

Minor Pentatonic	*1*		*mi3*	*P4*	*P5*		*mi7*
Natrual Minor	*1*	*ma2*	*mi3*	*P4*	*P5*	*mi6*	*mi7*
Dorian	*1*	*ma2*	*mi3*	*P4*	*P5*	*ma6*	*mi7*
Harmonic Minor	*1*	*ma2*	*mi3*	*P4*	*P5*	*mi6*	*ma7*

Next, let's take this information and transfer it to the fretboard using the Pattern IV Octave Shape. Take a look at the fretboard diagrams below.

- On the left is the Minor Pentatonic shell (for reference)
- To its right is the Natural Minor Scale
- To its right is the Dorian Scale
- On the far right is the Harmonic Minor Scale

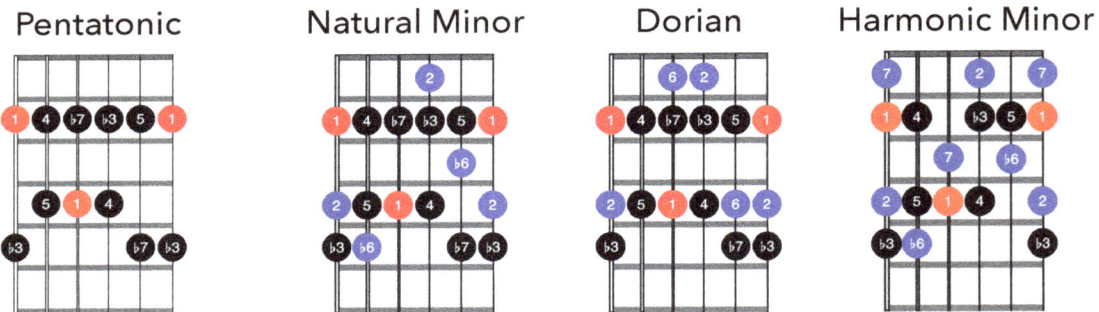

The point is that there is no need to see all of these as completely different shapes. They are derivatives of the pentatonic shell, or you could say, variations of the Natural Minor Scale.

Let's look at a progression in C minor. It's common for the primary harmonic and melodic orientation and the key signature to be to C Natural Minor and for single or small groups of chords and melody notes to be from the parallel Harmonic Minor and/or Dorian Minor Scales.

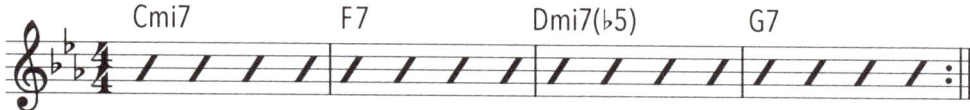

Let's analyze this example below to determine from what scale or scales each chord could have originated.

- Cmi7 is the I chord in both C Natural Minor and Dorian Minor.
- F7 is the IV7 in C Dorian Minor. It does not belong to C Natural Minor or C Harmonic Minor.
- Dmi7(♭5) is the IImi7(♭5) in both C Natural Minor and C Harmonic Minor.
- G7 is the V7 in C Harmonic Minor.

It's clear that there is no single minor scale that fits all of the chords. Some of the chords belong to Natural Minor and others to either Harmonic Minor or Dorian Minor. Some chords belong to two of the parallel minor scales and some to only one. To navigate this progression efficiently on the fretboard in the Improvisation Module, we need to first locate each of the scales in the same location on the fretboard. Under each chord of the progression is the diagram for its recommended scale and the in-position arpeggio.

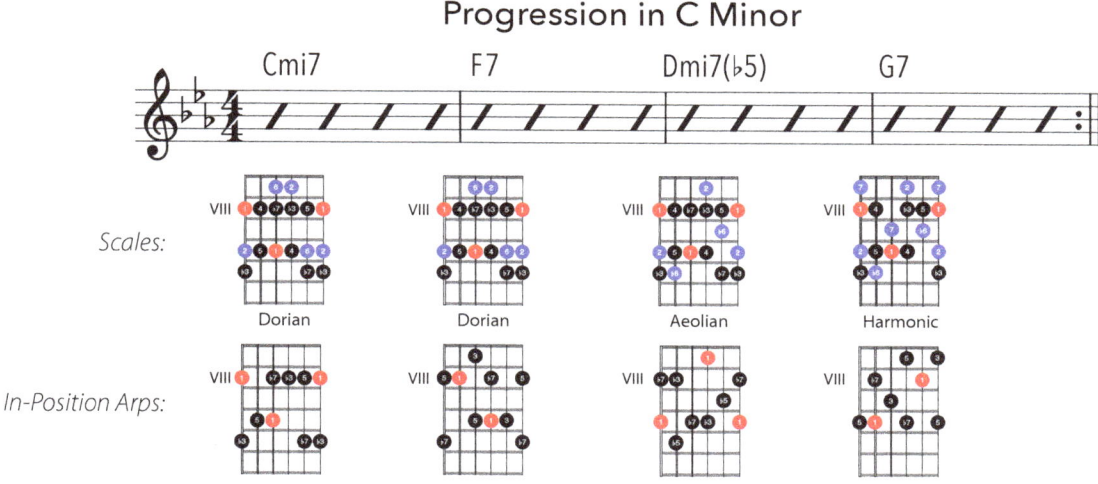

Notice that all theoretical options are not shown above, just the ones discussed as the best options. You'll use these shapes in the Improvisation Module coming up. It's also helpful to see the in-position arpeggios so you can target chord tones. It's important to remember that IV7 is the most commonly used chord from Dorian and V7 is the most commonly used chord from Harmonic Minor.

RHYTHM GUITAR

Creating Parts for Reggae Songs

You studied Reggae earlier in the Level 3 Rhythm Guitar modules. Remember that in this Rhythm Guitar Module, we have two objectives:

- Follow the chart
- Create a rhythm guitar part appropriate for the track

Like we did when creating parts for the Blues and Folk, let's approach this like we want to make a producer, musical director, or band leader happy. There are no exactly right or wrong parts but strive for having your part be one that fits. You may find it helpful to refer back to the Reggae rhythm guitar parts you created back in Level 3.

First, let's take a look at the road map in the following page and use your Chart-Reading Checklist.

Chart-Reading Checklist

1. Look at the top left corner where all the preliminary information is: Key signature, Time signature, Style
2. Note the Tempo
3. Scan the form
4. Seek out any figures that need to be played
5. Scan the chords for the ones that are new or difficult for you
6. Seek out more detailed instructions like dynamics, accents, and expression markings

As before, we will listen to the track from the perspective of what the song needs from you, the rhythm guitar player. Refer back to your Reggae rhythm vocabulary and put that to work. Put on your producer hat and listen to what this track needs.

In the Reggae Rhythm Guitar modules you learned about 'chop' parts for your fretting hand that primarily used triads, as well as popcorn-like riffs that live inside the pentatonic shells. You also learned parts that used muting and scratches. Remember that a popcorn riff or a line where you double the bass player may be a signature part of the song. There's usually room for a second or third guitar part in Reggae; maybe a combination of the chop and popcorn. It's a lot of fun to build a track by layering parts.

Reggae Song Chart

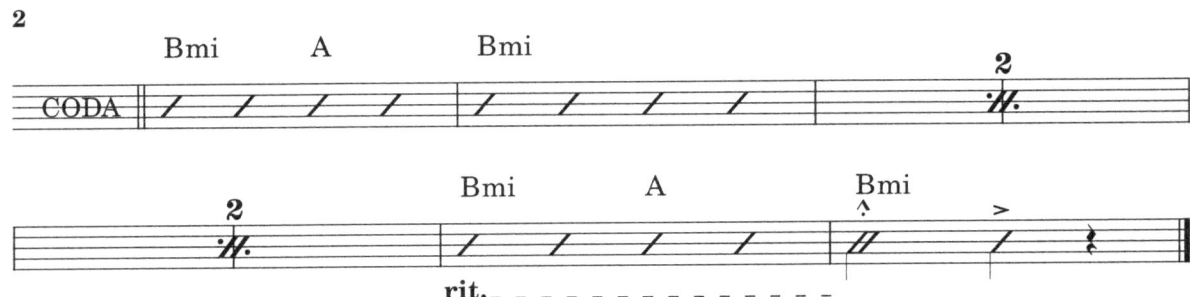

The Reggae Rhythm Guitar modules in Level 3 gave you a few suggestions as if I was the producer and wrote parts for you. Now you take on the role of a producer and listen for what the song needs from the rhythm guitar player. Create a part, record it, and listen back. Ask yourself, "would I want to hear this part on a recording?" Also ask yourself, "is there room for a second or even third rhythm guitar part?" If you can, share the part with other musicians you trust and see what they have to say. Once you have a part that sounds good to you, create another, then a third. Try layering parts.

Again, using the track for this Module, create some rhythm parts.

CHART WRITING

In this Module you'll finally get a chance to consolidate the chart by using the various repeat devices. But before we get started, let's quickly review the steps we have taken so far. Step one was the Form Chart. Step two was counting measures and creating the first draft of the crude first draft. Step three was writing down the chords. Step four was locating and notating rhythm figures and riffs.

Step Five

In step five, you will learn how to consolidate the measures of a song to reduce the number actually written on the page. To do this, think about the hierarchy of repeat signs:

- One-, two-, and four-bar repeats
- Opposing repeats
- Jump marks

In just a moment we'll work through the Crude Chord Chart looking for places to use one-, two-, and four-bar repeats first. That's the focus of this Module. The next couple of Modules will focus on start and end repeat bar lines, endings, and jump marks.

One-Bar Repeats

One-bar repeats mean to play what was played in the previous measure. They can save a bit of space if the measure that's being replaced has a lot of information. The diagonal line and two dots don't take up very much space.

One-Bar Repeat

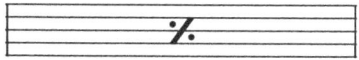

One-bar repeat in an example: this means to play the rhythm figure shown in the previous measure, even though the chord has changed from A to Bmi.

Another benefit of using the one-bar repeat is that it tells the reader to play what was just played without rewriting it. That seems obvious but here is the benefit: If the measure was written out a second, third, or even more times, the reader's mind has to concentrate that much more in the event that these subsequent measures have different information.

The reader won't know if it's new information until they read it. Then when they read they think, "oh, I just played that." That may seem like a small thing but from a reader's standpoint, it's one less thing to occupy brain space.

Here's a four-bar example written without using one-bar repeats.

Repeating Rhythm Figures without Repeats

Repeating Rhythm Figures with Repeats

Notice that because of the one-bar repeats the reader can see at a glance what to play for the entire four-bar phrase.

Two-Bar Repeats

Two-bar repeats mean to play what was played in the previous two measures. They can save space because the symbol (the vertical line and two diagonal lines) can use roughly the space of one measure.

Two-Bar Repeat

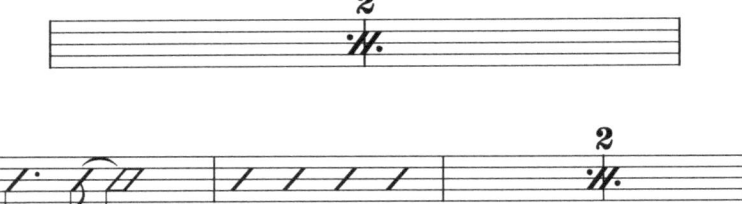

For example, if an eight-bar phrase is really a two-bar phrase played four times, bars one and two should be written out using a normal amount of space. The next three times the two-bar phrase is played can be written with three two-bar repeats. Each one of those uses the space of one measure. With the first two measures written out and the three two-bar repeats that each take the space of one measure, the entire eight-bar phrase can be written on one line using the space of five measures.

Eight-Bar Example without Two-Bar Repeats

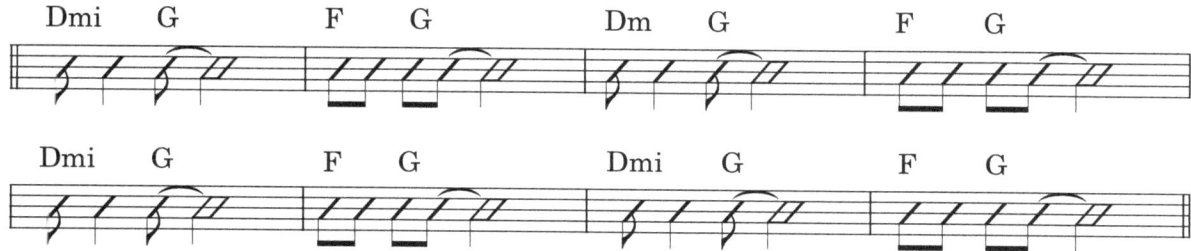

Eight-Bar Example with Two-Bar Repeats

At a glance, you can see what to play for the entire eight-bar phrase. This means the reader can absorb eight measures of music at a glance. That's important.

Four-Bar Repeats

Four-bar repeats are frowned upon by some musicians but as you learned in the Chart Reading modules, they are used often enough. They can save a lot of space because the symbol (the vertical line and four diagonal lines) can use roughly the space of one or two measures.

Four-Bar Repeat

For example, if a 16-bar phrase is really a four-bar phrase played four times, bars one, two, three, and four can be written out using a normal amount of space. The next three times the four-bar phrase is played can be written with three four-bar repeats. Each one of those uses the space of one measure, but usually it's best to use a little more space so it seems proportionate. With the first four measures written out and the three four-bar repeats that each take the space of one larger measure, the entire 16-bar phrase can be written on two lines using the space of seven measures.

You could, in extreme cases and if the content permits, fit the entire 16-bar phrase on one line. Keep in mind when you make this decision, you're balancing clarity and readability with saving space. There are some people who use this kind of symbol to repeat other numbers of bars, even odd-numbered phrases like three, five, or seven bars. This is usually frowned upon in most formal or professional chart writing environments.

Don't forget the simile tool. Simile simply means to perform a passage as you did before or, in a similar way. It can be used to cover a broad range of musical events, from melodies and riffs to rhythm figures or a specific articulation.

Now, Let's look at our second draft and check for opportunities to use one-bar, two-bar, and four-bar repeats. The brackets indicate one-bar or two-bar repeat markings.

The Form Chart for "A Good Chart Sets You Free"

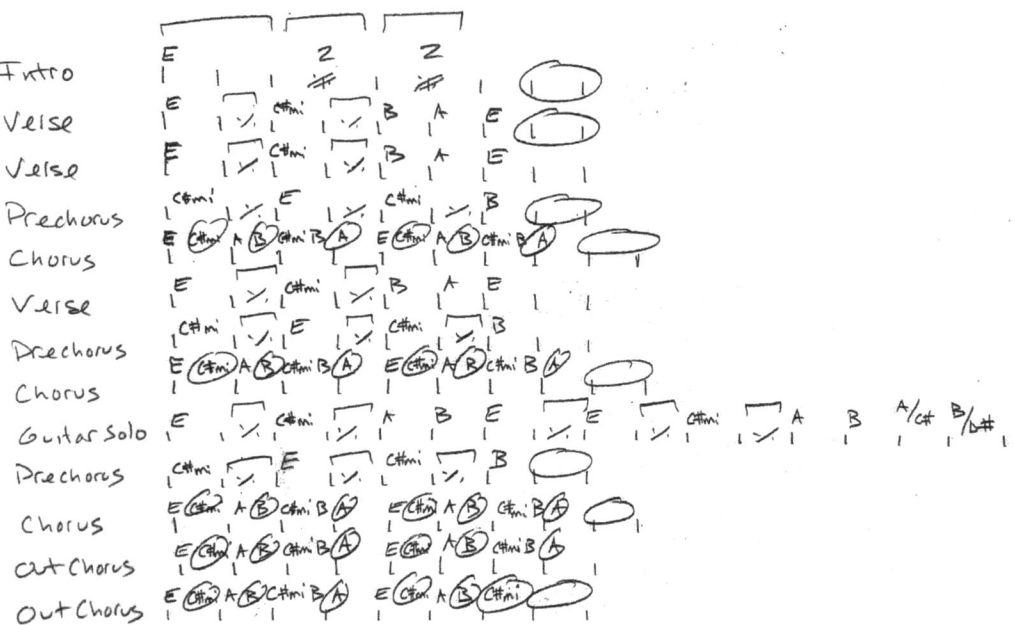

IMPROVISATION

You learned a lot of detail about using the Dorian Scale in the last Module. One of the most important things you learned is that IV7 and IImi7 are the most common chords from Dorian used in progressions. So when you are first scanning a progression for analysis clues, IV7 and IImi7 are strong indicators that the progression has chords from the Dorian world, at least momentarily. IV7 and IImi7 belong to Dorian.

Back in Level 5 you learned a lot of detail about using the Harmonic Minor Scale. One of the most important things you learned then is that V7 and VIIdim7 are the most common chords from Harmonic Minor used in minor modal interchange situations. So when you are first scanning a progression for analysis clues, V7 and VIIdim7 are strong indicators that the progression has chords from the Harmonic Minor world, at least momentarily: V7 and VIIdim7 are unique to Harmonic Minor.

You learned about Composite Minor progressions in the Theory Module for this Unit. Composite Minor is another word for modal interchange between parallel minor scales. And like in the modal interchange you studied in Level 4, where major keys borrow from their parallel minor, Composite Minor is so common and subtle that the shift is almost undetectable. The three scales involved in Composite Minor are identical up to the 5th scale degree. The only variation is in the 6th and 7th scale degrees.

We're going to put all of that knowledge to work in this Module and learn to solo through progressions with chords from parallel Natural Minor, Dorian Minor, and Harmonic Minor scales. This requires playing the right scales for each chord. And remember, the only difference is in the 6th and 7th scale degrees, so it's really not changing scales completely, but more adjusting the 6th and 7th scale degrees to accommodate certain chords. Keeping this in mind keeps this whole Composite Minor discussion in perspective.

Let's work on the same progression used in Theory and Fretboard Logic and we'll work within Pattern IV.

Progression in C Minor

First, listen to the track for this Module. I suggest playing some Pattern IV C Minor Pentatonic key-center ideas to get a feel for the sound of the progression. All the notes of the scale won't fit on G7 but that's OK for now. You could also mix in some Blues lines with the Minor Pentatonic Scale.

Next, let's get more specific with regard to scale and arpeggio choice:

- Cmi7 is the I chord in both C Natural Minor and Dorian Minor. We'll use C Dorian since it's followed by F7, that's IV7, which is from Dorian. So we'll use the same scale for the first two chords.
- Dmi7(♭5) is the IImi7(♭5) in both C Natural Minor and C Harmonic Minor, but we'll use Natural Minor to save B, the impactful leading tone, for the G7.
- G7 is the V7 in C Harmonic Minor so that's the best choice there.

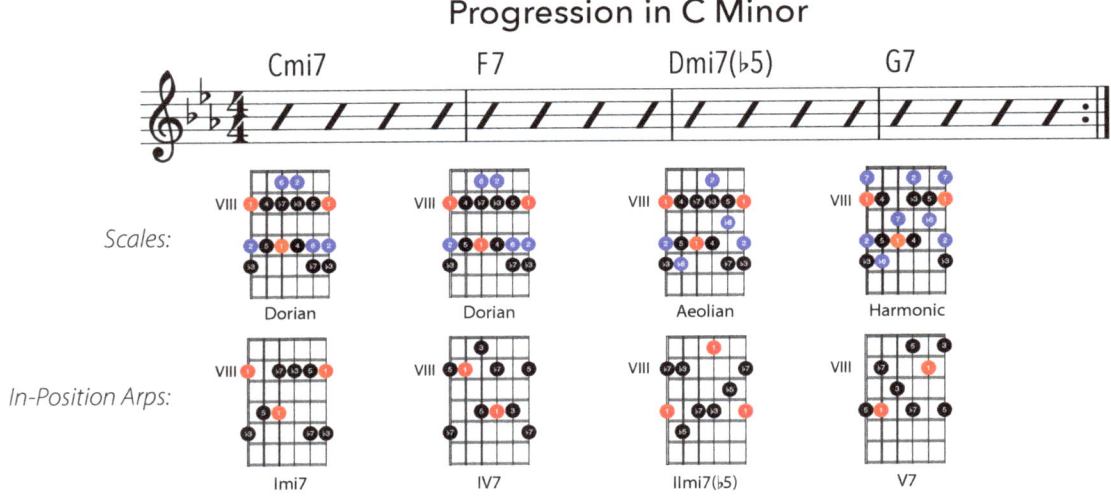

Play through the progression with the track, experimenting with the scales:
- C Dorian on Cmi7 and F7
- C Natural Minor on Dmi7(♭5)
- C Harmonic Minor on G7

Now listen to the demo and watch the transcription provided.

Level 6 Unit 5 • Composite Minor Demo 1

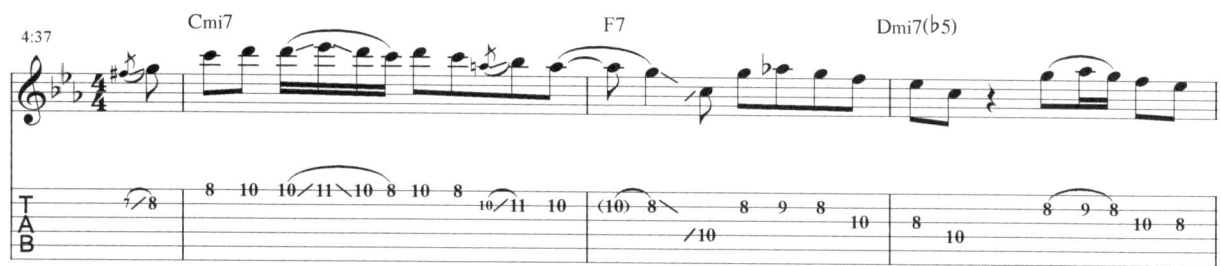
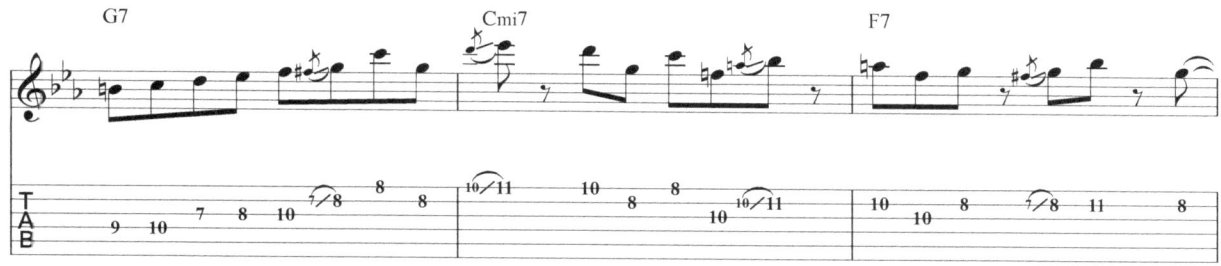
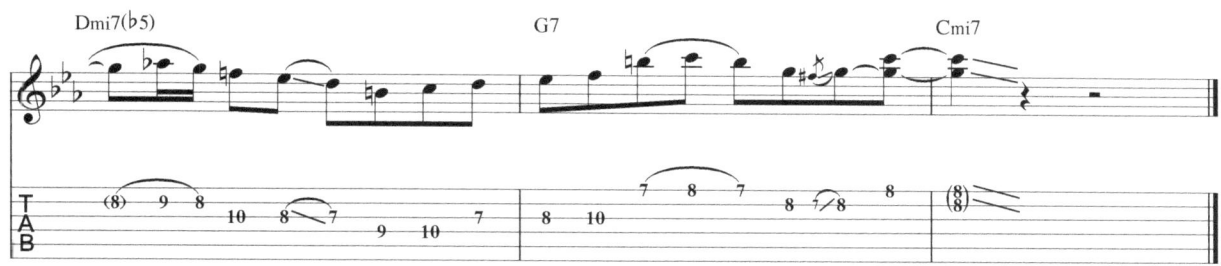

Next, let's zero in on the 6th and 7th scale degrees because that's the only difference between the three scales. Specifically, include the major 6th and minor 7th on Cmi7 and F7, the minor 6th and minor 7th on Dmi7(♭5), and the minor 6th and major 7th on G7.

Experiment with the track and focus your attention on where these notes are on the 2nd string. Listen to the demo and watch the transcription provided.

Level 6 Unit 5 • Composite Minor Demo 2

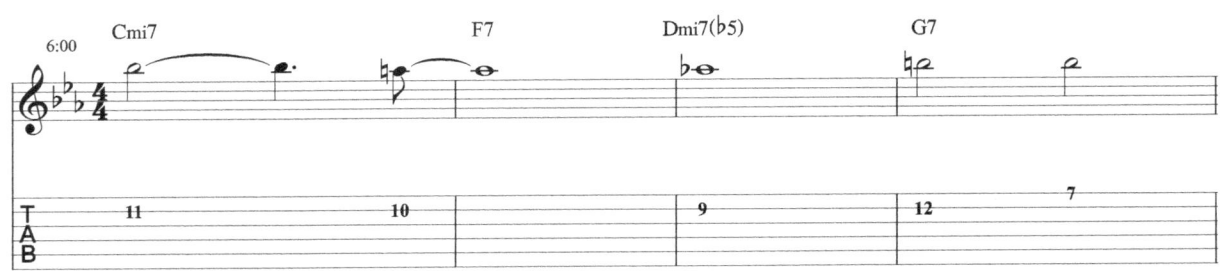

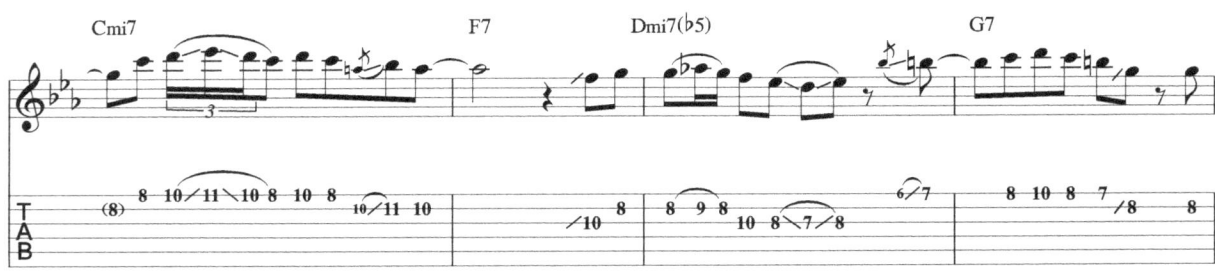

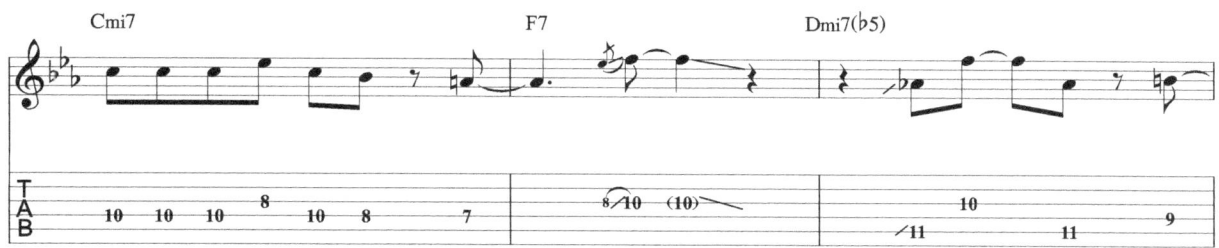
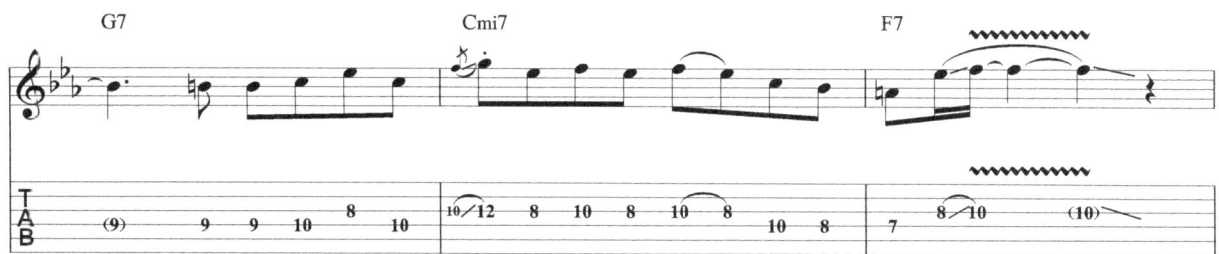
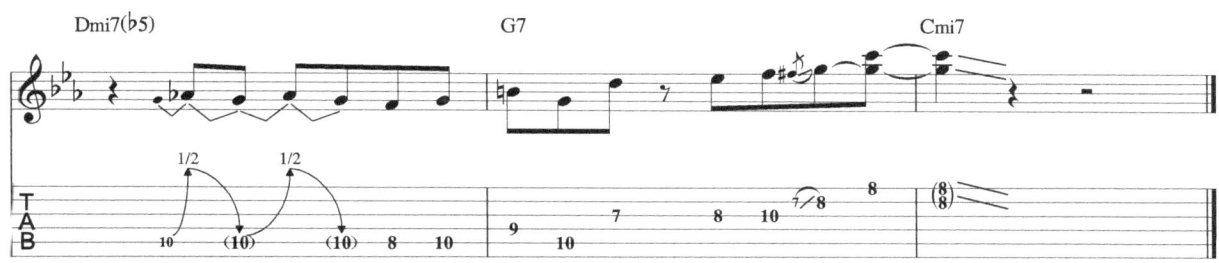

These various scales can help you accomplish something you have already done in previous Levels: playing chord tones.

Experiment blending the arpeggios and scales with the track. Listen to the demo and watch the transcription provided.

Level 6 Unit 5 • Composite Minor Demo 3

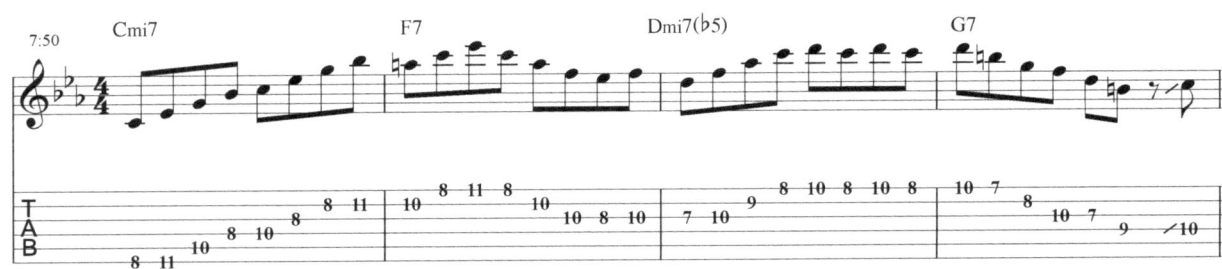

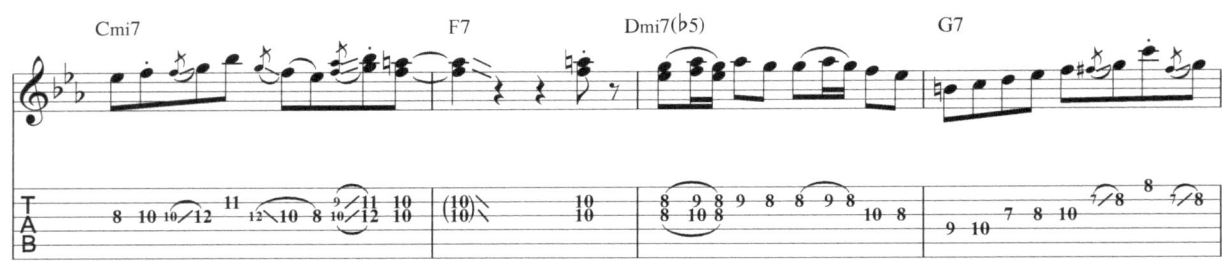

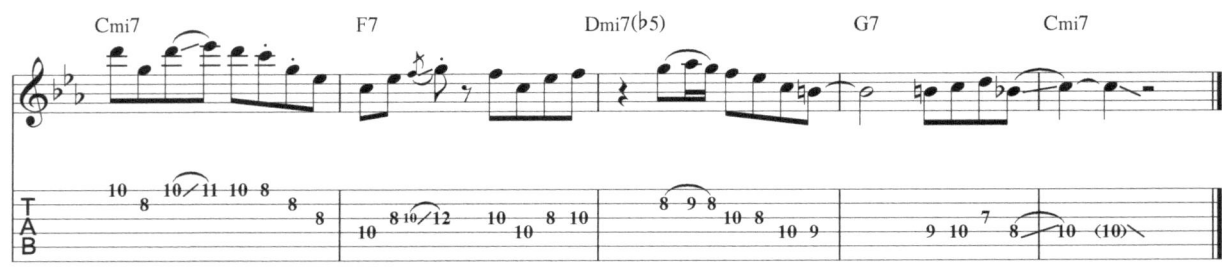

What should be coming into clear focus is how many scales and arpeggios can be found within an octave shape and Minor Pentatonic shell. By using the approach of starting with the pentatonic shell and making adjustments for each chord and/or scale, learning this becomes far more manageable from both a physical and mental standpoint. Remember that blending straight key-center Blues riffs is totally normal, accepted, and most of all, sounds great. Navigating with chord tones is important but it is just one tool in the tool box.

Experiment blending all of the arpeggios, various minor scales, and the Blues Scale with the track.

Level 6 Unit 5 • Composite Minor Demo 4

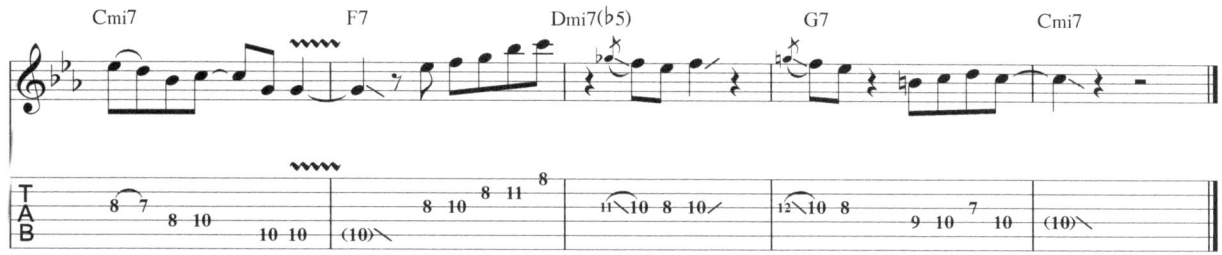

PRACTICE

Theory

- ❑ Understand the scale degrees that are the same and different between parallel minor scales.
- ❑ Understand the chord qualities built on each scale degree that are the same and different between parallel minor scales.
- ❑ Understand that a song in a single minor key could draw notes and chords from more than one minor scale built on the same tonic.

Fretboard Logic

- ❑ Learn to see and play the Pattern IV Minor Pentatonic, Natural, Dorian, and Harmonic Minor Scales within the Pattern IV Octave Shape.
- ❑ Learn to see that the only difference between the Natural, Dorian, and Harmonic Minor Scales is in the 6th and 7th scale degrees.
- ❑ Memorize the chords of the harmonized parallel minor scales.

Rhythm Guitar

- ❑ Follow the chart and create and record one or more rhythm guitar parts.

Chart Writing

- ❑ Recognize opportunities to use one-bar, two-bar and four-bar repeats on a chart. These are the first-tier space-saving devices.

Improvisation

- ❑ Practice soloing over the progression provided which shifts between the Natural, Dorian, and Harmonic Minor scales.

UNIT 6

Learning Modules

> **Theory** - Harmonic Analysis and Scale Application for Progressions with Composite Minor

> **Fretboard Logic** - Visualizing Parallel Minor Scales within the Same Octave Shape.

> **Rhythm Guitar** - Creating a Rhythm Guitar Part for a Country Song

> **Chart Writing** - Using Start and End Repeat Brackets and Endings

> **Improvisation** - Improvise over Progressions with Chords from Parallel Minor Scales

> **Practice** - Continue Practice Routine Development

The tracks for this Unit can be found at the following link:

https://fretboardbiology.com/book6/#u6

THEORY

In the last Theory Module you learned about Composite Minor. This Module focuses on harmonic analysis of progressions that use chords from parallel minor scales, in other words, from the world of Composite Minor. Harmonic analysis is important because it informs you about your note choices for melody, arrangement, and improvisation.

As you know, Composite Minor is a term to describe minor modal interchange because it's common for progressions in a minor key to draw upon one or more parallel minor scales for both chords and melody. Begin by reviewing the chords from harmonizing the three parallel scales we're using so far.

Composite Minor Harmonized 7th Chords

NAT MINOR:	Imi7	IImi7(♭5)	♭IIIma7	IVmi7	Vmi7	♭VIma7	♭VII7
	Cmi7	**Dmi7(♭5)**	**E♭ma7**	**Fmi7**	**Gmi7**	**A♭ma7**	**B♭7**
DORIAN:	Imi7	IImi7	♭IIIma7	IV7	Vmi7	VImi7(♭5)	♭VIIma7
	Cmi7	**Dmi7**	**E♭ma7**	**F7**	**Gmi7**	**Ami7(♭5)**	**B♭ma7**
HARMONIC:	Imi(ma7)	IImi7(♭5)	♭IIIma7(#5)	IVmi7	V7	♭VIma7	VII°7
	Cmi(ma7)	**Dmi7(♭5)**	**E♭ma7(#5)**	**Fmi7**	**G7**	**A♭ma7**	**B°7**

In the last Module we analyzed this progression in the key of C minor:

Progression in C Minor

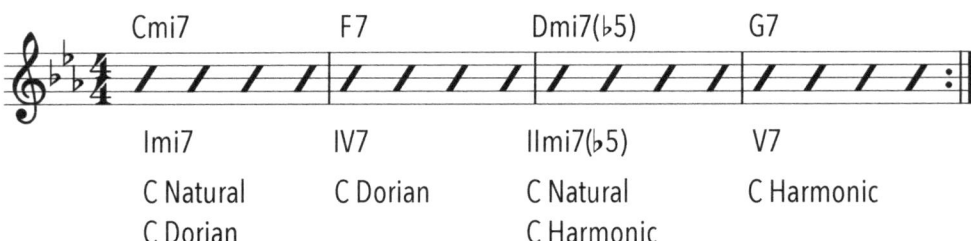

- Cmi7 is the I chord in both C Natural Minor and Dorian Minor.
- F7 is the IV7 in C Dorian Minor. It does not belong to C Natural Minor or C Harmonic Minor.
- Dmi7(♭5) is the IImi7(♭5) in both C Natural Minor and C Harmonic Minor.
- G7 is the V7 in C Harmonic Minor.

As you can see, there is no single minor scale that fits all of the chords. Some of the chords belong to Natural Minor and others to either Harmonic Minor or Dorian Minor.

Analyzing Progressions

Let's analyze some other progressions, writing the function of each chord using Roman numerals and specifying the qualities. Then under each chord function, we will also write in the minor scale or scales that fit the chord: Natural Minor, Dorian Minor, and/or Harmonic Minor scales. Remember that the most common chords from Dorian used in Composite Minor are IImi7 and IV7. The most common chords from Harmonic Minor used in Composite Minor are V7 and VIIdim7. Keep those chords front of mind and always be on the lookout for them in minor keys.

Let's analyze three progressions:

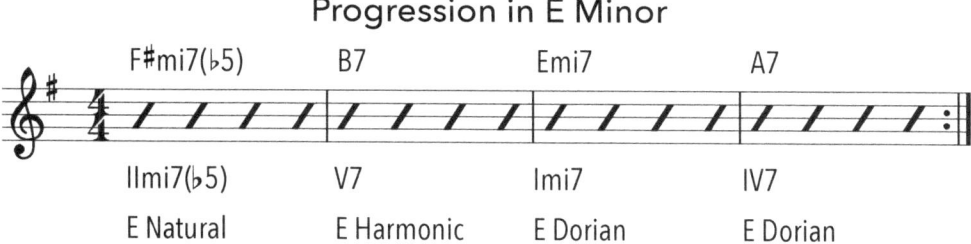

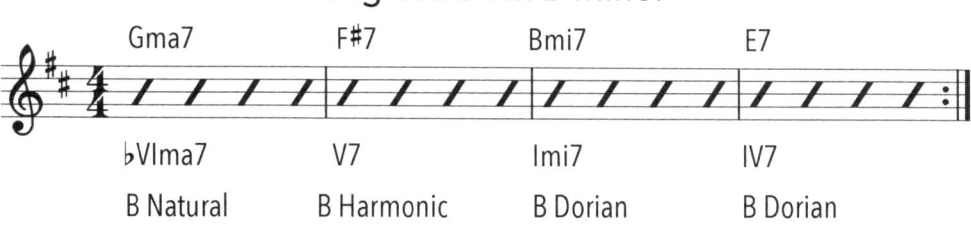

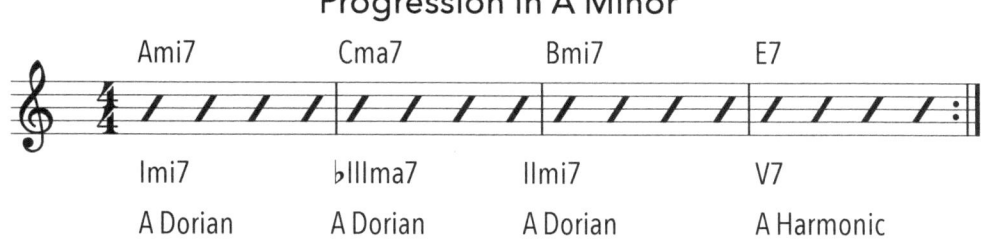

Here's something to be aware of: When Imi7 is followed by a chord from Dorian, such as IV7 or IImi7, it's normal to then play Dorian for both chords. The continuity just sounds better, but you should try for yourself. Try Natural Minor on Imi7 and Dorian on IV7 or IImi7. I think you'll agree that it sounds odd and Dorian for both is a better choice.

FRETBOARD LOGIC

In the last Fretboard Logic Module you learned the shared Composite Minor scale shapes in Octave Shape IV. You learned the Minor Pentatonic, Natural Minor, Dorian, and Harmonic Minor Scales that lay on the fretboard within the octave shape.

Let's transfer this same theoretical information to the fretboard using the Pattern II Octave Shape. And here's a reminder: Natural Minor, Dorian, and Harmonic Minor are identical to the 5th scale degree. It's only the 6th and 7th scale degree that vary.

Scales of Composite Minor

Minor Pentatonic	1		mi3	P4	P5		mi7
Natrual Minor	1	ma2	mi3	P4	P5	mi6	mi7
Dorian	1	ma2	mi3	P4	P5	ma6	mi7
Harmonic Minor	1	ma2	mi3	P4	P5	mi6	ma7

- On the left is the Minor Pentatonic shell (for reference)
- To its right is the Natural Minor Scale
- To its right is the Dorian Scale
- On the far right is the Harmonic Minor Scale

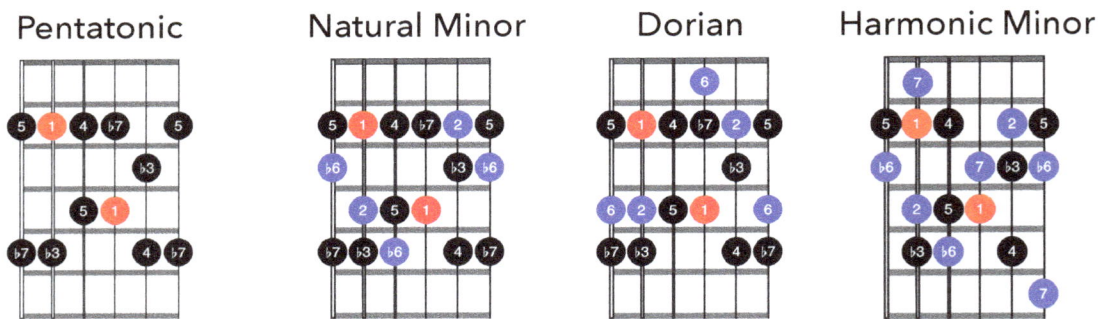

There's no need to see all of these as completely different scale patterns. They are derivatives of the pentatonic shell and/or variations of the Natural Minor Scale.

We'll work with the same progression we used in the last Logic and Improvisation Modules but this time in Octave Shape II. You have already done the analysis, so here it is under each chord.

- Cmi7 is the I chord in both C Natural Minor and Dorian Minor.
- F7 is the IV7 in C Dorian Minor. It does not belong to C Natural Minor or C Harmonic Minor.
- Dmi7(♭5) is the IImi7(♭5) in both C Natural Minor and C Harmonic Minor.
- G7 is the V7 in C Harmonic Minor.

It's clear that there is no single minor scale that fits all of the chords. Some of the chords belong to Natural Minor and others to either Harmonic Minor or Dorian Minor. To navigate this progression efficiently on the fretboard in the Improvisation Module, we need to first locate each of the scales in the same location on the fretboard. Under each chord of the progression is the diagram for its recommended scale within the Pattern II Octave Shape.

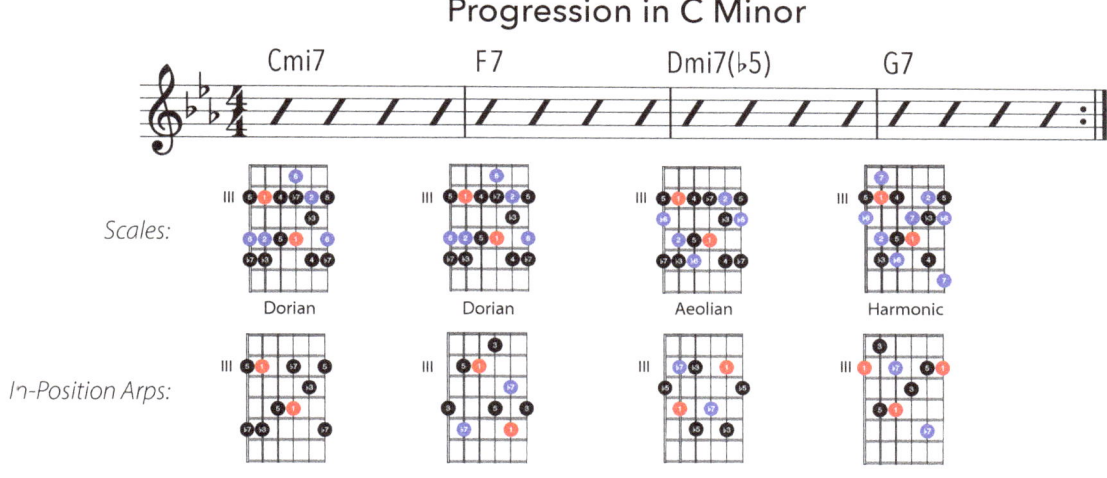

It's also helpful to see the in-position arpeggios so you can target chord tones. You will use these shapes in the Improvisation Module coming up. And again, always remember that IV7 is the most commonly used chord from Dorian and V7 is the most commonly used chord from Harmonic Minor. Please relate all of this to the Family Tree. It's important that you keep that connection going!

RHYTHM GUITAR

Creating Parts for Country Songs

In this Module, we are looking at Country rhythm guitar parts. You should have the hang of our approach by now, so let's look at the chart on the next page, and go through your Chart-Reading Checklist.

Chart-Reading Checklist

1. Look at the top left corner where all the preliminary information is: Key signature, Time signature, Style
2. Note the Tempo
3. Scan the form
4. Seek out any figures that need to be played
5. Scan the chords for the ones that are new or difficult for you
6. Seek out more detailed instructions like dynamics, accents, and expression markings

Now let's think like a producer and listen from the perspective of what rhythm parts this song needs. You recall that in the Country Rhythm Guitar modules, you learned parts for your fretting hand that use triads, and alternating bass parts for your picking hand that use strumming. You also learned some fingerpicking patterns and pedal-steel-like guitar parts.

Next, listen to see what kinds of parts fit with the track provided in the link below. Record your part and judge it from the perspective of a producer or musical director.

Is there room for a second or even third part? Usually there is but don't always feel obligated to fill every hole with something. Often open space is the right part.

Listen for places to leave space. This is often the hardest skill to acquire.

Country Song Chart

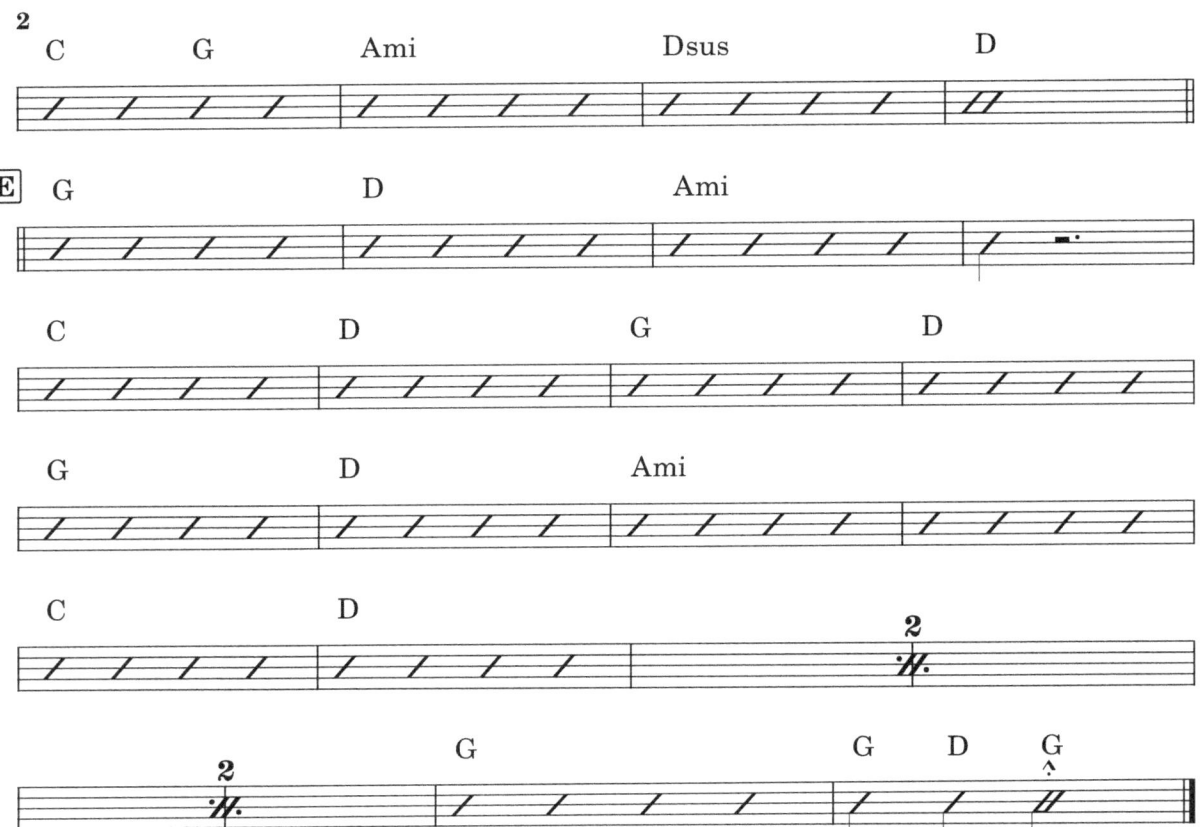

CHART WRITING

This Module focuses on using start and end repeat brackets as well as endings. But before we get started, let's once again review the steps we have taken so far.

- Step one was the Form Chart.
- Step two was counting measures and creating the crude first draft.
- Step three was writing down the chords.
- Step four was locating and notating rhythm figures and riffs.
- Step five was consolidating the chart by using one-, two-, and four-bar repeat devices.

Use what you now know about the basic Form Chart, as well as the number of measures, and the one-, two-, and four-bar repeats to find opportunities to use start and end repeat bar lines, as well as endings. Space permitting, try to start new sections at the left margin. This means to write the start repeat bar line there. Again, this is important because the musician's eyes are always moving back and forth from the music to their instrument and to the person leading the show. It is extremely helpful for the reader to know that a new section will always start on the left margin.

It's also helpful to arrange your measures so a section ends on the right margin. This makes it easier to start the next new section at the left margin. Also, if the number of bars per line works out, sections can be laid out so they begin on the left margin and end on the right margin. When the musician's eyes leave the page momentarily, it's very helpful for them to know that when they come back to the chart, they can find their place. Good organization of measures and sections makes this possible.

Here are some examples of good and bad ways to start and end sections. This makes finding your place after looking away from the chart much more comfortable.

Start and End Repeats at the Margins

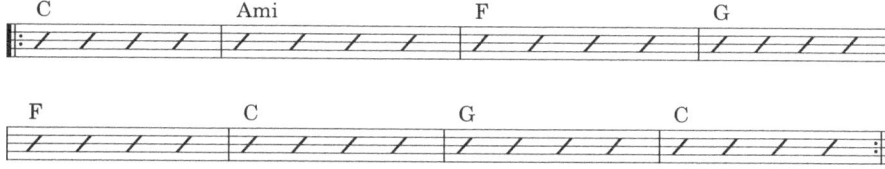

Reading a lot of chord charts will inform you about how to write them. You will encounter some that are good and many that are bad. Try to learn from what you see. You will see chart-organization problems which can be avoided with some simple page lay-out tactics.

In this next example, the start and end repeat bars are not at the margins. The subsequent section starts in the middle of the line. This makes finding your place after looking away from the chart much less comfortable.

Start and End Repeats in the Middle of the Line

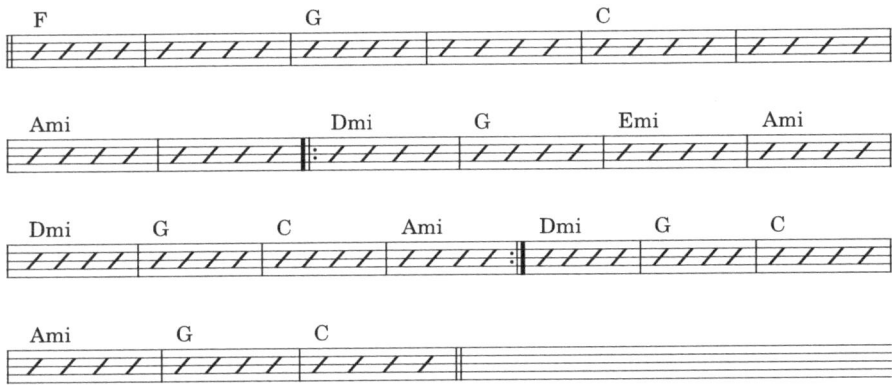

In this example the end repeat bars are not at the margin, but the subsequent section started at the left margin anyway. This makes looking away more comfortable but also wastes precious space. This is not optimal, but it's better than starting a new section in the middle of a line.

Start and End Repeats Not at the Margins

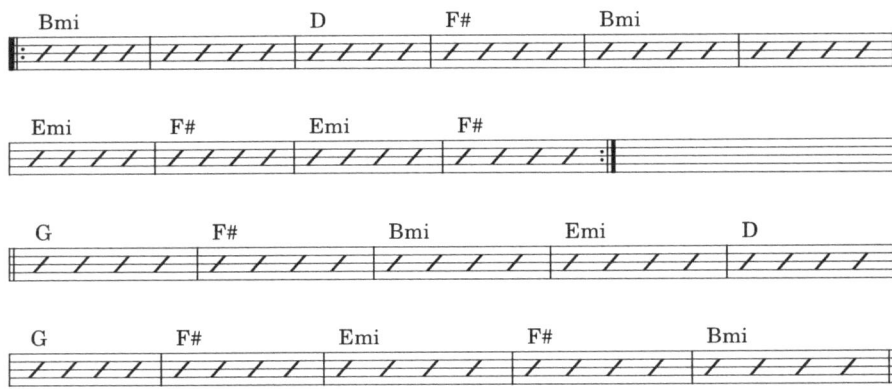

Let's discuss writing section endings. Often when the second time a section is played, it's not an exact replica of the first time. It's common for the last bar or two to be slightly different than the first time. Rather than writing it all out again, first and second endings can be used (and by the way, there are also third, fourth ending options, or more).

In this next example, there are two eight-bar phrases. They are identical up until the last measure.

Two Similar Sections with Different Endings

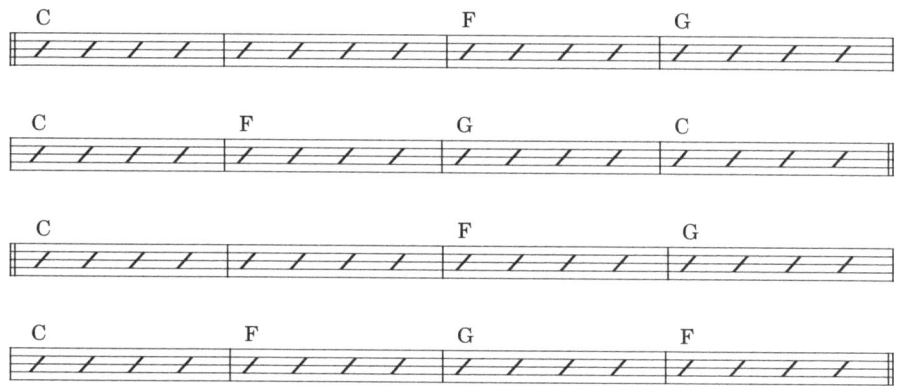

Rather than write the entire eight bars again, write out bars one through eight, but label the eighth bar as a first ending. When we get to the stage of putting this information on the actual chart, this is done with a two-sided box with '1st ending' written inside. Then add the end repeat bar line with two dots. This directs the reader's eye to go back to the start repeat bar line and play the section again. When reaching the end of bar seven on the second playing, the reader should skip the first ending and play the second ending, which is different. At that point they read on to the next section.

It's helpful to stack endings on the page for easy locating. If endings are stacked, the reader can read through the first ending, repeat, and on the second time they come to the place where the first ending is, their eyes can just drop down a line while keeping the same lateral eye movement going.

Repeating Sections with 1st and 2nd Endings (Stacked)

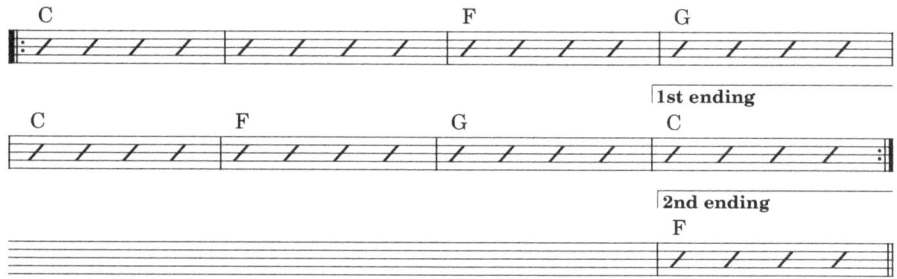

This is a great help, and the open space before the second ending helps separate the sections. But this also wastes all that space on the line where the second ending is. So the use of the stacked endings has to be considered based on the availability of space.

If you can't stack endings, at least try to have the second (or third or more) ending in line to the right of the first ending.

Repeating Sections with First and Second Endings (Same Line)

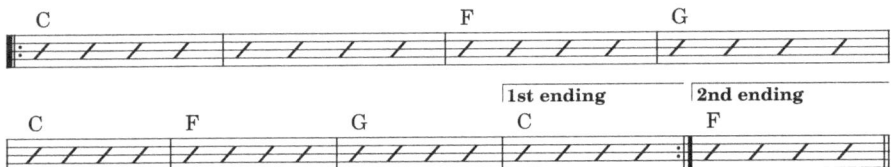

There are times, especially for solos and out choruses at the end of a song, where a section is repeated until someone cues the last time. If there is no difference in the last time, only 'repeat until cue' needs to be written. You can also write 'open'.

Repeating Until Cue (Open)

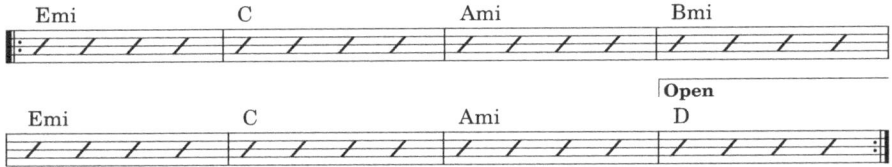

I suggest that instructions with words be written in and boxed in with either a two- or three-sided box. The open side of the box should be toward the staff that the written information applies to.

Fretboard Biology — Level 6 • Unit 6: Chart Writing

If the out choruses at the end of a song are repeated until someone cues, and if the end of the last time is different, you need to use endings. The first ending should be labeled to instruct 'open' or 'repeat until cue' or 'till cue'. The last ending should be labeled 'last ending', 'last x', or 'on cue'. These instructions need to be boxed in like any other ending or instructions.

Repeating Until Cue (Open) with Different Ending

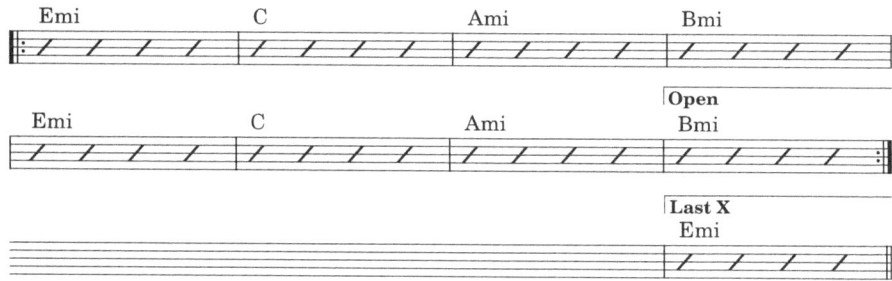

Look at our Form Chart second draft and look for opportunities to use start and end repeat bar lines.

Marking Start and End Repeats on the Form Chart

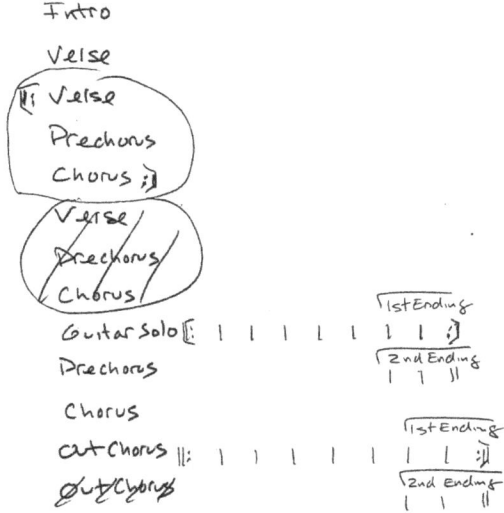

IMPROVISATION

In the last Improvisation Module you learned to solo through Composite Minor progressions with chords from parallel Natural Minor, Dorian Minor, and Harmonic Minor Scales using Pattern IV Octave Shape and referencing the Pattern IV Minor Pentatonic shell. Keeping in mind that navigating through these progressions requires playing the right scales for each chord, let's work on the same progression used in Theory and Fretboard Logic, but this time within the Pattern II Octave Shape.

First listen to the track for this Module again. As always, I suggest playing some Pattern II C Minor Pentatonic key-center to get a feel for the sound of the progression. All the notes of the scale won't fit on G7 but that's OK for now.

Next, get more specific with regard to scale choice. This will be the same as what you did in Pattern IV, but now, in Pattern II.

- Cmi7 is the I chord in both C Natural Minor and Dorian Minor. We'll use C Dorian since it's followed by F7, IV7, which is from Dorian. So we'll use the same scale for the first two chords.
- Dmi7(♭5) is the IImi7(♭5) in both C Natural Minor and C Harmonic Minor but we'll use Natural Minor to save B, the impactful leading tone for the G7.
- G7 is the V7 in C Harmonic Minor so that's the best choice there.

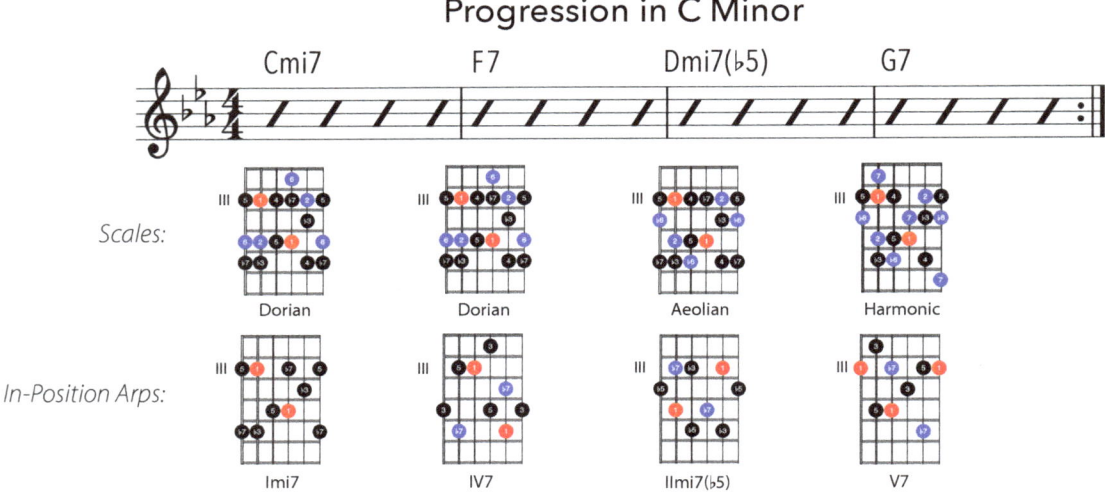

Play through the progression using the appropriate scales.

Level 6 Unit 6 • Composite Minor Demo 1

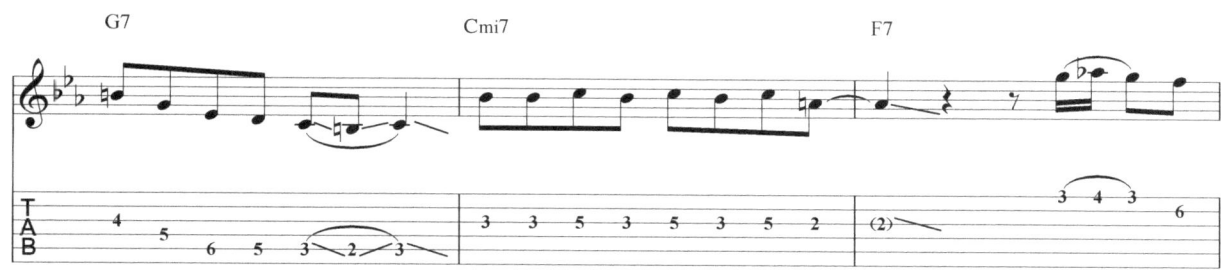

Next, zero in on the 6th and 7th scale degrees because that's the only difference between the three scales. Specifically, include the major 6th and minor 7th on Cmi7 and F7, the minor 6th and minor 7th on Dmi7(♭5), and the minor 6th and major 7th on G7. Be sure to review the scale comparisons in the Fretboard Logic Module if you don't understand why.

Listen to the demo and watch the transcription provided.

Level 6 Unit 6 • Composite Minor Demo 2

These various scales help you accomplish something you have already done in previous Levels: to play chord tones. So, let's lay out the arpeggios of these four chords, in position, withing the general Pattern II octave shape and minor pentatonic shell.

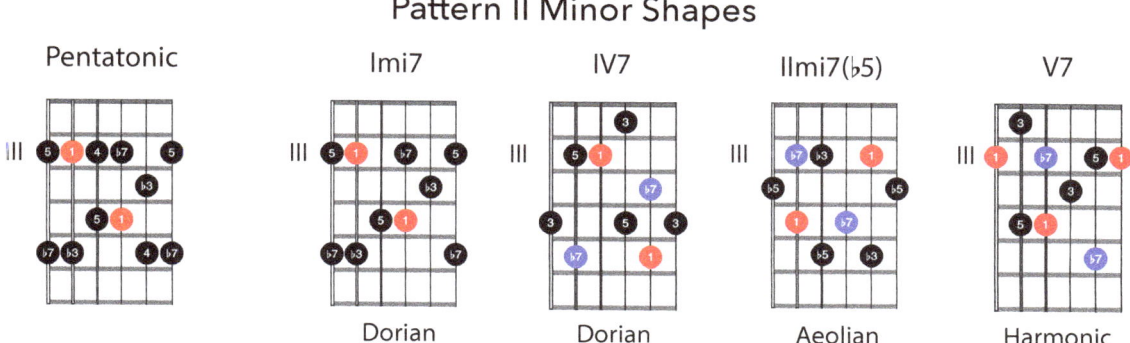

Experiment blending the arpeggios and scales with the track provided. Again, you can see how many scales and arpeggios can be found within the octave shape and Minor Pentatonic shell. By using the approach of starting with the shell and making adjustments for each chord and/or scale, learning and using them becomes far more manageable from both a physical and mental standpoint.

Practice blending the arpeggios, the various minor scales, and the Blues Scale with the track. And remember, when Imi7 is followed by a chord from Dorian, like IV7 or IImi7, it's normal to then play Dorian for both chords. There is continuity in that choice and it just sounds better, but you should try for yourself. Try Natural Minor on Imi7 and Dorian on IV7 or IImi7. I think you'll agree that it sounds odd and Dorian for both is a better choice.

Here are the three additional progressions we analyzed in the Theory Module. Included is the analysis and scale suggestions based on what you've learned about Composite Minor. These are all very common chord progression fragments. Over time, work in-position with the scales and arpeggios found within Octave Shapes IV and II that you learned in this Unit and the last.

This is a long-term practice item; don't expect to master this quickly, but you will get there if you follow the process. Work with the slower-tempo examples first so you have a chance to really focus on the detail. And don't feel obligated to play a lot of notes. Sparse is OK! Keep in mind that the differences in the three scales are just with the 6th and 7th scale degrees.

Progression in E Minor

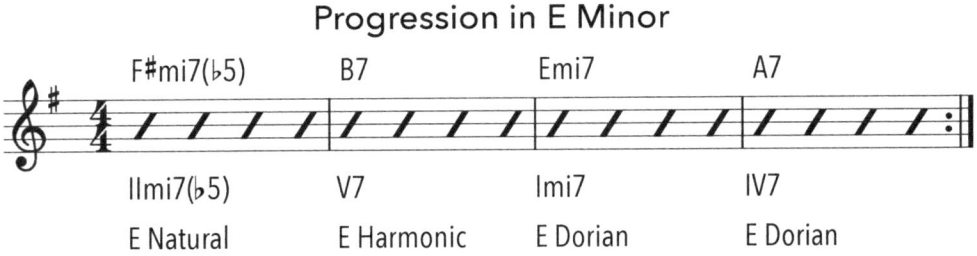

Listen to the demo and watch the transcription provided.

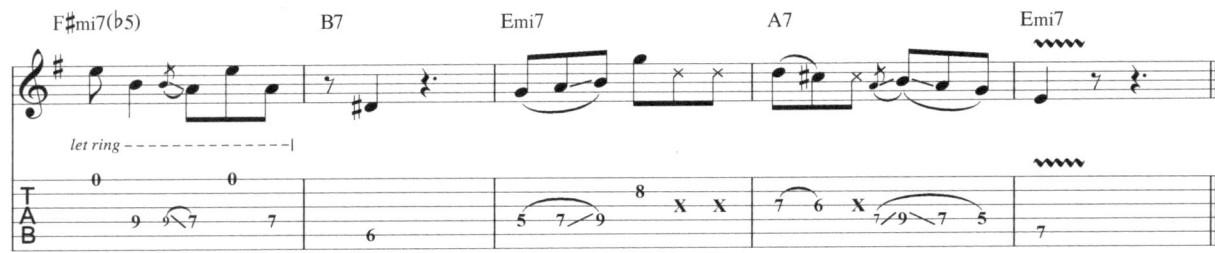

Level 6 • Unit 6: Improvisation

Progression in B Minor

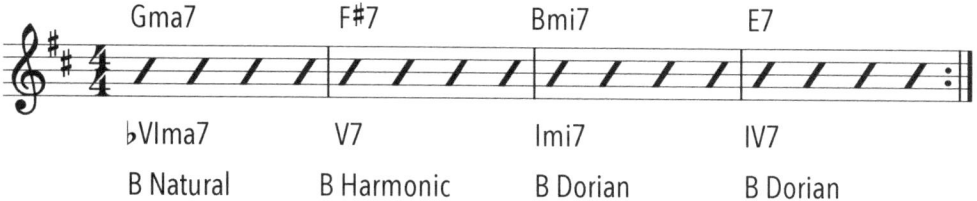

♭VIma7	V7	Imi7	IV7
B Natural	B Harmonic	B Dorian	B Dorian

Listen to the demo and watch the transcription provided.

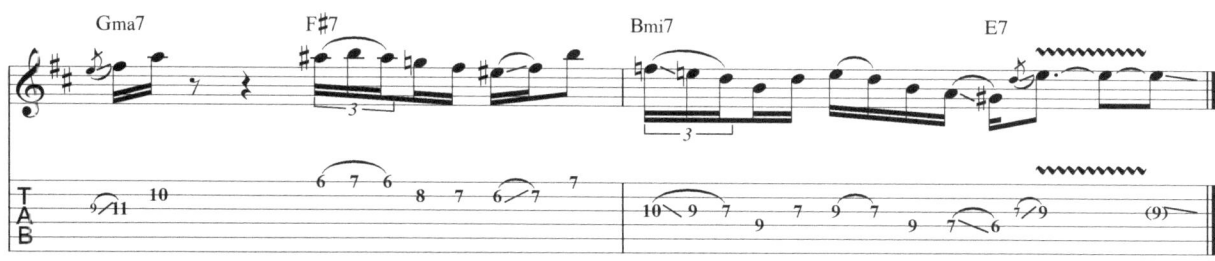

Progression in A Minor

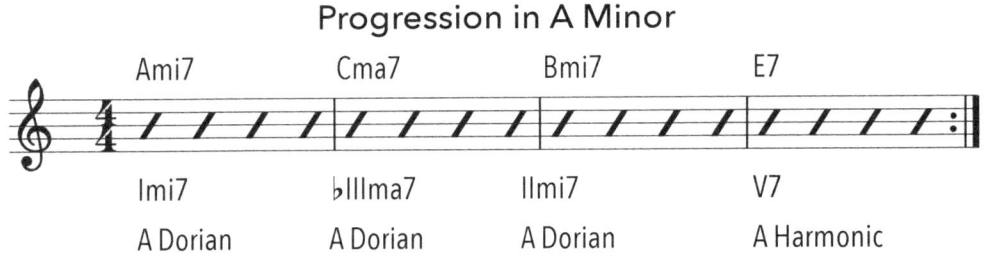

Listen to the demo and watch the transcription provided.

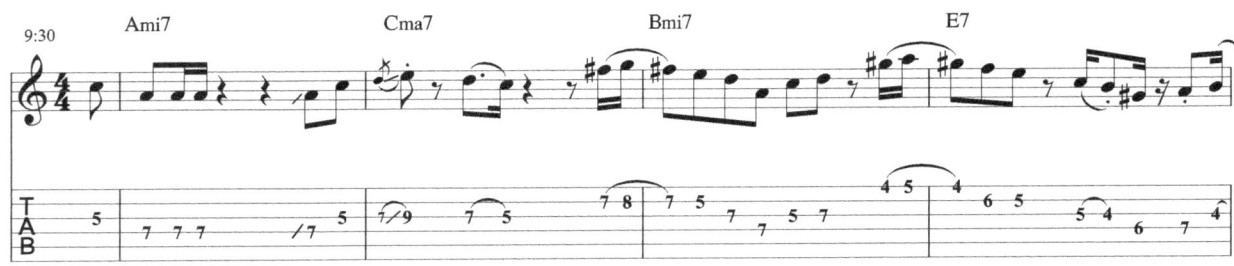

PRACTICE

Theory

- ❏ Be able to analyze progressions that use the chords from parallel minor scales.
- ❏ Know the appropriate scale choices for each of the chords in a progression that uses chords from parallel minor scales.

Fretboard Logic

- ❏ Learn to see and play the Pattern II Minor Pentatonic, Natural, Dorian, and Harmonic Minor Scales within the Pattern II Octave Shape.
- ❏ Learn to see that the only difference between the Natural, Dorian, and Harmonic Minor Scales is in the 6th and 7th scale degrees.

Rhythm Guitar

- ❏ Follow the chart and create and record one or more rhythm guitar parts.

Chart Writing

- ❏ Know how to start and end sections on the margins when possible.
- ❏ Know how to use start and end repeat brackets as well as first, second, and more endings.
- ❏ Know how to write additional instructions to the reader using a two- or three-sided box.

Improvisation

- ❏ Practice soloing over the progession provided which shifts between the Natural, Dorian and Harmonic Minor scales.

UNIT 7

Learning Modules

> **Theory** - The Most Common Progression Fragments in the Mixolydian Scale

> **Fretboard Logic** - Deriving Patterns of the Mixolydian Scale from the Major Pentatonic Scales, Common Mixolydian Progression Fragments

> **Rhythm Guitar** - Creating a Rhythm Guitar Part for a Funk Song

> **Chart Writing** - Using Jump Marks like DC, DS, and Coda Signs

> **Improvisation** - Using the Mixolydian Scale

> **Practice** - Continue Practice Routine Development

The tracks for this Unit can be found at the following link:

https://fretboardbiology.com/book6/#u7

THEORY

In an earlier module you learned that Modes can be harmonized just like the Major, Natural Minor, and Harmonic Minor Scales. One of the reasons for knowing the harmonized modes is that an entire song can be written in modes other than Ionian and Aeolian. If a mode can be used as the basis for a composition, the chords of the harmonized mode are what support the melody and make up the harmony of the song.

The Mixolydian Scale

In this Module, we'll work with the Mixolydian Scale. You may hear musicians use the terms Mixolydian Scale, Mixolydian Mode, or just Mixolydian. They all mean the same thing.

Let's review the construction of the Mixolydian Scale:

Mixolydian Mode Interval Pattern

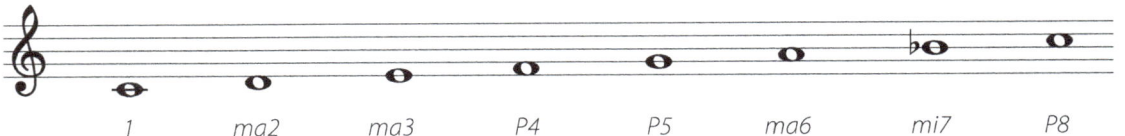

Tonic, major 2nd, major 3rd, perfect 4th, perfect 5th, major 6th, and minor 7th. Because it has a major 3rd, it is a major-sounding mode. Look at this comparison of the Major Pentatonic and Mixolydian Scales.

Mixolydian as a Derivative of the Major Pentatonic Scale

Major Pentatonic	*1*	*ma2*	*ma3*		*P5*	*ma6*	
Mixolydian Mode	*1*	*ma2*	*ma3*	*P4*	*P5*	*ma6*	*mi7*

You can think of the Mixolydian Scale as a Major Pentatonic Scale with an added perfect 4th and minor 7th.

Now look at this comparison of the Major (Ionian) Scale and Mixolydian Scales:

Mixolydian as a Derivative of the Major (Ionian) Scale

Ionian Mode	*1*	*ma2*	*ma3*	*P4*	*P5*	*ma6*	*ma7*
Mixolydian Mode	*1*	*ma2*	*ma3*	*P4*	*P5*	*ma6*	*mi7*

The Mixolydian Scale can also be seen as a Major Scale with minor 7th. The scale degree that distinguishes the Mixolydian from the Major Scale is the ♭7.

Chords

In Unit 3 you learned the chords of the harmonized Mixolydian Scale. They are:

Mixolydian Mode Chord Qualities

I7   IImi7   IIImi7(♭5)   IVma7   Vmi7   VImi7   VIIma7

Progressions

It's more common for the Mixolydian Scale to be used in situations that are harmonically inactive, meaning that the chord doesn't change. Another way to say 'harmonically inactive' is that the chord is 'static', as in, there is a 'static dominant 7th chord'. So when there's a static dom7 chord for any length of time in a song, most musicians hear the Mixolydian Scale as the most appealing sound.

Let's check for avoid tones in the Mixolydian Scale. Examine the E Mixolydian Scale. The chord tones of an E7 are highlighted.

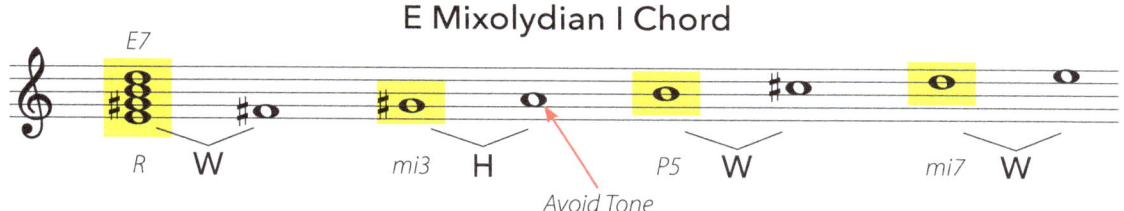

Note that the scale degrees above each note of E7 are a whole step higher except for the 4th, which, like in the Major Scale, is a half-step higher, and therefore, an avoid tone.

However, while it's still an avoid tone, our ears are more tolerant of the 4th against a 3rd of a dom7 chord than of the 4th against a 3rd of a ma7 chord. Perhaps that's because a dominant chord already has some built-in dissonance from the tritone between the major 3rd and minor 7th. Remember a tritone is a diminished 5th (or flat 5th) and augmented 4th (or ♯4). We're used to hearing some dissonance in the chord already.

It's helpful to look at the most common short progressions from the Mixolydian Scale. The following progressions are signature Mixolydian progression fragments. This first two-chord Mixolydian progression fragment is the most classic and commonly used. It's been the basis for many songs and is easily recognizable when you hear it. There are songs where this two-chord combination makes up the entire song. In other cases, this fragment may be just a section of the song. It is I7 to Vmi7.

Progression in E Mixolydian

Listen to the track for this Module to hear the E Mixolydian scale played over this progression.

The signature sound in this progression is the voice that moves from the major 3rd of the I7 to the minor 7th of the Vmi7. In E Mixolydian, the major 3rd of the E7, that's G#, moves up a half step to the minor 7th of the Bmi7. That's A.

The 3rd Moves to the Minor 7th

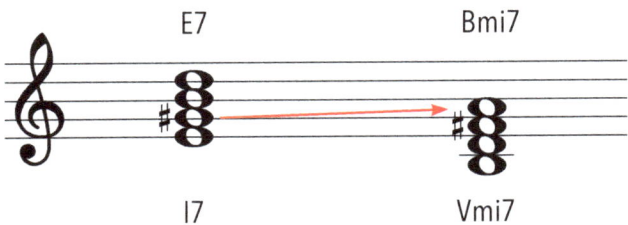

It's worth noting that this is the reverse of a classic Dorian progression you learned earlier. If the progression was Bmi7 to E7, and you perceived B as the tonic, you would hear this as Imi7 to IV7, a classic Dorian progression where the Bmi7 is Imi7 and the E7 is IV7. And by the way, the notes in B Dorian and E Mixolydian are exactly the same. They both have three sharps and can be related to A major.

This next Mixolydian progression fragment is common, too. It's been the basis for many songs as well. It is Ima to bVIIma.

Progression in C Mixolydian

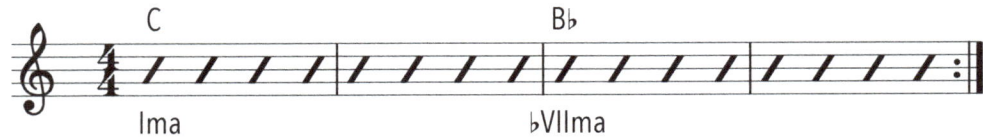

The signature sound in this progression is essentially that all of the voices of the chord move by step.

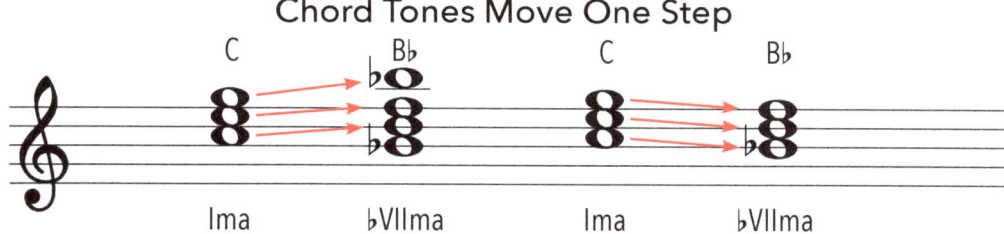

See the direction of the moving voices:
- The root of C, the I chord, can move up a whole step to D, the 3rd of the B♭ chord.
- The root of C, the I chord, can also move down a whole step to B♭, the root of the B♭ chord.
- The 3rd of C, E, can move up a half step to F, the 5th of the B♭ chord.
- The 3rd of C, E, can move down a whole step to D, the 3rd of the B♭ chord.
- The 5th of C, G, can move up a minor 3rd to B♭, the root of the B♭ chord.
- The 5th of C, G, can move down a whole step to F, the 5th of the B♭ chord.

This progression may look familiar to you from Level 4 which addressed modal interchange. C to B♭ was analyzed as Ima to ♭VIIma there, too, but ♭VII was analyzed as being borrowed from the parallel minor, C minor.

Analyzing the progression as all C Mixolydian or interpreting the B♭ as borrowed from the parallel C minor are both correct but they sound different. The written melody will dictate which way the progression should be heard and analyzed. Try both options when you get to the Improvisation Module.

All of these progression scenarios will be addressed from a performance standpoint in the Improvisation Module.

FRETBOARD LOGIC

This Module focuses on the Mixolydian Mode. You know how to create the modes by adding notes to the pentatonic shells, and we'll do that here.

The goal in this Module is to learn all five patterns of Mixolydian by adding two notes to the five Major Pentatonic shells. By deriving the Mixolydian Scale from the Major Pentatonic Scale, the muscle memory you have already developed there will make Mixolydian feel and sound much more natural, and sooner.

To create the Mixolydian Scale from a Major Pentatonic shell, add a perfect 4th and a minor 7th. That's it.

Mixolydian as a Derivative of the Major Pentatonic Scale

Major Pentatonic	*1*		*ma2*	*ma3*		*P5*	*ma6*	
Mixolydian Mode	*1*		*ma2*	*ma3*	*P4*	*P5*	*ma6*	*mi7*

It's important to have a clear understanding of the correlation between the following shapes: the Major Pentatonic and Mixolydian scales and the chord and arpeggio built on the 1st scale degree.

Pattern I

Let's look at Pattern I. The diagram on the left is the Pattern I Major Pentatonic shell. To its right is the same shell with a perfect 4th and a minor 7th added. This is the Pattern I Mixolydian Mode. To its right is the dominant 7 chord voicing built on the 1st scale degree and on the far right is the dominant 7 arpeggio built on the 1st scale degree.

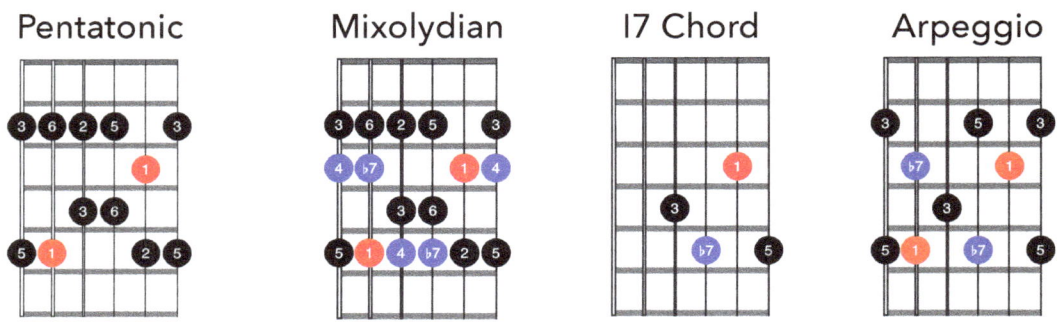

Pentatonic   Mixolydian   I7 Chord   Arpeggio

Pattern II

Let's look at Pattern II. The diagram on the left is the Pattern II Major Pentatonic shell. To its right is the same shell with a perfect 4th and a minor 7th added. This is the Pattern II Mixolydian Mode. To its right is the dominant 7 chord voicing built on the 1st scale degree and on the far right is the dominant 7 arpeggio built on the 1st scale degree.

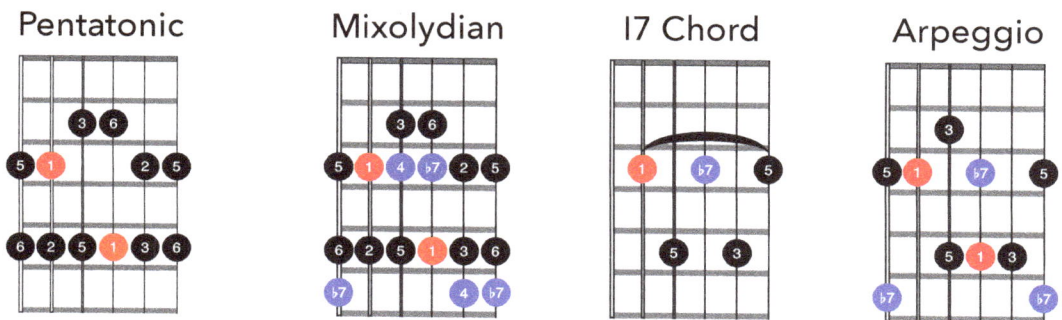

Pattern III

Let's do the same with Pattern III. Add a perfect 4th and a minor 7th to the Pentatonic to create the Pattern III Mixolydian Mode. Again, the dominant 7 chord voicing built on the 1st scale degree and the dominant 7 arpeggio built on the 1st scale degree are to the right.

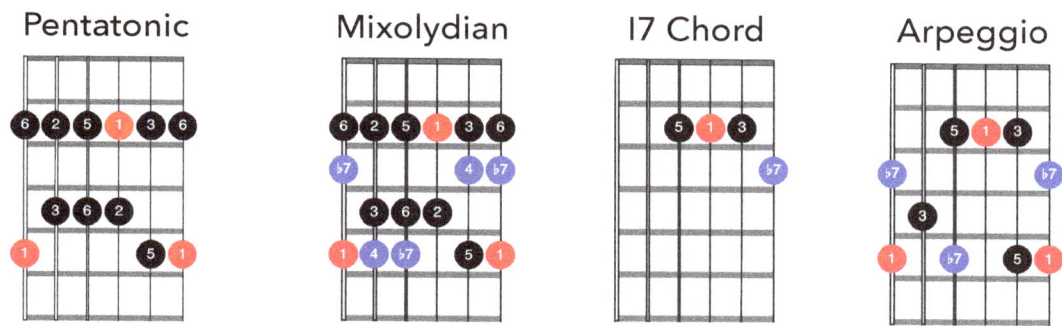

Pattern IV

Same process with Pattern IV. Add a perfect 4th and a minor 7th to the Pentatonic to create the Mixolydian Mode. The chord voicing and arpeggio are both built from the tonic.

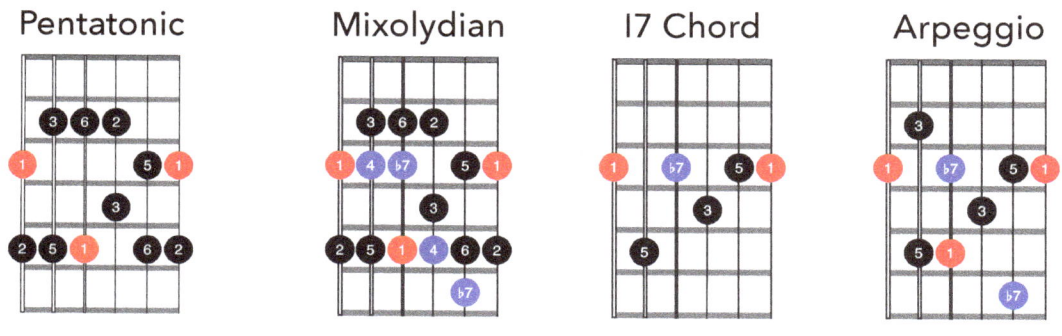

Pattern V

Let's look at Pattern V. The diagram on the left is the Pattern V Major Pentatonic shell. To its right is the same shell with a perfect 4th and a minor 7th added. This is the Pattern V Mixolydian Mode. To its right is the dominant 7 chord voicing built on the 1st scale degree and on the far right is the dominant 7 arpeggio built on the 1st scale degree.

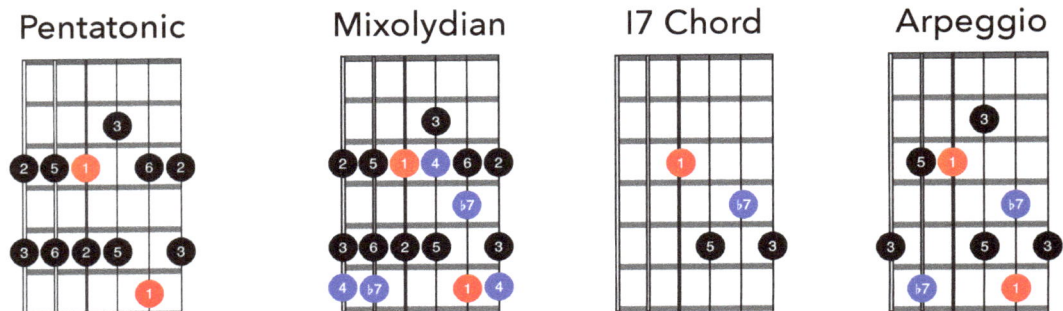

And again, don't feel like you need to memorize all these dots immediately. Understanding the process is far more important. Remember that most guitarists find a couple patterns that become their go-to places on the fretboard. Over time you can add other patterns to your arsenal.

Mixolydian Harmony

Let's move on to Mixolydian harmony. It's important to get a feel for the progressions that clearly present the sound of Mixolydian. Here are a couple of the progression fragments that were presented in Theory that will also be used in the Improvisation Module.

Practice playing chords on these progressions a few ways with whatever groove you like, or play along with Improv tracks. You can use barre chords, shell voicings, and in some cases, open chords. Here are two short progressions.

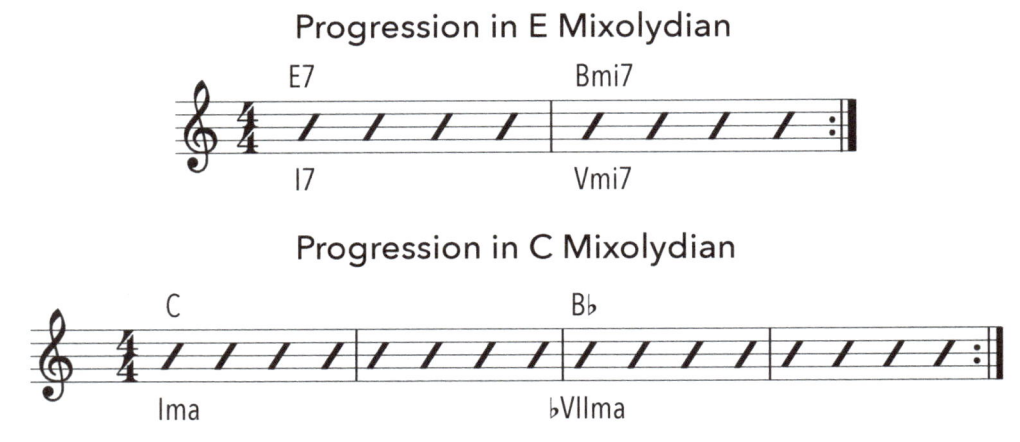

Please relate all of this to the Family Tree to keep that connection going!

RHYTHM GUITAR

Creating Parts for Funk

You studied Funk rhythm guitar in the Level 4 Rhythm Guitar modules. In this Module, you will put your rhythm guitar vocabulary to work to create new parts.

First, let's take a look at the road map on the following pages and use your Chart-Reading Checklist.

Chart-Reading Checklist

1. Look at the top left corner where all the preliminary information is: Key signature, Time signature, Style
2. Note the Tempo
3. Scan the form
4. Seek out any figures that need to be played
5. Scan the chords for the ones that are new or difficult for you
6. Seek out more detailed instructions like dynamics, accents, and expression markings

Next, think like a producer and listen for a part that fits with the band. Consider the instrumentation so you know how busy or sparse you should be, and what kind of voicings should be used and in what register.

- Make sure that you are part of fabric of the groove. That's a requirement.
- Get the right guitar sound.
- Be as consistent as possible. Your band mates are counting on you to be and stay in your lane. Good time is critical.

In the Funk Rhythm Guitar modules you learned chordal comping parts and popcorn parts for a variety of grooves and chord qualities. If you haven't been actively using the comping vocabulary you learned back then, it might be a good idea to go back and review that material. Don't assume all those parts will work in every song. Some may, some may need some modification, and some may not work at all. And there may be room for two parts so keep that in mind.

Funk Song Chart

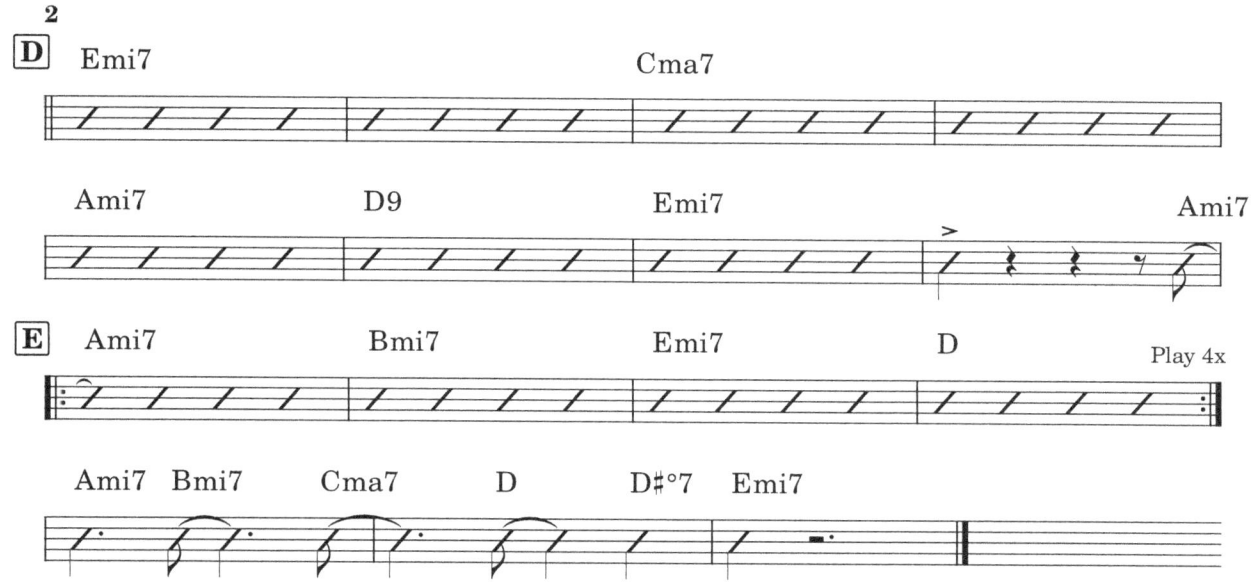

Record your part and listen with a critical ear. Funk parts need to feel right, and that's usually an intangible that is hard to express with words. Judge it from the perspective of a listener. Does it feel good? Does it sound right? Does it move the listener? It needs to or you need to keep working at it. Nobody said this groove stuff was going to be easy, but it sure is rewarding when you play music that feels good.

There is often room for a second or even third part, but don't forget the value of open space. Understanding where and how to create space comes from experimentation. Record a lot—as much as you can. Expect to invest time in this. This should be fun. Keep trying new ideas.

CHART WRITING

This Module focuses on using jump marks like DC, DS, and Coda. But before we get started, review the steps we have taken so far. Step one was the Form Chart. Step two was counting measures and creating the crude first draft. Step three was writing down the chords. Step four was locating and notating rhythm figures and riffs. Step five was consolidating the chart by using one-bar, two-bar, and four-bar repeat devices. Step six was about start and end repeats.

Step Seven

After you've exhausted the opportunities to use start and end repeat signs, and have a situation where the song repeats several successive sections, jump marks like DC and DS can be used. These jump marks allow you to avoid rewriting huge chunks of music. In Level 5, we discussed jump marks in the Chart Reading modules. Let's do a quick review:

- DC is used when the form returns to the very first note written.
- DS is used when the form returns to any place other than the first note played. The location is marked with a 𝄋 sign.

That part of understanding the DC and DS marks is pretty simple. What happens after the return to the very first note played (DC) or to the sign (DS) requires more explanation.

There are three different ways the eye travels through the chart after a DC or DS.

1. DC (and nothing written with it) or DS (and nothing written with it):
   After repeating to the top (DC) or to the sign (DS), the eye follows the chart until it reaches the location where DC or DC is written. At that point, it continues on to the next section. No special notation is required for this.

2. DC AL CODA and DS AL CODA:
   After repeating to the top (DC) or to the sign (DS), the eye follows the chart until it reaches the coda sign. Coda means ending. This directs the eye to a place later in the chart where the word CODA is written. The coda section is placed after the point where the DC or DC are written and if possible, either write the label CODA in the staff and indent the first measure, and/or skip a whole line and begin writing out the actual Coda. This helps the eye find it in the heat of the moment. A coda is usually not a big section but there are exceptions.

3. DC AL FINE and DS AL FINE:
   If the chart shows DC AL FINE or DS AL FINE, after repeating to the top or to the sign, the eye follows the chart until AL FINE is written. The AL FINE could be before or after where the DC or DS marking was in the body of the song. The place where AL FINE is written is the end of the song. There's usually a definitive rhythm figure in the body of the tune that makes a good ending.

Both DC and DS as well as any of the other instructions, like AL CODA or AL FINE, are best written below the staff in a two- or three-sided box, but it is sometimes written above the staff as well. The open side of box should be toward the staff it applies to.

Repeat signs are usually not played on a DC or DS unless it is explicitly stated with the DC or DS markings. Sometimes this will be written on a chart: 'DC al Coda (no repeats)'. This is redundant, but many people don't know the rule that repeats are not played unless otherwise stated. Sometimes charts will write 'DC al Coda with repeats' (or 'w/rpts)', which is important for people who do know the rule. Whether you use these extra words of clarification is a personal choice, but I normally choose to be explicit and write DC w/rpts, DC no rpts, DS w/rpts, or DS no rpts.

It's also common and acceptable to write instructions at the location where the repeat in question is. It can read 'REPEAT GOOD ON DC' (or 'ON DS') or 'NO REPEAT ON DC' (or 'ON DS') or other language like that. And again, this is best written below the staff in a two- or three-sided box with the open side of box toward the staff it applies to.

Let's look at our second draft and look for opportunities to use jump marks.

Jump Marks on the Form Chart

So how many measures have we saved ourselves from writing by using all of the repeat devices? Do the math: it's 50. And if we average writing four measures per line, we have saved writing about 13 lines of music which would require two pages. Using all the repeat devices is important to consolidating a lot of music on the page.

IMPROVISATION

Mixolydian Mode

You had a taste of playing the Mixolydian Scale over a static dominant 7 chord in the Unit 2 Improvisation Module. And in the Unit 3 Module, you played only the Major Pentatonic Scale over a track that would normally use the Mixolydian Scale. The idea was to just get a feel for the sound. In this Module we will dig deeper into the Mixolydian Scale.

Remember that all of the scales and arpeggios you learn are your tools and you need to know how they work. Each note in every scale or arpeggio has a personality and an effect on the listener. At the very least, get to know how each note makes you feel against the chord.

I suggest that you think of Mixolydian, and all the other modes, as a pentatonic shell with two notes added. As we have discussed, relating the modes to the Major Scale patterns comes with some troublesome muscle memory issues that result in the modes sounding vague. If you relate the modes to pentatonic shells, you benefit from the muscle memory you've already developed from using the pentatonic scales.

We'll be working in the Pattern III Mixolydian Scale in this Module because it's derived from the Pattern III Major Pentatonic Scale, which is a pattern most guitarists are very comfortable with. But everything we discuss in this Module can be used in any of the five patterns of the Mixolydian Scale.

Hearing the Mixolydian Sound

Let's start by playing the Pattern III E Major Pentatonic Scale over the static E7 vamp. Now play the Pattern III Mixolydian Scale to hear what that sounds like.

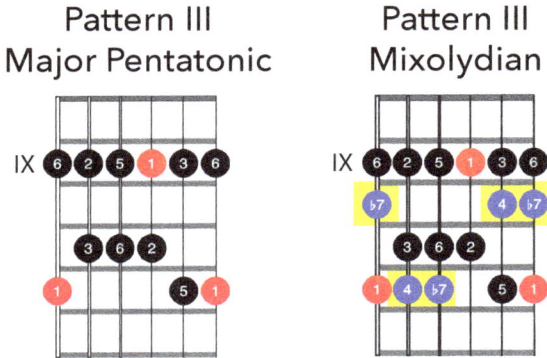

They both sound major, they both fit nicely, and they have the five notes of the Major Pentatonic Scale in common. The Mixolydian Scale, however, has the added perfect 4th and minor 7th. These two notes are the notes that distinguish Mixolydian from Major Pentatonic. The minor 7th is the note that distinguishes Mixolydian from the Major Scale.

Identify the chord tones within the scale. There are four: the root, major 3rd, perfect 5th, and minor 7th. And there are seven notes in the scale. The notes other than the chord tones are the major 2nd, perfect 4th, and minor 7th.

Mixolydian Mode Interval Pattern

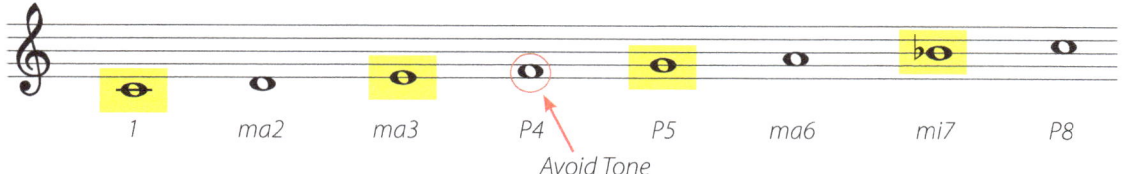

The major 2nd is a whole step above the root. The perfect 4th is a half step above the major 3rd and the major 6th is a whole step above the perfect 5th. So the Mixolydian Scale has one avoid tone, the perfect 4th.

Each note in every scale or arpeggio has a personality and an effect on the listener. Play each note of the scale against the static chord with the track. The exercise is to dwell on every note of the scale and experience how each one makes you feel when played over the chord. Come up with your own adjectives to describe how you hear each note of the scale against the chord and work at remembering them. If you know the 'personality' of a note, you can use it to set a mood to start a phrase with or perhaps find a note to dwell on in a solo.

Practice soloing on a static dominant 7 chord sampling the unique effect of each scale tone. Experiment with combinations, too.

Progressions in Mixolydian

Next, let's look at some short progression fragments. In the Theory Module you learned some of the standard progression fragments that represent Mixolydian. Let's review the chords of the harmonized Mixolydian Scale.

Mixolydian Mode Chord Qualities

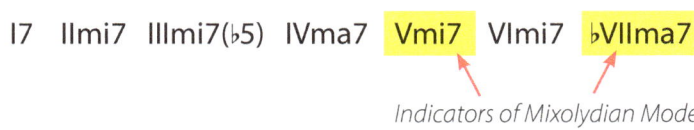

Indicators of Mixolydian Mode

Of these, Vmi (or Vmi7) and ♭VIIma are the most common chords from Mixolydian. Be cautious with ♭VIIma because we also know that from the study of modal change as a possible borrowed chord from the parallel minor, right? If you don't remember that, go back to Level 4 and review. It's important to solo on the most common short progressions from the harmonized Mixolydian Scale.

This first two-chord Mixolydian progression fragment is the most classic and commonly used. It's been the basis for many songs and is easily recognizable when you hear it. There are songs where this two-chord combination makes up the entire song. In other cases, this fragment may be just a section of the song. It is I7 to Vmi7.

Progression in E Mixolydian

Play it so you know what it sounds like, and play the E Mixolydian Scale over it using the tack for this Module.

Level 6 Unit 7 • Mixolydian Demo 1

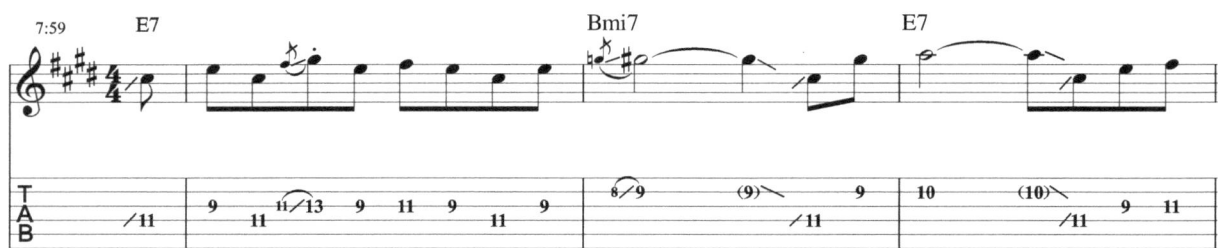

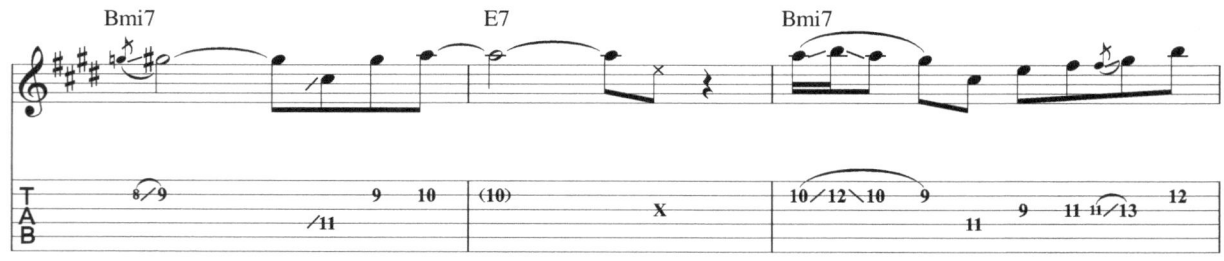

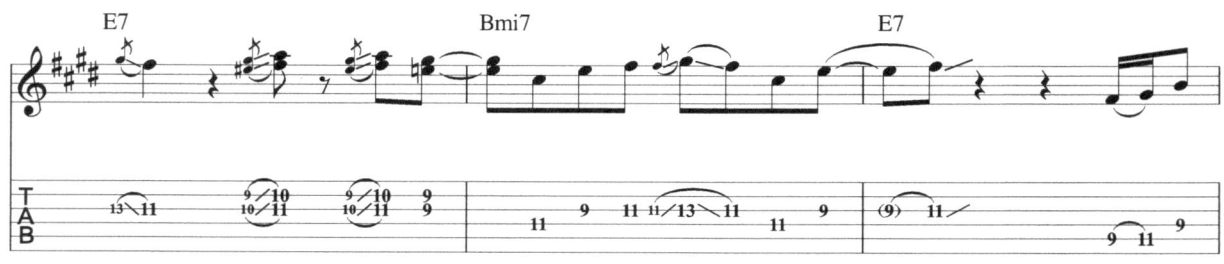

The signature sound in this progression is the voice that moves from the major 3rd of the I7 to the minor 7th of the Vmi7. In E Mixolydian, the major 3rd of the E7, that's G#, moves up a half step to the minor 7th of the Bmi7. That's A.

The Major 3rd Moves to ♭7

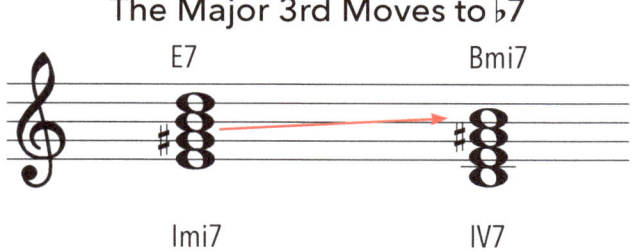

It's worth noting that this is the reverse of a classic Dorian progression you learned earlier. If the progression was Bmi7 to E7, and you perceived B as the tonic, you would hear this as Imi7 to IV7, a classic Dorian progression. Remember, the notes in B Dorian and E Mixolydian are exactly the same. They both have three sharps and can be related to A major.

Work on exploiting that little move over the progression. Target chord tones when you exploit the G# to A.

What other chord tones can you take advantage of? It's helpful to see both arpeggios together in-position. On the left is the Pattern III Mixolydian Scale. To its right is E7, which is I7 and Bmi7, which is Vmi7, all in-position.

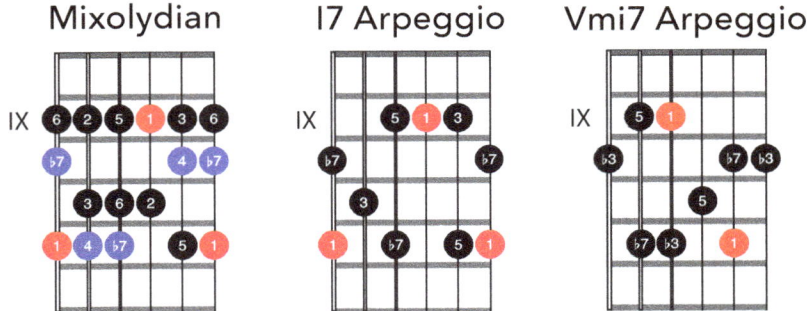

Practice soloing over this vamp blending the Mixolydian Scale and the arpeggio of each chord.

Level 6 Unit 7 • Mixolydian Demo 2

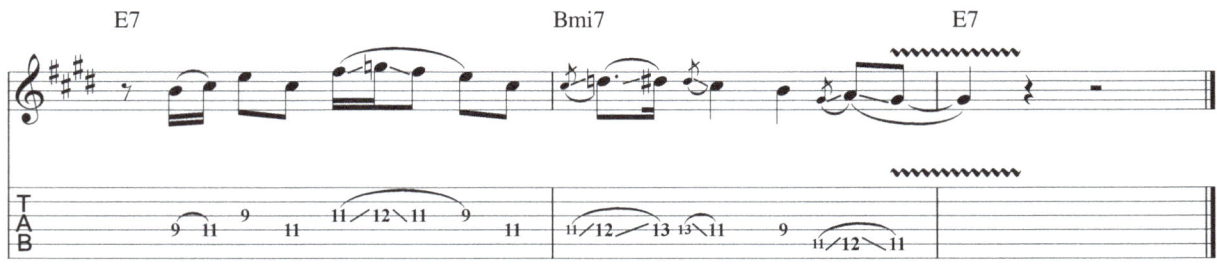

What notes are common between the two chords? B and D. That means they can be used on either chord or held over both. What notes are not in both chords? E and G# from the E7, and F# and A from the Bmi7. Those notes can mark the changes, but don't feel like you need to avoid any scale tone on either chord.

This next Mixolydian progression fragment is common, too. It's been the basis for many songs as well. It is Ima to ♭VIIma.

Progression in C Mixolydian

Practice playing the C Mixolydian scale over the track.

Level 6 Unit 7 • Mixolydian Demo 3

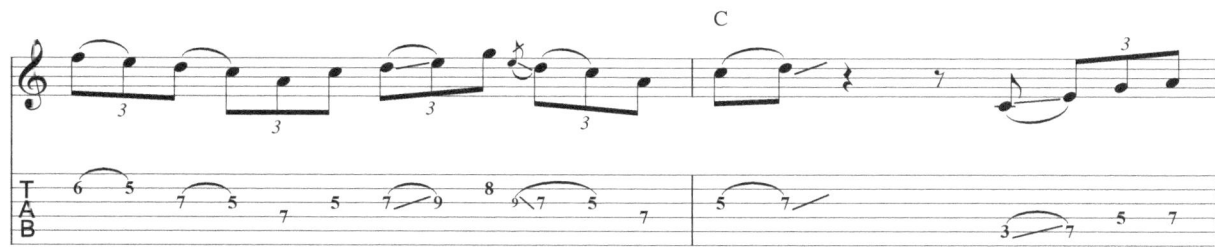

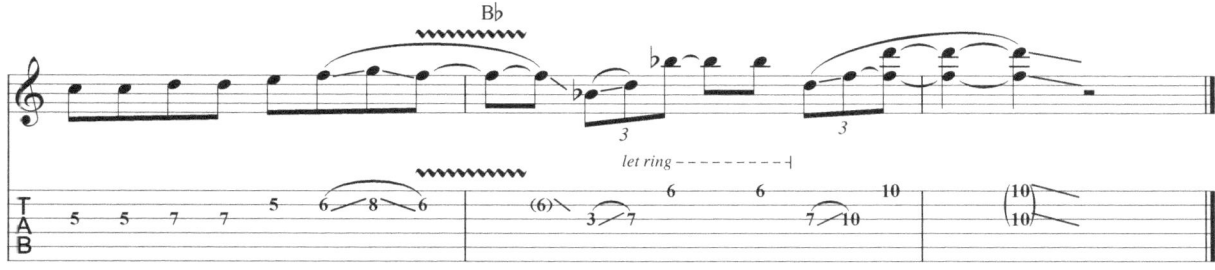

The signature sound in this progression is essentially all of the voices which move by half and whole steps from chord to chord. See the direction of the moving voices:

- The root of C, the I chord, can move up a whole step to D, the 3rd of the B♭ chord.
- The root of C, the I chord, can also move down a whole step to B♭, the root of the B♭ chord.
- The 3rd of C, E, can move up a half step to F, the 5th of the B♭ chord.
- The 3rd of C, E, can down a whole step to D, the 3rd of the B♭ chord.
- The 5th of C, G, can move up a minor 3rd to B♭, the root of the B♭ chord.
- The 5th of C, G, can move down a whole step to F, the 5th of the B♭ chord.

Chord Tones Move One Step

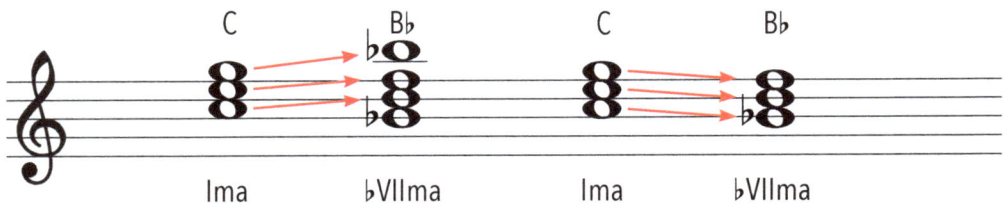

Work on exploiting those movements. You're playing chord tones when you exploit these moving voices.

Fretboard Biology — Level 6 • Unit 7: Improvisation

Level 6 Unit 7 • Mixolydian Demo 4

What other chord tones can you take advantage of? It's helpful to see both arpeggios together in-position. On the left is the pattern III Mixolydian scale. To its right is the C7 arpeggio, which is I7 and the Bbma arpeggio, which is bVIIma, all in-position.

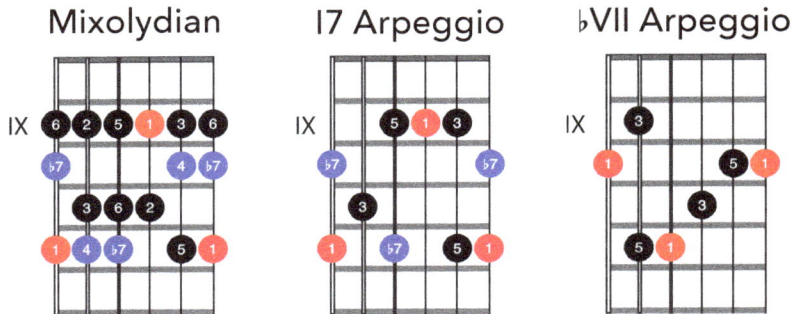

Practice soloing over this vamp blending the Mixolydian Scale and the arpeggio of each chord.

Level 6 Unit 7 • Mixolydian Demo 5

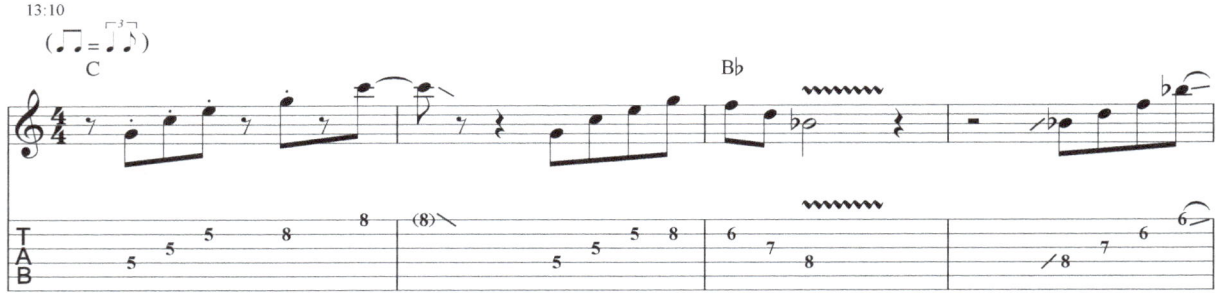

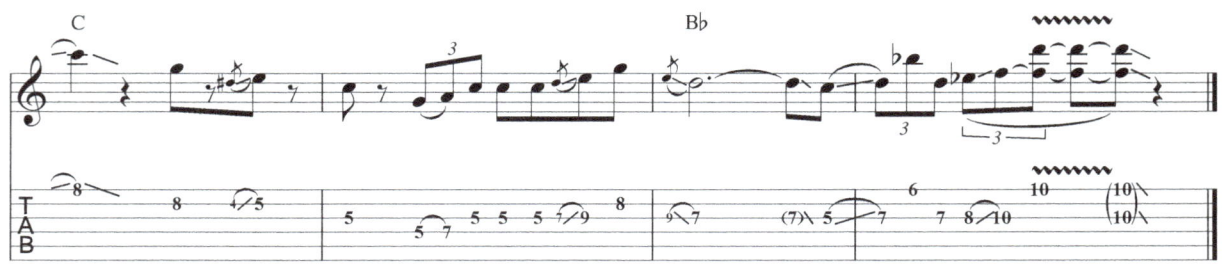

What notes are common between the two chords? Only B♭, if you consider the I chord C, which is I7. That means it can be used on either chord or held for some time.

What notes are not in both chords? C, E, and G from the C7, and D and F from the B♭. Those notes can mark the changes but don't feel like you need to avoid any scale tone on either chord. The chord tones simply mark the change.

This progression may look familiar to you from Level 4 which addressed modal interchange. C to B♭ was analyzed as Ima to ♭VII there, too. But ♭VII was analyzed as being borrowed from the parallel minor. The two analyses are both correct but have a different sound and the written melody will dictate how the progression should be heard. Try both options.

Level 6 Unit 7 • Mixolydian Demo 6

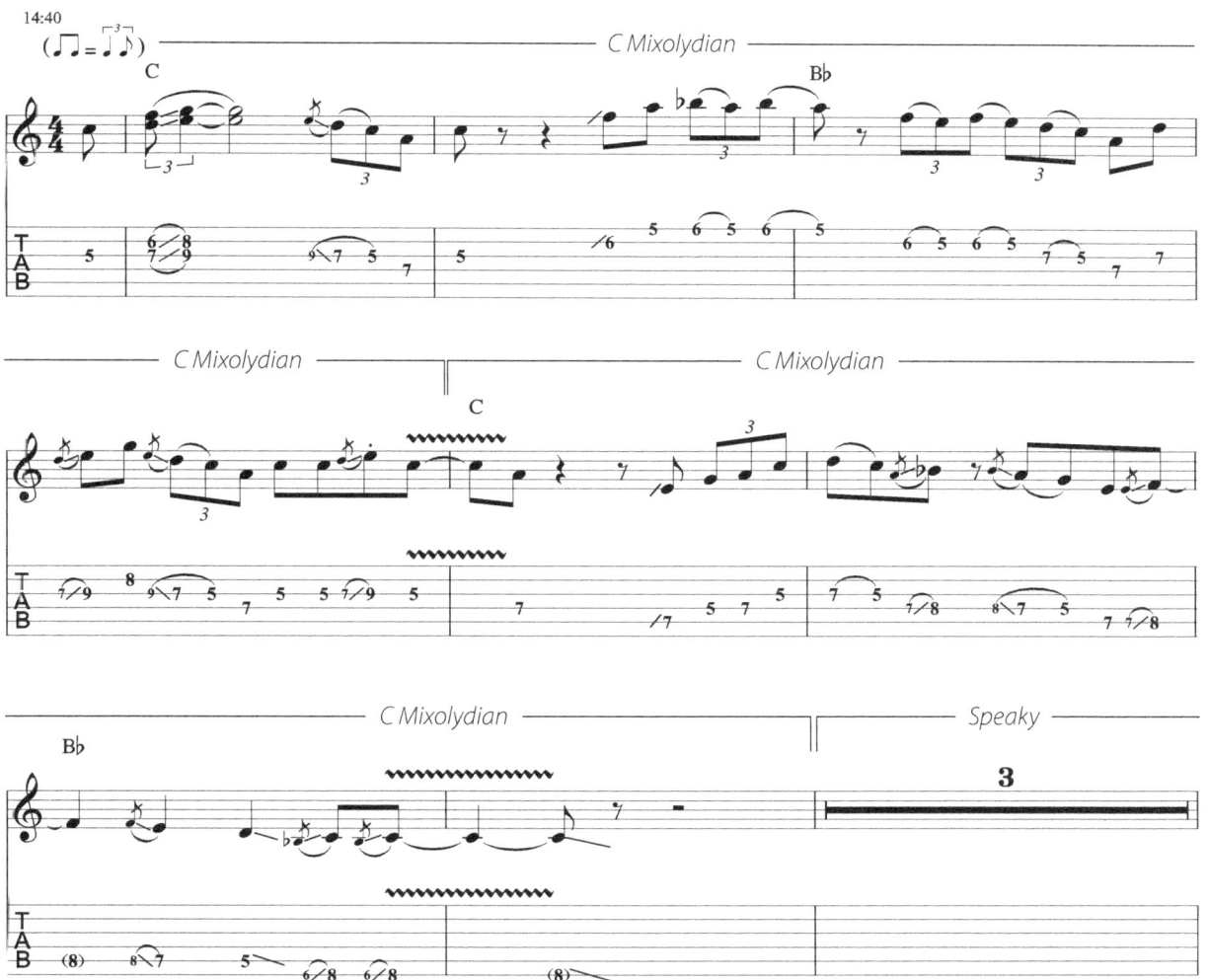

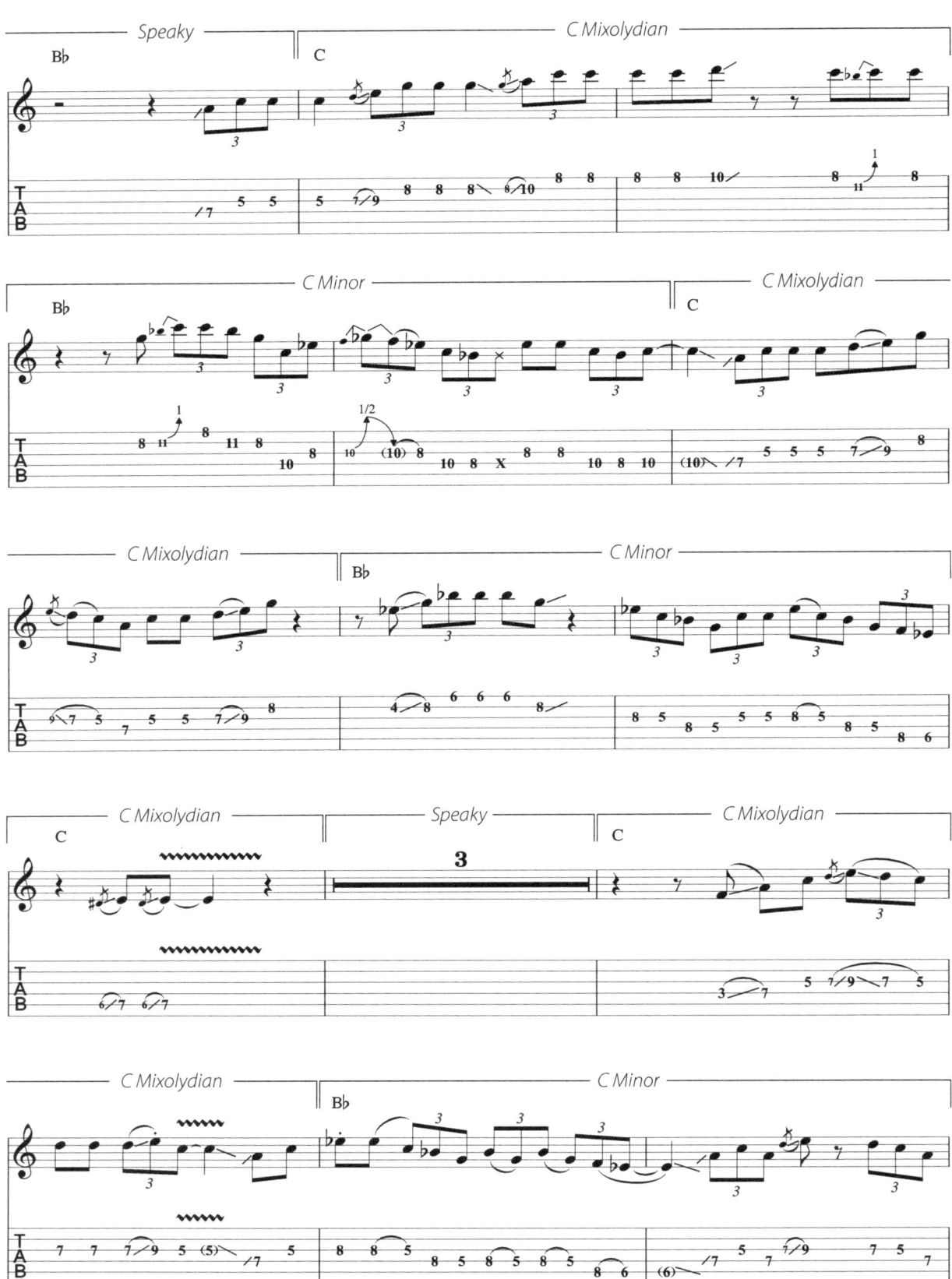

Fretboard Biology — Level 6 • Unit 7: Improvisation

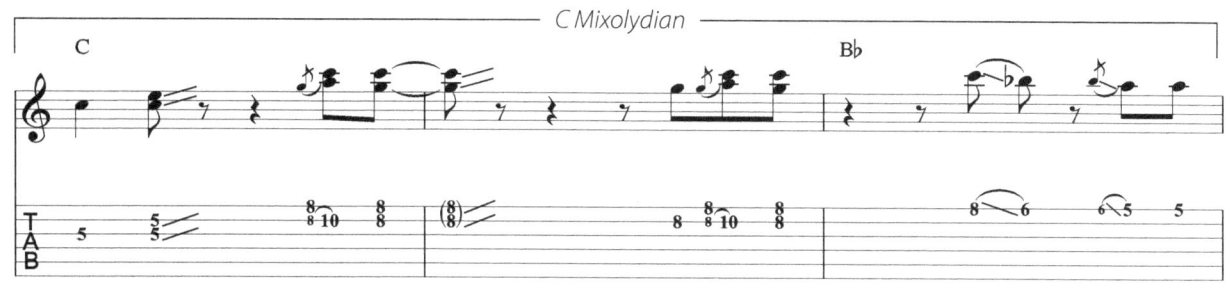

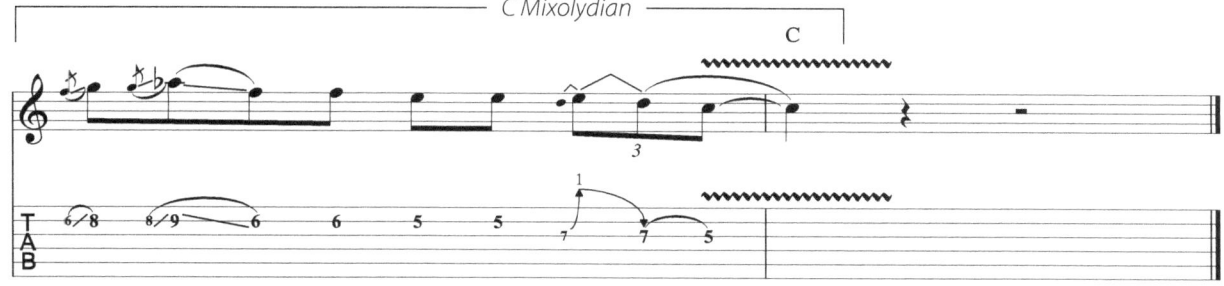

PRACTICE

Theory

- ☐ Learn the common progression fragments in the Mixolydian Scale.
- ☐ Learn the important moves of the voices within the common Mixolydian progression fragments.

Fretboard Logic

- ☐ Know the process of how to derive five patterns of the Mixolydian Scale from the Major Pentatonic Scales by adding a perfect 4th and minor 7th.
- ☐ Become familiar the common Mixolydian progression fragments.

Rhythm Guitar

- ☐ Follow the chart and create and record one or more rhythm guitar parts.

Chart Writing

- ☐ Know the appropriate way to use the jump marks like DC, DS, and Coda signs.

Improvisation

- ☐ Know the personality of each note in the Mixolydian Scale when played over a static dominant 7th chord.
- ☐ Be familiar with soloing over the common progression fragments from the Mixolydian Scale.

UNIT 8

Learning Modules

> **Theory** - The Most Common Progression Fragments in the Lydian Scale
> **Fretboard Logic** - Deriving Patterns of the Lydian Scale from the Major Pentatonic Scales, a Common Lydian Progression Fragment
> **Rhythm Guitar** - Creating a Rhythm Guitar Part for a Classic R&B Song
> **Chart Writing** - Placing all the Information on the Page
> **Improvisation** - Using the Lydian Scale
> **Practice** - Continue Practice Routine Development

The tracks for this Unit can be found at the following link:

https://fretboardbiology.com/book6/#u8

THEORY

The Lydian Scale

In this Module, we'll work with the Lydian Scale. You will hear musicians use the terms Lydian Scale, Lydian Mode, or just Lydian. They all mean the same thing.

Review the construction of the Lydian Scale:

Lydian Mode Interval Pattern

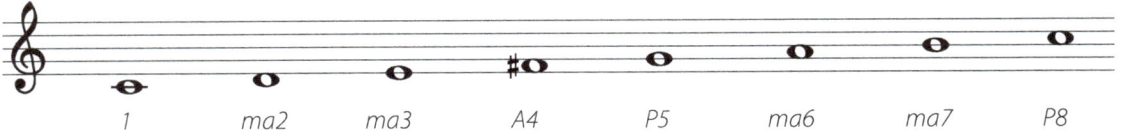

| 1 | ma2 | ma3 | A4 | P5 | ma6 | ma7 | P8 |

Tonic, major 2nd, major 3rd, augmented 4th, perfect 5th, major 6th, and major 7th. Because it has a major 3rd, it is a major-sounding mode. The 4th in the scale is referred to several ways: augmented 4th, raised 4th, sharp 4. They all mean the same thing.

Look at this comparison of the Major Pentatonic and Lydian Scales:

Lydian as a Derivative of the Major Pentatonic Scale

Major Pentatonic	1	ma2	ma3		P5	ma6	
Lydian Mode	1	ma2	ma3	A4	P5	ma6	ma7

The Lydian Scale can be seen as a Major Pentatonic Scale with an added augmented 4th and major 7th. Next, look at this comparison of the Major and Lydian Scales:

Lydian as a Derivative of the Major Scale

Ionian Mode	1	ma2	ma3	P4	P5	ma6	ma7
Lydian Mode	1	ma2	ma3	A4	P5	ma6	ma7

The Lydian Scale can be seen as a Major Scale with an augmented 4th.

Chords

In Unit 3 you learned the chords of the harmonized Lydian Scale. They are:

Lydian Mode Chord Qualities

Ima7   II7   IIImi7   IVmi7(♭5)   Vma7   VImi7   VIImi7

Progressions

The common-sense approach to learning Lydian is to look at the most common harmonic situations in which it's used in popular music. When there's a static ma7 chord for any length of time in a song, one option is to use the Lydian Scale as the prevailing sound, as opposed to the Major Scale which is the Ionian Mode. The raised 4th (augmented 4th) keeps the ma7 chord sounding buoyant, contrary to the Ionian Mode, which in Western Music most people hear as a strong and anchored tonic sound and 'final' sounding.

It's important to emphasize the effect of the Lydian Scale when used as a chord scale for a ma7 chord. We'll call this sense of temporary attachment and buoyancy the Lydian effect. As I mentioned, the Major Scale (Ionian Mode) is usually the sound associated with an anchored major tonal center. The Lydian Scale, with its raised 4th, tends to make the ma7 chord sound less grounded, and almost as a temporary harmonic landing spot. Lydian clearly fits a ma7 chord, but the Lydian effect is that of a temporary attachment. This is useful in many situations where a chord scale is needed for a ma7 chord that is not the I chord, and where you don't want a feeling of grounded resolution.

Let's check the C Lydian Scale for avoid tones. The chord tones of a Cma7 are highlighted. Note that the scale degrees above each note of Cma7 are whole steps, meaning there are no avoid tones. However, the raised 4th is often described as an exotic sound.

Lydian I Chord (ma7)

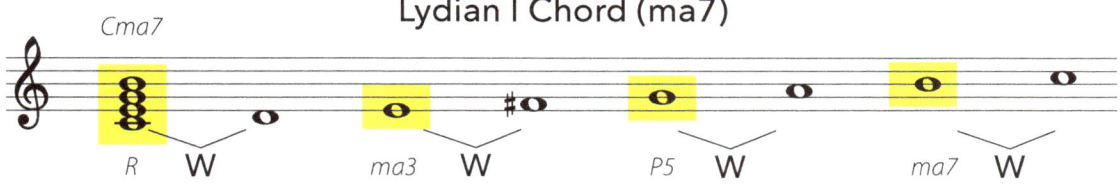

There are no avoid tones in the Lydian Scale.

This two-chord progression fragment is common in Jazz-influenced music. It's been used in many songs and is easily recognizable when you hear it. It is Ima7 to bIIma7.

Progression in C Lydian

In the key of C major, Dbma7 is not diatonic. The signature sound in this progression is the parallel movement of all the chord tones. They all move up a half step.

Chord Tones Move Up Half Step

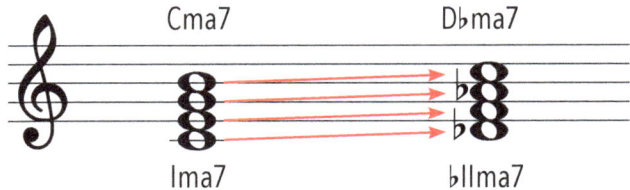

C is the tonic and Cma7 is the I chord. Therefore the Ionian Mode (Major Scale) is an appropriate sound. The Dbma7 is not the tonic and the song did not change keys. A chord scale is needed and the common choice is Lydian, and in this case that would be Db Lydian.

Why Db Lydian on Dbma7? Remember that the Lydian effect is a sense of temporary attachment, whereas Db major would sound too permanent, as if the song had changed keys from C to Db.

FRETBOARD LOGIC

This Module focuses on the Lydian Mode. You know how to create the modes by adding notes to the pentatonic shells.

The goal in this Module is to learn all of the patterns of the Lydian Mode by adding two notes to the five Major Pentatonic shells. By deriving the Lydian Scale from the Major Pentatonic Scale, the muscle memory you developed there will make Lydian feel and sound much more natural, and sooner.

To create the Lydian Scale from a Major Pentatonic shell, add an augmented 4th and major 7th. That's it.

Lydian as a Derivative of the Major Pentatonic Scale

Major Pentatonic	1	ma2	ma3		P5	ma6	
Lydian Mode	1	ma2	ma3	A4	P5	ma6	ma7

It's important to have a clear understanding of the correlation between the following shapes: the Major Pentatonic and Lydian Scales and the chord and arpeggio built on the 1st scale degree.

Pattern I

Let's look at Pattern I. The diagram on the left is the Pattern I Major Pentatonic shell. To its right is the same shell with an augmented 4th and a major 7th added. This is the Pattern I Lydian Mode. To its right is the ma7 chord voicing built on the 1st scale degree and on the far right is the ma7 arpeggio built on the 1st scale degree.

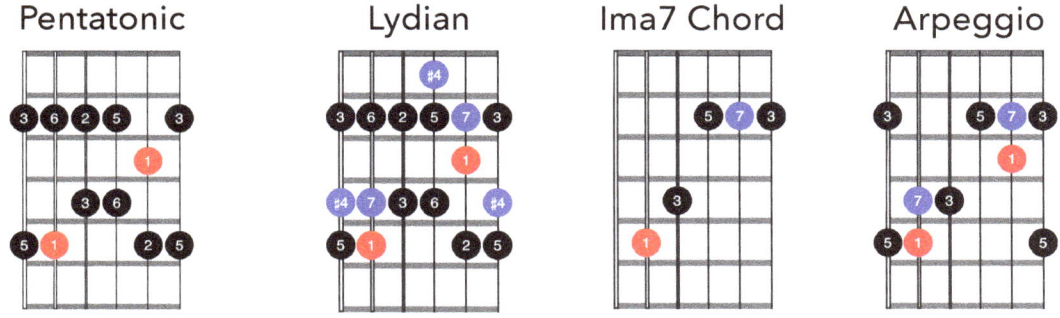

Pentatonic · Lydian · Ima7 Chord · Arpeggio

Pattern II

Let's look at Pattern II. The diagram on the left is the Pattern II Major Pentatonic shell. To its right is the same shell with an augmented 4th and a major 7th added. This is the Pattern II Lydian Mode. To its right is the ma7 chord voicing built on the 1st scale degree and on the far right is the ma7 arpeggio built on the 1st scale degree.

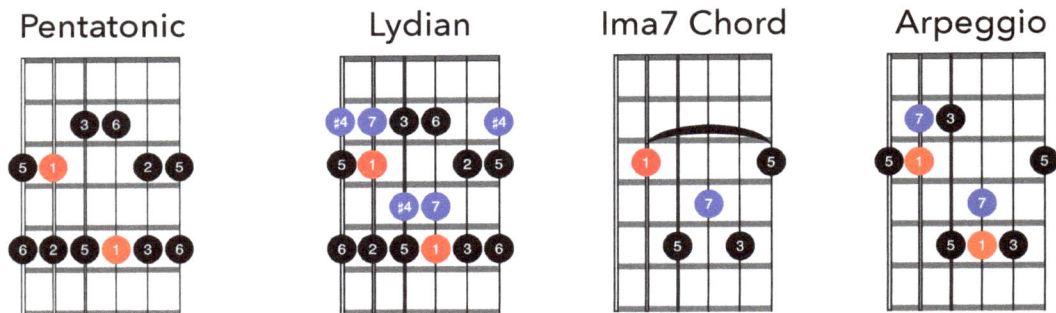

Pattern III

Let's do the same with Pattern III. Add an augmented 4th and a major 7th to the Pentatonic Scale to create Pattern III Lydian Mode. Again, the ma7 chord voicing built on the 1st scale degree and the ma7 arpeggio built on the 1st scale degree are to the right.

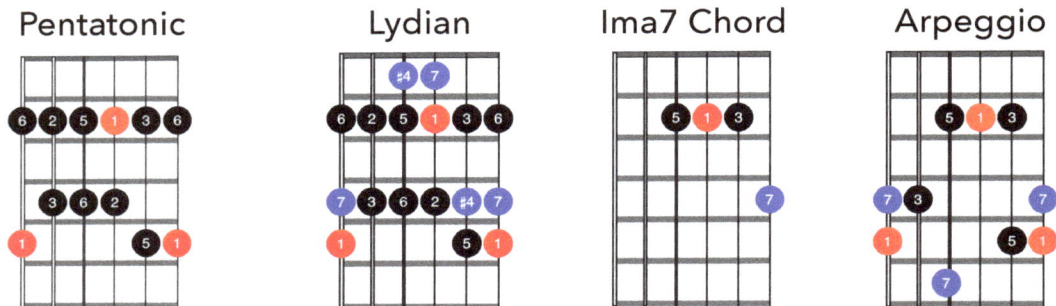

Pattern IV

Same process with Pattern IV. Add an augmented 4th and a major 7th to create the Pattern IV Lydian Mode. The chord voicing and arpeggio are both built from the tonic.

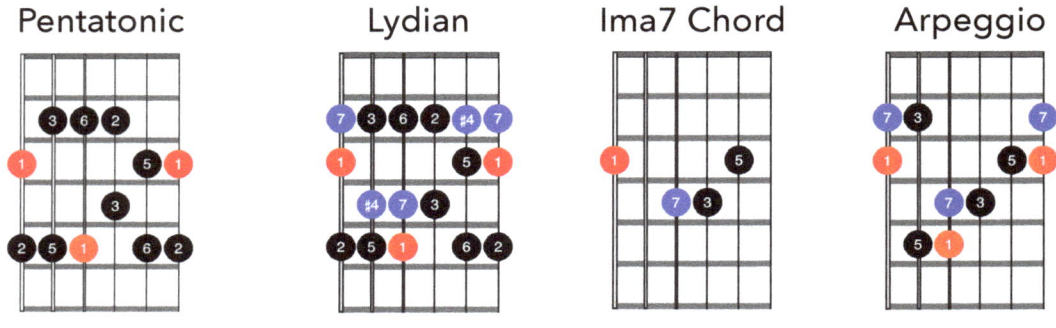

Pattern V

Let's look at Pattern V. The diagram on the left is the Pattern V Major Pentatonic shell. To its right is the same shell with an augmented 4th and a major 7th added. This is the Pattern V Lydian Mode. To its right is the ma7 chord voicing built on the 1st scale degree and on the far right is the ma7 arpeggio built on the 1st scale degree.

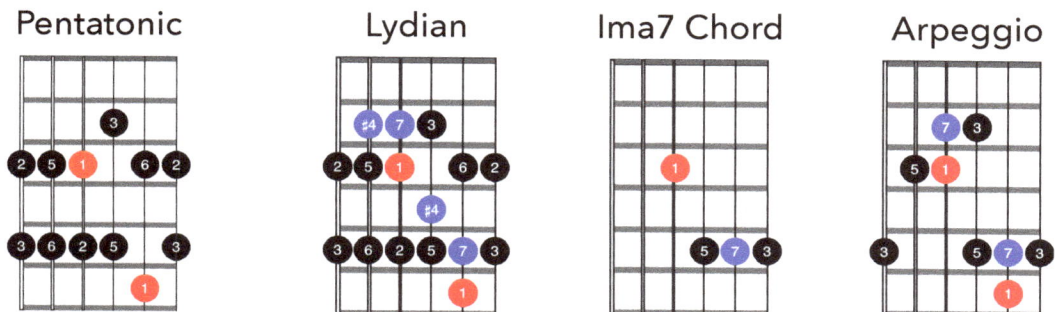

Again, don't feel like you need to memorize all these dots. Memorize the principle.

Lydian Harmony

Let's move on to Lydian harmony. It's important to get a feel for a progression that clearly presents the sound of Lydian. Let's use the same progression fragment that was presented in the Theory Module. This will also be used in the Improvisation Module.

Practice playing the chords of this progression in a few ways with whatever groove you like or play along with the Improv track provided in the link for this Module. You can use barre chords, shell voicings, or an open chord on Cma7.

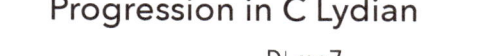
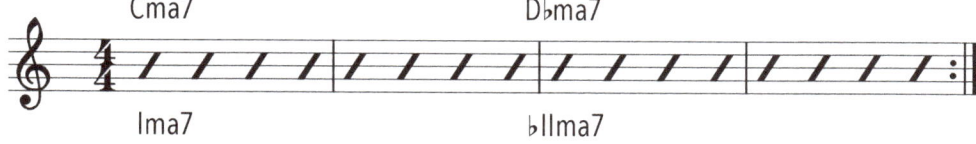

Please relate all of this to the Family Tree. It's important that you keep that connection going!

RHYTHM GUITAR

Creating Parts for Classic R&B

Maybe more than any other style, Classic R&B has guitar parts that clearly feel like they define the sound of the genre. R&B, Blues, Funk, and even Country borrow vocabulary from each other. But how that vocabulary is incorporated into a song can define a genre.

First, let's take a look at the road map on the following page and use your Chart-Reading Checklist.

Chart-Reading Checklist

1. Look at the top left corner where all the preliminary information is: Key signature, Time signature, Style
2. Note the Tempo
3. Scan the form
4. Seek out any figures that need to be played
5. Scan the chords for the ones that are new or difficult for you
6. Seek out more detailed instructions like dynamics, accents, and expression markings

You learned several of the signature R&B rhythm guitar devices, like moving chord voicings, popcorn parts, and the major pentatonic money makers. These can all combine to create a good rhythm guitar part that supports the lead vocal or instrument.

I hope you logged away the material you learned previously because we are going to put that vocabulary to work now.

Listen to the track for this Module again and think like a producer.

You're listening for a part that fits with the band, so consider the instrumentation and what voicings you should use and in what register. Like in the previous units:

- Make sure your part is supportive of the lead vocal or instruments. That's your job.
- Get the right guitar sound.
- Be as consistent as possible and stay in your lane.

Classic R&B Song Chart

Joe Elliott

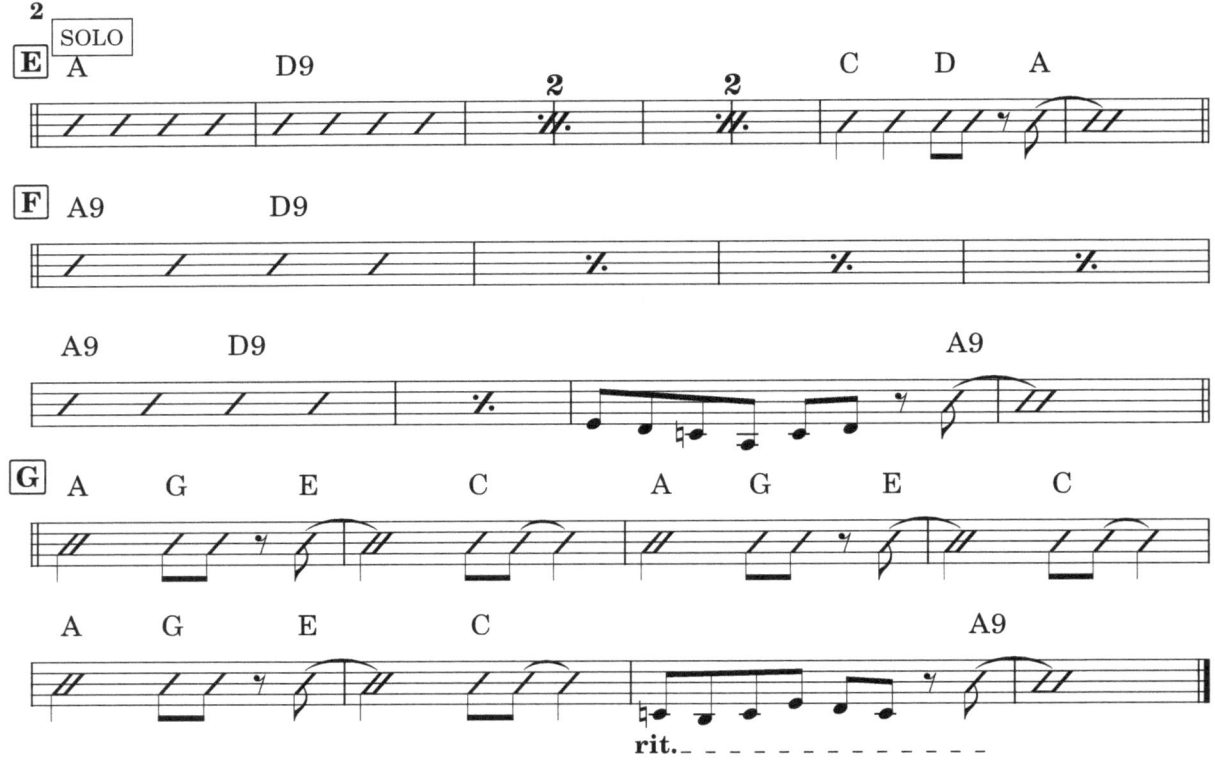

Record your part and ask yourself, "would I want to hear this part on a recording?" If you can, share the part with other musicians you trust and see what they have to say.

Also ask yourself if there's room for a second or even third part. Usually the answer is yes, but don't forget the importance of space, too.

If you haven't been actively using the comping vocabulary you learned back in Level 4, it might be a good idea to go back and review that material. Don't assume all those parts will work in every song. Some may, some may need some modification, and some may not work at all. And there may be room for two parts so keep that in mind.

I hope this is fun and you revisit this chart and track from time to time.

CHART WRITING

Step Eight

In this Module you'll start putting the information on the real chart. But before we get started, let's once again review the steps we have taken so far.

- Step one was the Form Chart.
- Step two was counting measures and creating the crude first draft.
- Step three was writing down the chords.
- Step four was locating and notating rhythm figures and riffs.
- Step five was consolidating the chart by using one-bar, two-bar, and four-bar repeat devices.
- Step six was about start and end repeats and endings.
- Step seven was about using jump marks like DC, DS, and Coda.

All of the steps you learned in Units 1 through 7 led you to the point where you can create a chord chart that's friendly to the reader. In other words, you have planned ahead and now you're ready to write the real chart.

Before you start writing the final draft, it's a good idea to examine the Form Chart and the rough draft together to the get lay of the land. Look at the rough draft and be sure that it is clear about where all the repeat devices are to be used. Cross out the bars or sections you won't need to write. Referencing the form map on the next page, you should cross out the content you won't need to write out (because of repeat devices and jump marks) on the rough draft of the chart.

Also, count how many lines will be needed for each section. A general suggestion is to have the space of four bars per line. Trying to cram in too many bars makes for a chart that's hard to read. The goal is to not have the measures be too crowded together, and that especially goes for measures with a lot of information written in them. In other words, a measure with a figure or riff might need more space than a measure with a whole note, or one with four slash marks. This is the stage where you think about all of that.

As you count the number of actual bars you need, write the number of bars and lines for each section off to the side. The crossed out lines show the ones that don't need to be written.

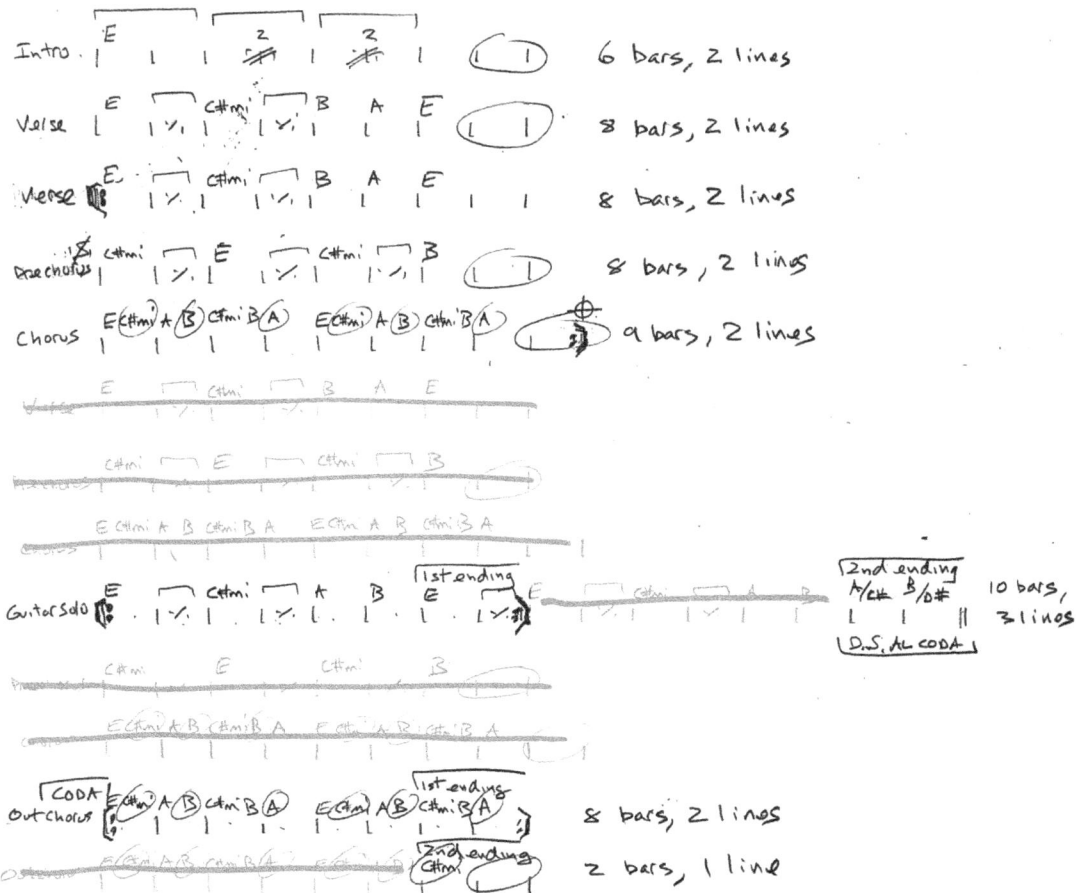

Now that you know how many lines will be needed (16 lines in this example), you know whether it will fit on one page or whether you'll need two or three pages, depending on the number of lines on the paper you are using.

There have been many instances where I can't make a chart fit on one page and I only need one or two lines of the second page. In these cases, I can relax the first page a little and perhaps stack first and second endings or use two or more lines for a section. Charts that are crowded with information can be hard to read. So if there is room to spread it out, I usually take advantage of it.

There are a few things to keep in mind as you put the information down on the page as the 'real version' for you and your bandmates:

- Minimize clutter.
- Charts should read themselves.
- Music should look the way it sounds.

Fretboard Biology — Level 6 • Unit 8: Chart Writing

Transferring the Form Chart to the Page

Here's the big moment. Use a pencil unless you're entering the information on your computer. Begin putting the information on the page. I normally use the top line for the title, but you may prefer to write the title in the upper margin and begin the music on the top line. Either way, begin by writing in the "get started" instructions.

The top left area of a chord chart or any piece of music has important preliminary information that gets you ready to play. Write the title in the margin or on the top stave. Write the style directly below the title. This could be a one-word description like Rock, Swing, Shuffle, Samba, or multiple-word descriptions like 16-Note Shuffle. You can even reference another song or band as in "a la Stones" or "a la Cowboys Don't Cry".

Write in the tempo in the upper left area directly below the song title to the right of the indication of style. It's shown in the form of an equation.

Write the name of either the songwriter or artist off to the right or above somewhere.

Write in the clef sign. You need to make decision about which one. Sometimes it's a treble clef but sometimes a bass clef. The decision is based on what kind of figures may be written into the song and by whom they are played.

For example, if there's a signature bass riff that the song relies on, it's appropriate to use a bass clef. If there's a signature guitar riff that the song relies on, it's appropriate to use a treble clef. Same with keyboards. And it is OK to change the clef sign as needed from section to section. If the same riff is played in different octaves by the bass and guitar, pick one clef or the other; one person will have to read in a different clef than they're used to.

For this song, I'm going to use treble clef since we're guitar players.

Next, write the key signature directly to the right of the clef sign. Next, write in the time signature directly to the right of the key signature. Now it's time to write in the actual measures and music.

The first line is always a place to be careful. For starters, the clef sign, key signature and time signature use a significant amount of space on the line so you have to plan accordingly if you need to fit four measures into the remaining space. This assumes four measures per line is a standard. I usually make that a goal.

I normally wait until the bar lines are written, the chord symbols and rhythm figures are in, and any riffs are notated before writing in section letters, DC, or DS markings, Codas, or anything else. This is because you may need to fit these markings in and around the chord symbols. But every situation is different and as you gain experience, you learn to anticipate potential competition for space on the page. When notating by hand, I use a pencil with a good eraser and I don't hesitate to use it.

I suggest you write the barlines in for an entire line first, then write slash marks or any rhythm figures or riffs. This is before any chord symbols go on the chart. Once all that is completed for a line, you can put the chord symbols in above the staff. It's up to you, but I often wait until all bar lines, slash marks, rhythm figures, and riffs are in before I put chord symbols in. The benefit is that it helps keep your penmanship consistent.

When you do write in any information on the chart, try to keep the horizontal corridor right above the staff clear for the chord symbols. This is the main place the reader's eye is focused on and having other notation mixed in with the chord symbols only adds stress.

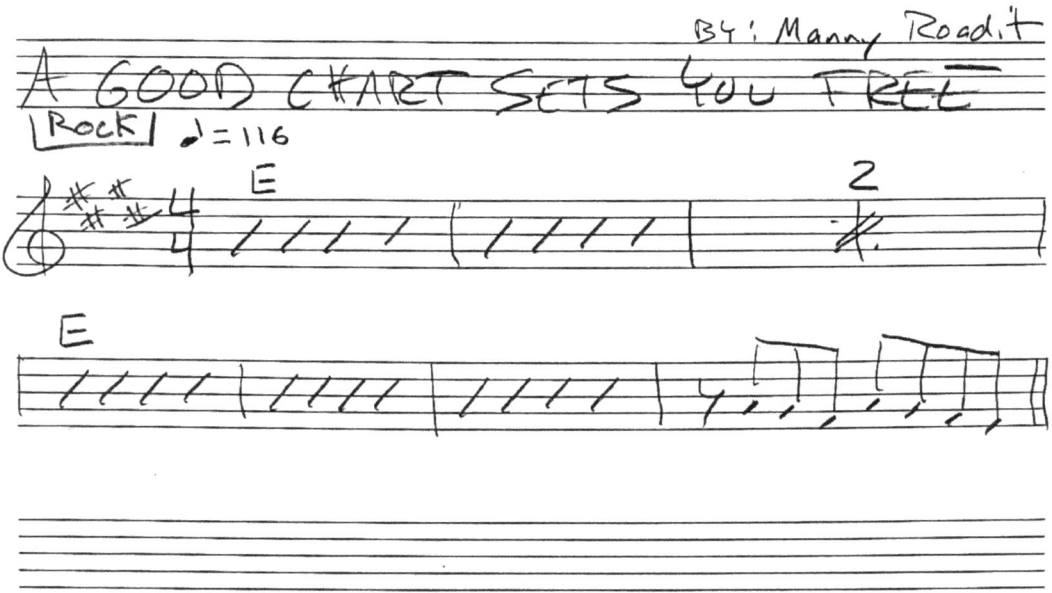

Now work through the entire chart, line by line. Remember to wait on the section markings and everything else until you're finished with this stage. Once you have this step completed, go back through the chart and add the first and second ending markings. Then go through to add rehearsal letters. Next, work through and add the DS and CODA signs.

Next, work through adding any of the other helpful information. This can include information about a solo or perhaps some lyric cues, or pretty much any other notes that will help the performance.

Once this is done, take a look and let your eye travel through the chart while listening to the recording. Is it easy or do you struggle to keep your place? More importantly, will someone who hasn't been working on writing the chart for several hours be able to follow the road map? That's what's important.

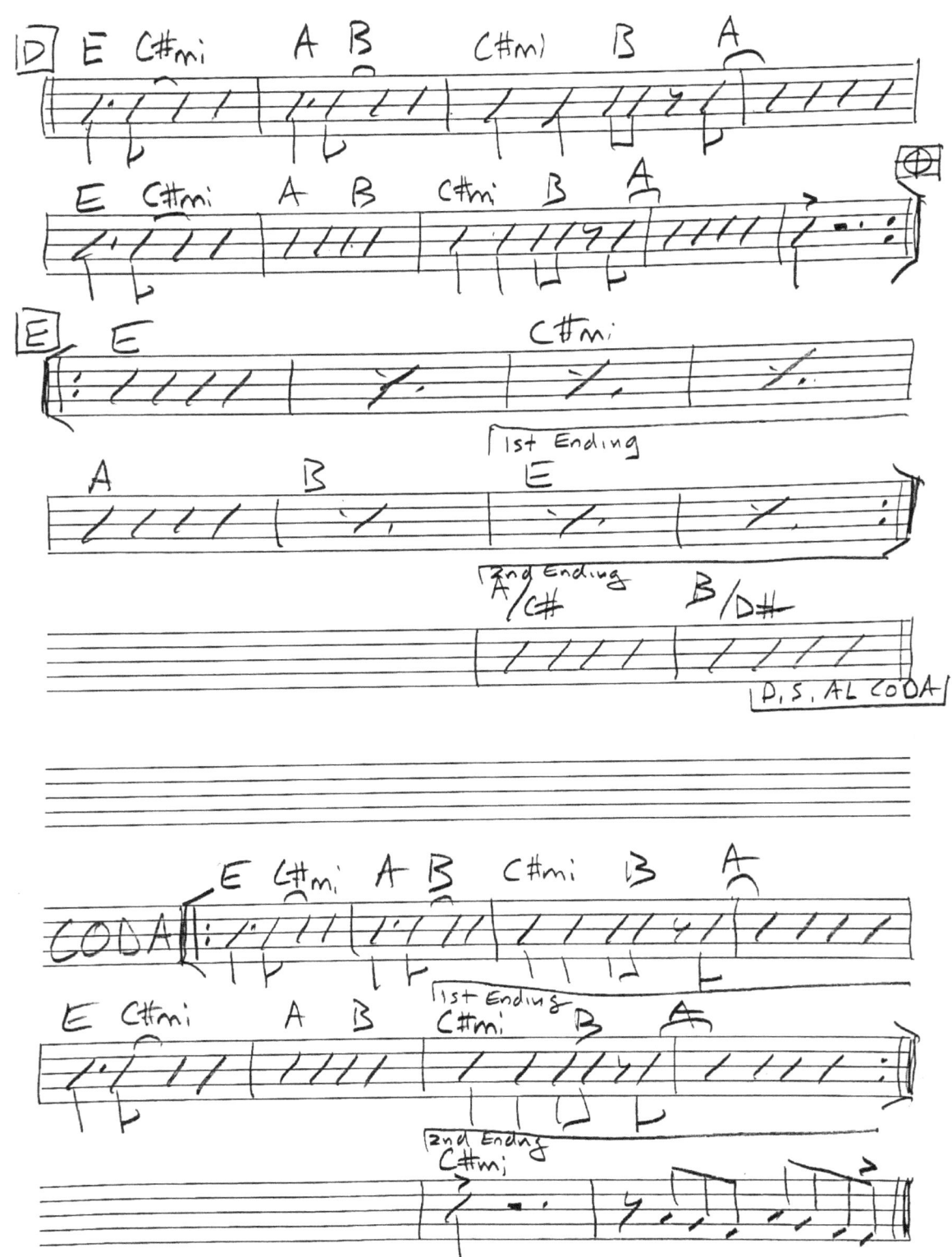

IMPROVISATION

Lydian Mode

You had a little experience playing the Lydian Scale over a static ma7 chord in the Unit 2 Improvisation Module. The idea was to just get a feel for the sound. In this Module we'll get into some finer detail about the Lydian Scale.

Remember that all of the scales and arpeggios you learn are tools and it's important to know how they work. Each note in every scale or arpeggio has a personality and an effect on the listener. Get to know how each note makes you feel against the chord.

Remember that we're thinking of Lydian and all the modes as pentatonic shells with two notes added. By relating modes to pentatonic shells, you benefit from the muscle memory you've already developed from using the pentatonic scales.

We'll start by working in Pattern III in this Module because it's derived from the Pattern III Major Pentatonic Scale, which is a pattern most guitarists are very comfortable with. But everything we discuss in this Module can be used in any of the five octave shapes, pentatonic shells ,and patterns of the Lydian Scale.

Hearing the Lydian Sound

Let's start by playing the Pattern III Major Pentatonic Scale over a static Cma7 vamp. Then play the Pattern III Lydian Scale over the same static Cma7 vamp.

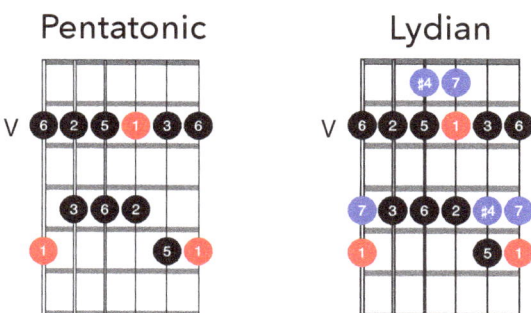

They both sound major, they both fit nicely, and they have the five notes of the Major Pentatonic Scale in common. The Lydian Scale, however, has the added augmented 4th and major 7th. These two notes are the notes that distinguish Lydian from Major Pentatonic. The augmented 4th and ma7 are also the two notes that distinguish Lydian from the Major Scale.

As before, let's Identify the chord tones within the scale. There are four: the root, major 3rd, perfect 5th, and major 7th. And there are seven notes in the scale. The notes other than the chord tones are the major 2nd, augmented 4th, and major 6th. There are no avoid tones in Lydian mode.

Notes of the Lydian Scale

1 — ma2 — mi3 — A4 — P5 — ma6 — mi7 — P8

Unique tone of the Lydian Mode

Each note in every scale or arpeggio has a personality and an effect on the listener. Play each note of the scale against the static chord vamp with the track. The exercise is to dwell on every note of the scale and experience how each one makes you feel when played over the chord. Come up with your own adjectives to describe how you hear each note of the scale against the chord and work at remembering them. If you know the personality of a note, you can use it to set a mood to start a phrase with or perhaps find a note to dwell on in a solo.

Spend some time soloing on a static ma7 chord and listen to the unique effect of each scale tone. Experiment with combinations, too. Remember, Lydian has no avoid tones. That's one reason it's a popular scale, but it's also well-suited for ma7 chords in progressions that are not the tonic chord.

Progressions in Lydian

Next, let's talk about the Lydian Scale used in progressions. One of the common uses of the Lydian Scale is a little different than that of the Dorian and Mixolydian Modes. Consider the following about the Dorian and Mixolydian modes.

With the Dorian mode, we sampled progressions with chord movement, where the mi7 chord was clearly the I chord and other chords from the harmonized scale were used. But a strong sense of I was established.

With the Mixolydian Mode, we sampled progressions with chord movement, where the I7 chord was clearly the I chord and other chords from the harmonized scale were used. But again, a strong sense of I was established.

While it's possible for Lydian to offer a sense of I when it's used for a static ma7 chord, it's usually used as a chord scale for a ma7 chord that is not the I chord.

This is illustrated in this two-chord progression fragment you saw in both the Theory and Fretboard Logic Modules. This is common in Jazz-influenced music but it's heard in pop songs, too, and you'll recognize it when you hear it. It is Ima7 to bIIma7, and it's written here in C major. Imagine that C has been established as the tonic and therefore Cma7 is clearly the I chord.

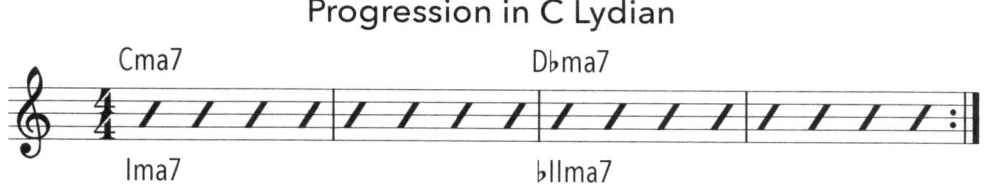

In the key of C major, Dbma7 is not diatonic. Is it modal interchange? From what we have studied so far, no. The sound of the parallel movement of all the chord tones in this progression should stand out. They all move by a half step.

C is the tonic and Cma7 is the I chord; therefore the Ionian Mode (Major Scale) is an appropriate sound. The Dbma7 is not the tonic chord and the song did not change keys. A chord scale is needed for it and the common choice is Lydian. In this case, that is Db Lydian. Why Lydian? Remember that the Lydian effect gives a sense of temporary attachment, whereas the sound of Db major on the Dbma7 chord would sound too permanent, as if the song had changed keys from C to Db.

Compare the C Major Scale to Db Lydian. Are there any common tones?

C Major	C	D	E	F	G	A	B	C	
Db Lydian	Db	Eb		F	G	Ab	Bb	C	Db

Yes. F, G, and C, although F is an avoid tone for Cma7. C and G, however, sound great when held over each chord. So in this case and others, the Lydian Scale is used as a chord scale solution for a ma7 chord that is not the tonic chord.

Play the C major scale over Cma7 and the Db Lydian scale over Dbma7. Use the Pattern IV C Major Scale and the Pattern IV Db Lydian Scale. You can exploit the common tones, C, F, and G, as well as the chord tones that move by half step from chord to chord.

Now listen to the demo and watch the transcription provided.

Level 6 Unit 8 • Lydian Demo 1

Lydian is sometimes used over Ima7 which is normally an 'Ionian setting'. This has a colorful and exotic effect but still is not usually used in the context of a whole song or passage of a song unless it's written using chords from the harmonized Lydian Scale.

Let's take a look at another possibility. Look at this progression and listen to the track.

Progression in E Minor

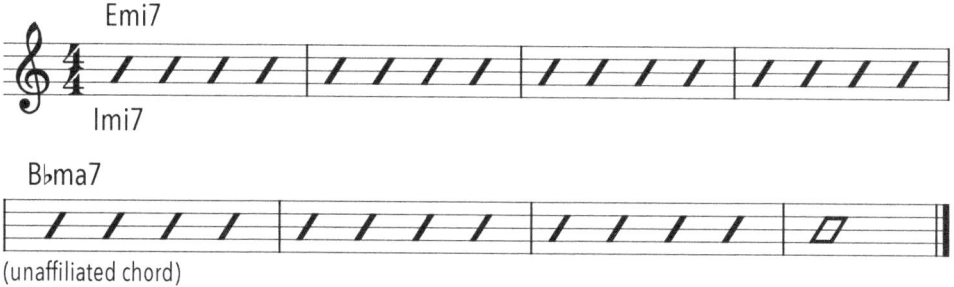

(unaffiliated chord)

This repeating 8-bar vamp seems to established E minor as the key center to start. But then in moves to a B♭ma7 chord which really has nothing to do with the key of E minor, and that includes Natural Minor, Dorian Minor and Harmonic Minor. The duration of these chords as 'static' is pretty long: 4 bars each. And that's enough time to almost create a tonal world around each, although, when Emi7 returns, you feel a strong attachment to it as the 'real' tonic chord. But what about B♭ma7? Where did it come from? Actually, it doesn't have to have come from anywhere.

One beautiful thing about writing music is that you don't have to follow the rules if you don't want to. If you like that way something sounds, it's your prerogative to write what you want into a song and then figure out what to play over it later.

Recall in your introduction to Lydian as a chord scale that is an excellent choice to play over a ma7 chord that you don't want to sound like a tonic chord. The raised 4th offers that 'Lydian effect' which is a sound of temporary attachment. If you were to play the B♭ major scale over B♭ma7 it would sound like you had modulated to B♭. B♭ Lydian, however, checks all the boxes as the right scale choice. It has all the chord tones of B♭ma7, it has no avoid tones and it doesn't make you feel like you've modulated to B♭.

Experiment playing an E Dorian over the Emi7 and B♭ Lydian over the B♭ma7. This kind of two chord vamp can be addictive in practice sessions because you have so much time to develop ideas on each chord.

Level 6 Unit 8 • Lydian Demo 2

PRACTICE

Theory

- ❏ Learn the most common progression fragment in the Lydian Scale.
- ❏ Learn the important moves of the voices within the common Lydian progression fragments.

Fretboard Logic

- ❏ Know the process of how to derive five patterns of the Lydian Scale from the Major Pentatonic Scales by adding an augmented 4th and major 7th.
- ❏ Become familiar with the most common Lydian progression fragment.

Rhythm Guitar

- ❏ Follow the chart and create and record one or more rhythm guitar parts.

Chart Writing

- ❏ Know how to place the information from your draft charts onto the page.

Improvisation

- ❏ Know the personality of each note in the Lydian Scale when played over a static major 7th chord.
- ❏ Be familiar with soloing over the most common progression fragment that uses the Lydian Scale.

UNIT 9

Learning Modules

> **Theory** - The Most Common Progression Fragments in the Phrygian Scale

> **Fretboard Logic** - Deriving Patterns of the Phrygian Scale from the Minor Pentatonic Scales, the Most Common Phrygian Progression Fragments

> **Rhythm Guitar** - Creating a Rhythm Guitar Part for an Afro-Latin Song

> **Chart Writing** - Adding Helpful Information to a Chart

> **Improvisation** - Using the Phrygian Scale

> **Practice** - Continue Practice Routine Development

The tracks for this Unit can be found at the following link:

https://fretboardbiology.com/book6/#u9

THEORY

The Phrygian Scale

In this Module, we'll work with the Phrygian Scale. You will hear musicians use the terms Phrygian Scale, Phrygian Mode, Phrygian Minor, or just Phrygian. They all mean the same thing.

Let's review the construction of the Phrygian Scale.

Phrygian Mode Interval Pattern

1   mi2   mi3   P4   P5   mi6   mi7   P8

Tonic, minor 2nd, minor 3rd, perfect 4th, perfect 5th, minor 6th, and minor 7th. Because it has a minor 3rd, it is a minor-sounding mode. The minor 2nd in the scale is referred to several ways: flat 2nd, lowered 2nd, flat 2. They all means the same thing.

Look at this comparison of the Minor Pentatonic and Phrygian Scales:

Phrygian as a Derivative of the Minor Pentatonic Scale

Minor Pentatonic	1		mi3	P4	P5		mi7
Phrygian Mode	1	mi2	mi3	P4	P5	mi6	mi7

The Phrygian Scale can be seen as a Minor Pentatonic Scale with an added minor 2nd and minor 6th.

Next, let's look at this comparison of the Natural Minor (Aeolian) and Phrygian Scales:

Modes as Derivatives of the Minor (Aeolian) Scale

Aeolian Mode	1	ma2	mi3	P4	P5	mi6	mi7
Phrygian Mode	1	mi2	mi3	P4	P5	mi6	mi7

The Phrygian Scale can also be seen as a Natural Minor Scale with a minor 2nd.

Chords

In Unit 3 you learned the chords of the harmonized Phrygian Scale. They are:

Phrygian Mode Chord Qualities

Imi7   bIIma7   bIII7   IVmi7   Vmi7(b5)   bVIma7   bVIImi7

Progressions

The common-sense approach to learning the Phrygian Mode is to look at the most common harmonic situations in which it's used in popular music. When there's a static mi7 chord for any length of time in a song, one option is to use the Phrygian Scale as the prevailing sound. The minor 2nd is the exotic sounding note, but also an avoid tone when played over the I chord. The rest of the scale is constructed like the Natural Minor Scale which means it also has a minor 6th, which is another avoid tone. You'll recall that an avoid tone can be played in passing so its effect on the listener is felt in a flash, but the impression is made nonetheless.

C Phrygian I Chord

This two-chord progression fragment is recognizable when you hear it. It is Imi to bIIma. This is in A Phrygian Minor.

Progression in A Phrygian

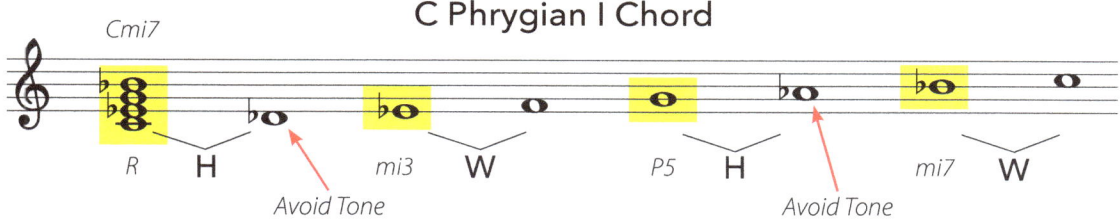

The signature sound in this progression is the parallel movement of most of the chord tones.

Chord Tones Move Up Half Step

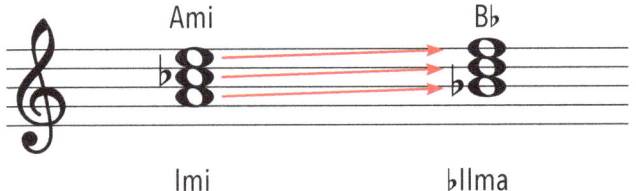

Here's another two-chord progression. It is Imi7 to ♭VIImi7.

Progression in A Phrygian

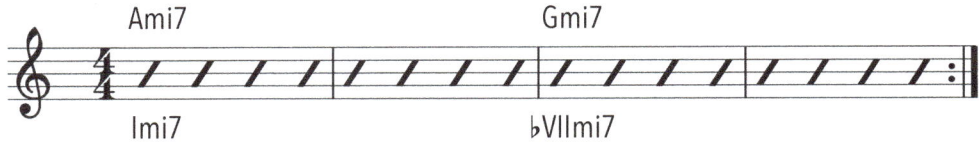

The signature sound in this progression is the parallel movement of all of the chord tones.

Chord Tones Move Down One Step

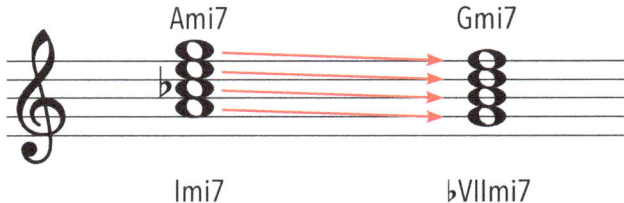

These progression scenarios will be addressed from a performance standpoint in the Improvisation Module.

FRETBOARD LOGIC

Our focus in this Module will be on the Phrygian Mode. You know how to create the modes by adding notes to the pentatonic shells.

The goal is to learn all of the patterns of Phrygian by adding two notes to each of the five Minor Pentatonic shells. By deriving the Phrygian Scale from the Minor Pentatonic Scale, the muscle memory you developed there will make Phrygian feel and sound much more natural, and sooner.

To create the Phrygian Scale from a Minor Pentatonic shell, add a minor 2nd and a minor 6th. That's it.

Phrygian as a Derivative of the Minor Pentatonic Scale

Minor Pentatonic	*1*		*mi3*	*P4*	*P5*		*mi7*
Phrygian Mode	*1*	*mi2*	*mi3*	*P4*	*P5*	*mi6*	*mi7*

It's important to have a clear understanding of the correlation between the following shapes: the Minor Pentatonic and Phrygian Scales and the chord and arpeggio built on the 1st scale degree.

Pattern I

Let's look at Pattern I. The diagram on the left is the Pattern I Minor Pentatonic shell. To its right is the same shell with a minor 2nd and a minor 6th added. This is the Pattern I Phrygian Mode. To its right is the mi7 chord voicing built on the 1st scale degree and on the far right is the mi7 arpeggio built on the 1st scale degree.

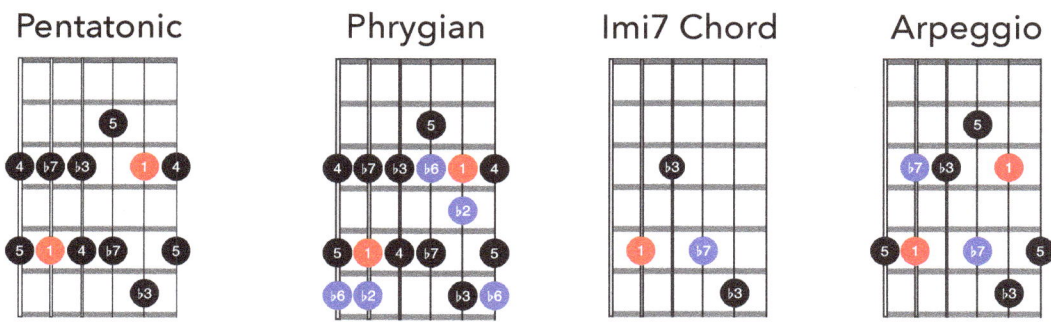

Pattern II

Here's Pattern II. The diagram on the left is the Pattern II Minor Pentatonic shell. To its right is the same shell with a minor 2nd and a minor 6th added. This is the Pattern II Phrygian Mode. To its right is the mi7 chord voicing built on the 1st scale degree and on the far right is the mi7 arpeggio built on the 1st scale degree.

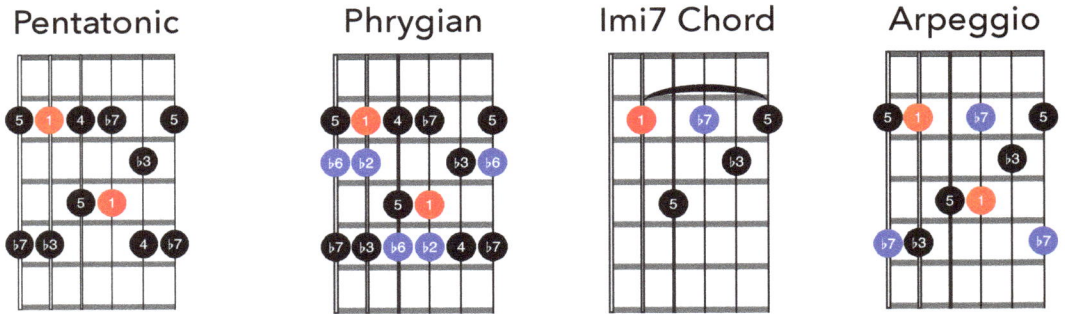

Pattern III

Let's do the same with Pattern III. Add a minor 2nd and a minor 6th to the pentatonic scale to create the Pattern III Phrygian Mode. The mi7 chord voicing built on the 1st scale degree and the mi7 arpeggio built on the 1st scale degree are to the right.

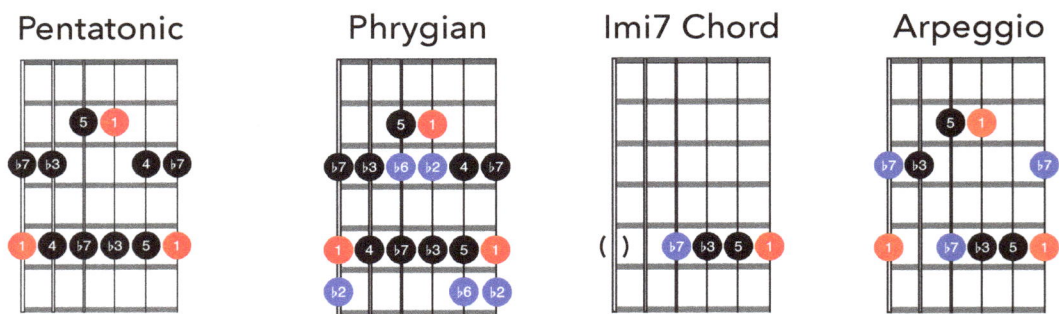

Pattern IV

Same process with Pattern IV. Add a minor 2nd and a minor 6th to create the Pattern IV Phrygian Mode. The chord voicing and arpeggio are both built on the 1st scale degree.

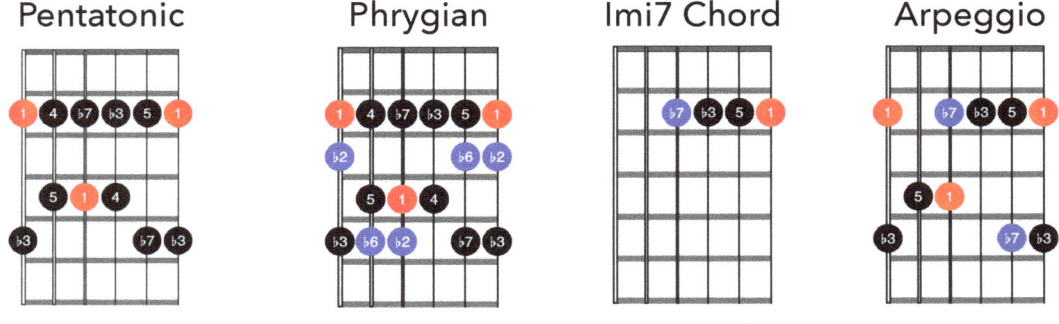

Pattern V

Here's Pattern V. The diagram on the left is the Pattern V Minor Pentatonic shell. To its right is the same shell with a minor 2nd and a minor 6th added. This is the Pattern V Phrygian Mode. To its right is the mi7 chord voicing built on the 1st scale degree and on the far right is the mi7 arpeggio built on the 1st scale degree.

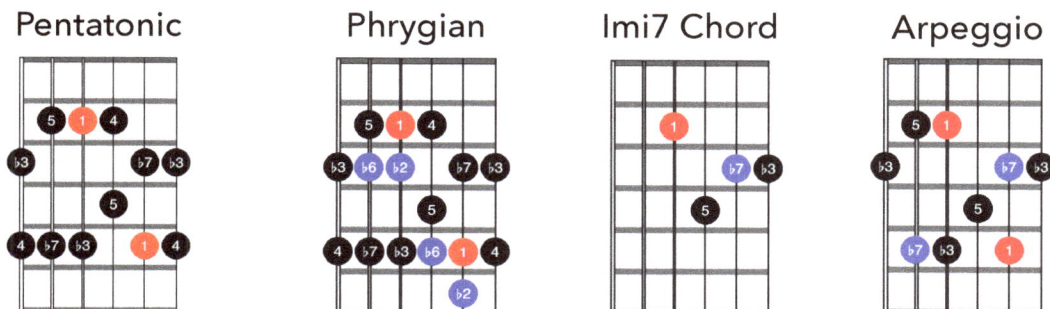

As before, there is no need to memorize all these dots right away. Understanding the process is far more important.

Phrygian Harmony

Let's move on to Phrygian harmony. It's important to get a feel for a progression that clearly presents the sound of Phrygian. We will use one of the progression fragments that was presented in the Theory Module that will also be used in the Improvisation Module.

Practice playing chords in a few ways with whatever groove you like or play along with the track for this Module. You can use barre chords, shell voicings, or an open chord on Ami.

Progression in A Phrygian

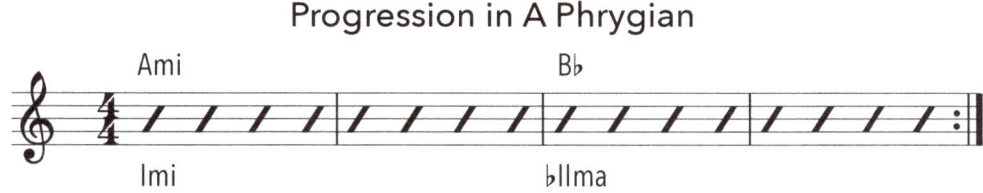

As always, be sure to relate all of this to the Family Tree. It's important that you keep that connection going!

RHYTHM GUITAR

Creating Parts for Afro-Latin Songs

In Unit 1 of Level 5, you studied rhythm guitar parts for Bossa Novas. Now let's look at a chart for a Bossa tune and come up with a rhythm part. As always, let's first take a look at the road map on the following page and use your Chart-Reading Checklist.

Chart-Reading Checklist

1. Look at the top left corner where all the preliminary information is: Key signature, Time signature, Style
2. Note the Tempo
3. Scan the form
4. Seek out any figures that need to be played
5. Scan the chords for the ones that are new or difficult for you
6. Seek out more detailed instructions like dynamics, accents, and expression markings

Listen to the track provided for this Module, and again, it's time to think like a producer. That means to listen from the perspective of what the song needs from a rhythm guitar player. This is a Bossa Nova and if you need to, go back and review the Level 5 Unit 1 Rhythm Module that introduced you to the groove.

Now listen to the track again and create a rhythm part. Record your part and ask yourself if it blends. Would you want to hear this part on a recording?

Normally there isn't room for a second part in a Bossa, but sometimes there is. If you were to add a second part, it would probably be a part that was sparse and in a high register.

Make this feel good! That's the most important thing. As before, share your recordings with other musicians you trust to see what they have to say.

Just a quick reminder that a G13 chord is just a G7 chord with extensions and can be treated as a G7 chord. We will discuss chord extensions in Level 7.

Latin Song Chart

Step Nine

Rules about chart-writing notation vary from region to region, genre to genre, and person to person. In fact, we shouldn't call everything you have learned in this series of modules 'rules'. The better term may be 'best practices' because what is important is to present the basic elements of a song on paper or screen in the best way for the musician to read. Clarity for the reader is your priority at all times, and as you may recall, the goal is to have the chart read itself.

In this Module we will talk about some additional topics that can make your charts more readable. I'll offer some reasons why you might use them and, for each one, in what circumstances they will be helpful.

Let's talk about a few form notation ideas that have to do with how the form of a song appears on the page.

Numbering

The first is the use of numbering. Numbering every measure of a song, if done neatly and discretely can really speed up locating a specific location in a song at a rehearsal. It's like having exact latitude and longitude coordinates on map. There a few places you can position the numbers but I suggest placing them below the staff and at the very beginning of the measure the number applies to.

A Good Chart Sets You Free

Rehearsal Letters and Section Terms

Next is the use of rehearsal letters and/or section terms. There are various ways to mark sections. Rehearsal letters are very common. But some musicians who perform a lot of music with vocals prefer to write the name of the section in the same place where a rehearsal letter would go. You can use descriptive words like Intro, Verse 1, Prechorus, Chorus, Bridge, Solo, Interlude, Ending, and so on. It's always advisable to surround words with boxes to set them apart from chord symbols. I have seen many sloppy charts where a letter in a word could be confused for a chord symbol.

For a reader, any uncertainty diverts focus from playing the music, and that's bad for the performance. Here's something to consider: Many singers don't refer to song form or structure in terms of rehearsal letters. They imagine the song structure in terms of verse, prechorus, chorus, and so on. Don't fight it, just go with that way to notate your chart if that's what will work best in that situation.

A Good Chart Sets You Free

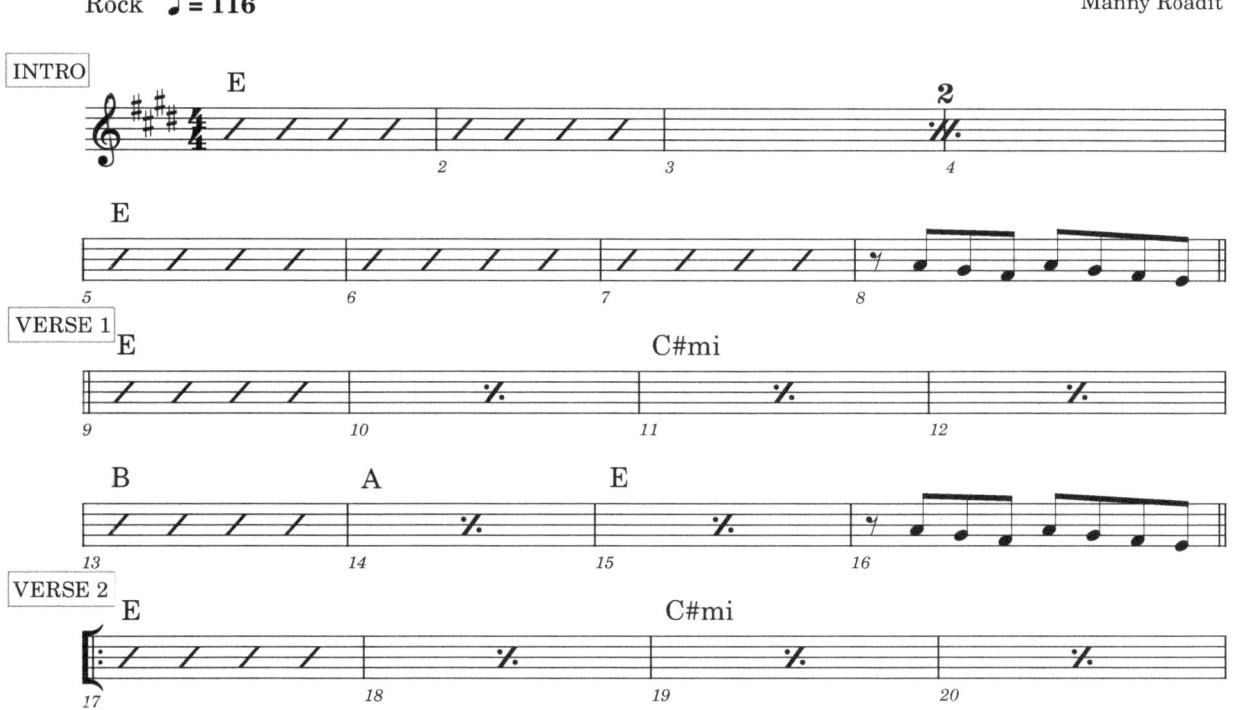

It's not unusual to use both rehearsal letters and descriptive words at the beginning of a section. So, for example, letter A might also be marked '1st verse' and so on. Be careful to not clutter the page. For a reader, any clutter can confuse and that distracts and diverts focus from playing the music.

Section Numbers

Now let's talk about using section numbers. Sections can also be marked by the number of the measure the section begins with. For example, if the section you might otherwise label letter A is the 9th measure, box in a '9' and place that in the same place where a rehearsal letter would go. This is common in lengthy charts where you might otherwise use up a lot of letters of the alphabet.

A Good Chart Sets You Free

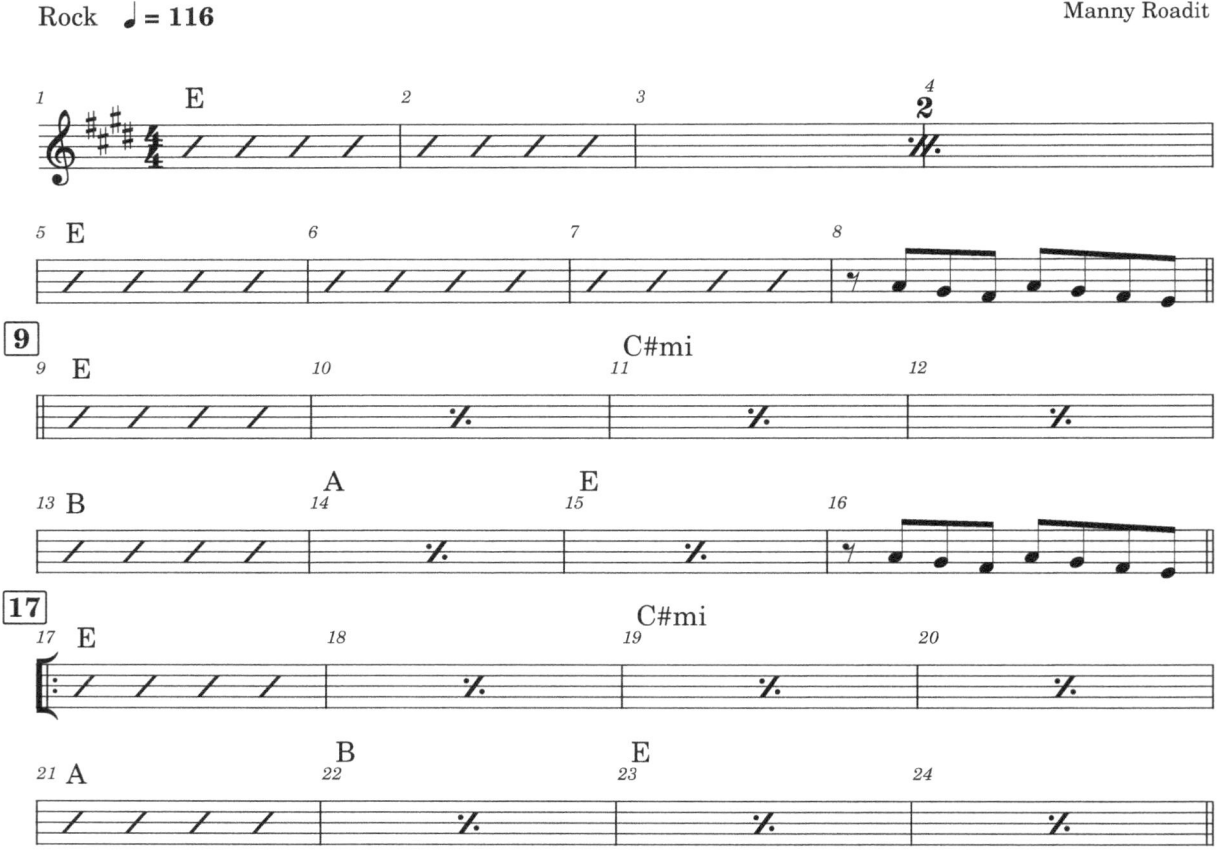

Form Summary

Whether you use rehearsal letters or words, it's always helpful to have a 'Form Summary' somewhere on the page. That can be next to or in the margin above the title or at the very bottom of the last page. It's basically a list of the sections.

A summary might look like this: A A B C A B C D A B C C C

If the reader is a quick learner, they can see what the overall structure of the song is at a glance. If they memorize the chords within each section and then memorize the form summary, they can memorize a song quickly. Even though the chart we've been working on has 13 sections, it's really only four unique sections performed in the order shown. It's much easier to learn four sections than 13.

Form Summary: A A B C A B C D A B C C C

Pick-Up Notes

Next, let's talk about pick-up notes. Pick-up notes are chords or melody, bass, or riff notes that precede and lead into a section. If these pick-up notes are to be present for a repeated section, they need to be notated in the final bar before the repeat. These can be set apart with parentheses or with a message written above or below saying '1stx only' or something to that effect.

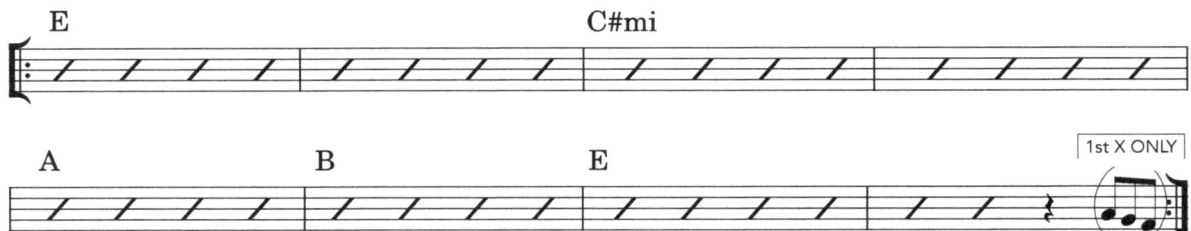

If pick-up notes are the very first notes played in a song, and you want to use the jump mark 'DC' from a location later in the song, the DC is normally interpreted as starting where the body of the first section is, meaning after the pick-up notes. If you want to be a stickler, you can use DS instead and place the sign above the measure after the pick-up notes.

Lyric Cues

You can also use what are called lyric cues. Lyric cues can be very helpful with repetitive vocal music where it's easy for the reader to get lulled into a little nap. Just a few words of the beginning of a vocal phrase can save the reader if they lose their place in one of these repetitive situations. It's saved me countless times.

Again, remember that many singers think of the song structure in terms of verse, prechorus, chorus, and so on, and not in terms of rehearsal letters. Don't fight it, just go with marking the sections with words if you feel that is appropriate, and add a few lyrics here and there for safety's sake.

Special Instructions

Next, we are going to take a look at a few ideas for notating special instructions on chord charts. These include things like notating written instructions, slight variations, who is supposed to play a particular figure, and warnings and attention-grabbers.

Let's start with how to put written language on a chart. Whenever English is written on the chart, I suggest capitalizing the letters and for most instructions, boxing them with a two- or three-sided box. Like with form names, boxing sets the words apart from the chord symbols and can help prevent avoidable confusion. Let's look at an example.

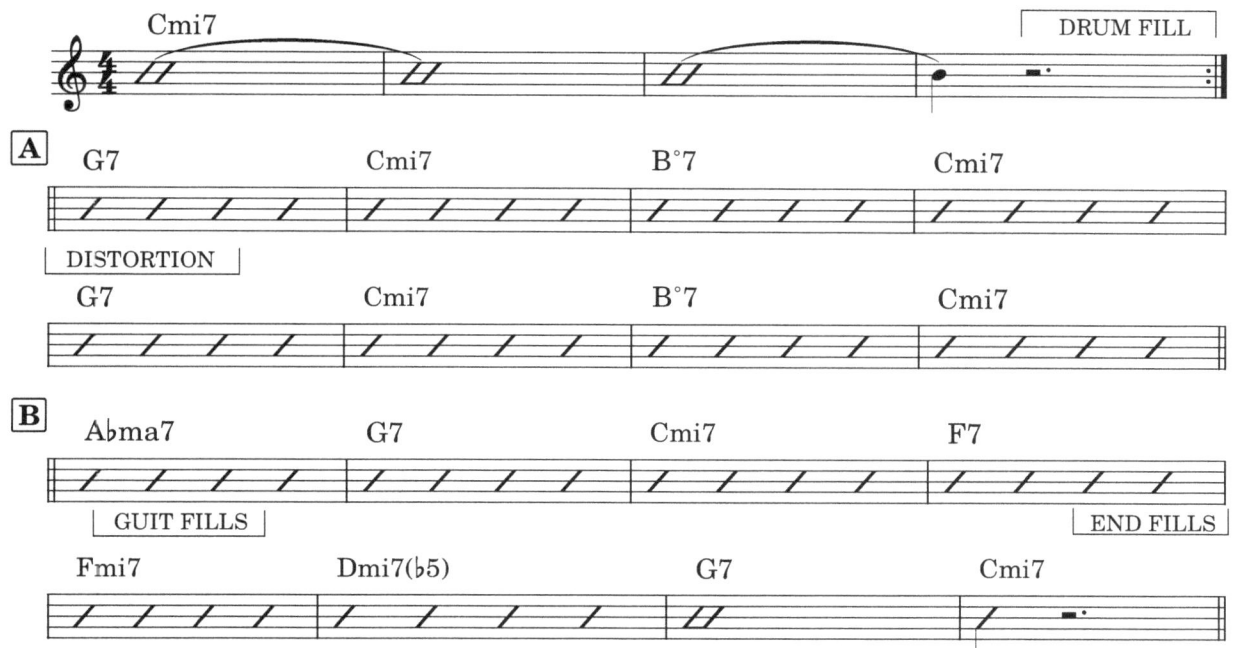

Notating Slight Variations

Next, we'll look at how to notate slight variations on a chart. Sometimes there is a slight variation in repeated sections that doesn't justify rewriting the whole section. It may be an additional chord, riff, or rhythm hit, and if you were to follow all of the suggestions you've learned thus far, you'd use another two or three or more lines just to notate that slight variation.

It is common practice to write in the variation and draw attention to it one of a couple of ways. Sometimes the creator of a chart will put the variation in parentheses and write instructions like, "2nd x only" or "don't play 1st x". You could also write the figure with a slightly smaller font so that it shows it's different. If it is a rhythm figure only, it can be written with smaller-than-normal slash marks that are placed higher in the staff or even above the staff. In my opinion, if it's clear and understandable, it's OK. Keep in mind that this is a chord chart which is a minimal representation of the song. You are not taking a test at school. The only test is whether the reader is successful at reading your chart.

You can help the reader avoid confusion by clearly notating who plays a particular section or figure and who doesn't. Sometimes a figure that may only apply to one or a couple of the instruments can be notated. There are a couple of common practice ways to instruct the band. Sometimes the creator of a chart will put the name of the instrument in parentheses and say "GUITAR ONLY" or DRUMS ONLY".

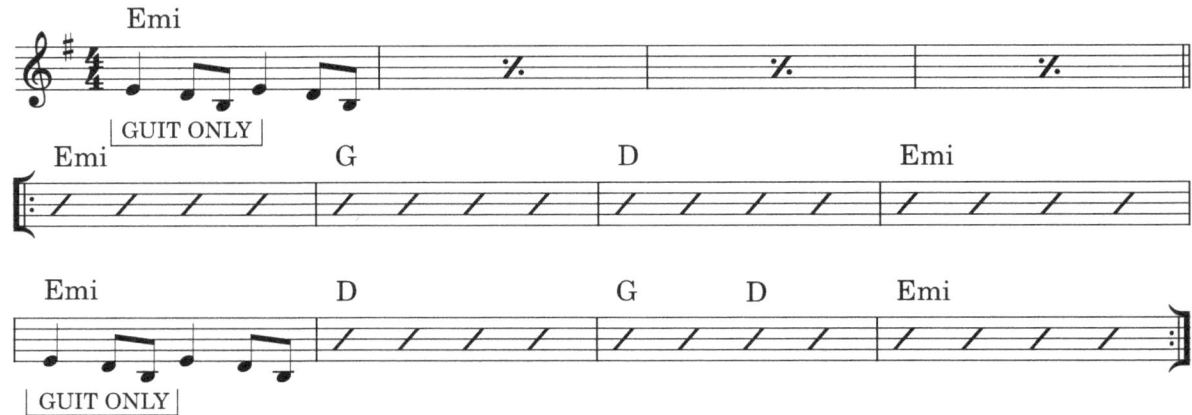

Warnings and Attention-Grabbers

Let's briefly talk about the use of warnings and attention-grabbers. Chord charts can include warnings that a hard part or odd form event is about to happen. I've seen a lot of charts with a little picture of glasses that act as a flashing light to pay extra special attention. I've seen charts with the word "LOOK" written above the staff as another way to warn the reader.

A Few More Tips

Lastly, let's discuss a few simple tips to help your charts look clean and organized. These are not so much about adding information to the page, but rather about making all the information on the page prettier to look at and easier on the eyes.

Here are a few extra tips you might want to try:

1. The first one I want to talk about is the use of a ruler for handwritten charts. Handwritten charts are only as good as your writing. Using a small ruler is a big help. You can use it for bar lines, creating an even line for the bottom of your chord symbols or any words that need to be written. A ruler helps make the boxes you draw around words or rehearsal letters look a lot better, too.

2. The next tip is the option of not using slash marks and leaving open bars. I've written many charts where I have intentionally not used slash marks and have left the staff between the barlines and below the chord symbols blank. This is effective in instances where you give the charts to the band members in advance of the rehearsal or gig so that the entire band can read from the same road map, but know

that each member will want to write in specific things for themselves in the staff where the slash marks would normally be. This works great in situations where the band members do their homework. Every band member has the same road map with the same section markers and repeat devices and all other chart marks, but each chart can be personalized by each musician.

3. The last tip I want to share is the use of color in your chart. Using colors to highlight start and end repeats, jump marks, or any other instructions that you want to draw attention to is really effective but has to be done by hand in most cases. Keep in mind that some shades of colored highlighters disappear under stage light colors. Experiment with the ones you can find at a store.

As we said in the beginning, rules about chart-writing notation vary from region to region, genre to genre, and person to person. Make clarity for the reader your priority at all times and you'll always be appreciated by them. Remember, the goal is to have the chart read itself. The more charts you read, the more ideas you'll get about what works and what doesn't. Don't be afraid to experiment. There are best practices and there are rules. Consider notating rhythms, single notes, and chords more as rules you should follow. And consider the arrangement of the content on the page (in other words, the road map), as best practices.

IMPROVISATION

Phrygian Mode

You had a brief experience playing the Phrygian Scale over a static mi7 chord in the Unit 2 Improvisation Module. The idea at that point was to just get a feel for the sound. This Module spends more time with the Phrygian Scale.

Each note in every scale or arpeggio has a personality and an effect on the listener. Get to know how each note makes you feel against the chord.

Remember the approach we are using for seeing the modes shapes on the fretboard is to add two specific notes to a pentatonic shell. By relating modes to these shells, you benefit from the muscle memory you've already developed from using the Pentatonic Scales.

We'll be working in Pattern IV Phrygian Scale in this Module because it's derived from the Pattern IV Minor Pentatonic Scale, which is a pattern most guitarists are very comfortable with. But everything we discuss in this Module can be used in any of the five octave shapes.

Hearing the Phrygian Sound

Let's start by playing the Pattern IV Minor Pentatonic Scale over the static Ami7 track provided in the link for this Module. Then play the Pattern IV Phrygian Scale over the same static Ami7 vamp. The minor 2nd is very distinct and after hearing the Minor Pentatonic Scale, the minor 6th stands out, too.

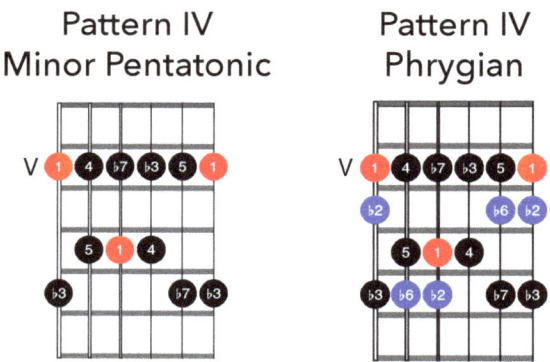

They both sound minor, they both fit, and they have the five notes of the Minor Pentatonic Scale in common. The Phrygian Scale, however, has the added minor 2nd and minor 6th. These two notes are the notes that distinguish Phrygian from Minor Pentatonic.

As with the other modes, there are four chord tones within the scale: the root, minor 3rd, perfect 5th, and minor 7th. And there are seven notes in the scale. The notes other than the four chord tones are the minor 2nd, perfect 4th, and minor 6th. The minor 2nd is the note that distinguishes the Phrygian Scale from the Natural Minor Scale and is really the defining note of the scale.

The Phrygian Scale has two avoid tones. The minor 2nd is a half step above the root or 1 and the minor 6th is a half step above the perfect 5th. So the minor 2nd and minor 6th are avoid tones.

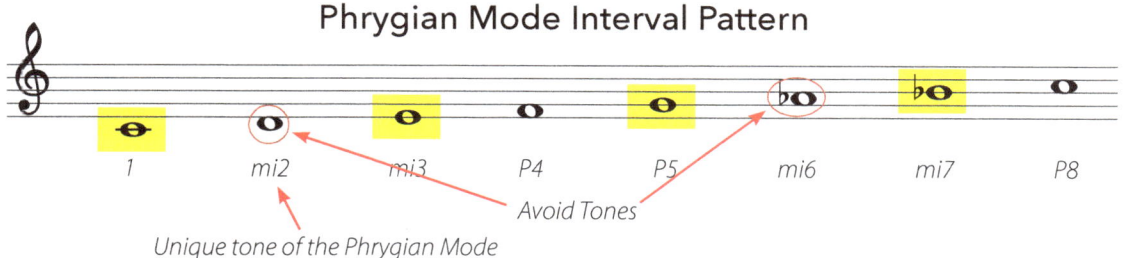

Each note in every scale or arpeggio has a personality and an effect on the listener. Play each note of the scale against the static chord vamp with the track. The exercise is to dwell on every note of the scale and experience how each one makes you feel when played over the chord. Come up with your own adjectives to describe how you hear each note of the scale against the chord and work at remembering them. Now you need one for the minor 2nd. It is impactful.

Spend some time soloing on a static mi7 chord sampling the emotional effect of each scale tone. Experiment with combinations of chord tones, too.

When there is a static mi7 chord for any length of time in a song, one option is to use the Phrygian Scale as the prevailing sound instead of any other minor scale. The minor 2nd is the exotic sounding note, but also an avoid tone, so be aware that this will grab the listener's attention. The rest of the scale is constructed like the Natural Minor Scale, which means it also has a minor 6th, another avoid tone.

And keep in mind that on a mi7 chord played for an extended period of time, the sound established by the ♭2 in Phrygian is so strong that it's hard to transition out of it. It's a bit like having a very strong taste in your mouth and then eating something that tastes completely different. The first taste may linger. Experiment changing from Phrygian Minor to any of the other parallel minor scales over a static mi7 vamp and see what you think.

Progressions in Phrygian

In the Theory Module you learned some of the standard progression fragments that highlight the most commonly-used chords from the harmonized Phrygian Scale. First, review the chords of the harmonized Phrygian Scale. They are:

Phrygian Mode Chord Qualities

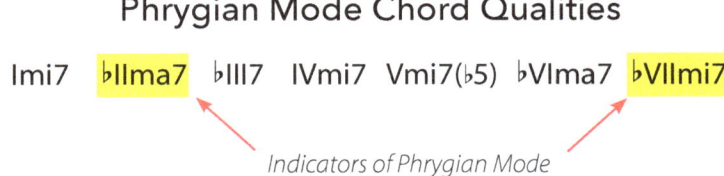

Indicators of Phrygian Mode

Of these, bIIma7 (or bIIma), and bVIImi7 (bVIImi) are the most common chords and are unique to Phrygian.

Here are two harmonic situations where you will see the Phrygian Scale used. This two-chord progression fragment is recognizable when you hear it. It is Imi to bIIma. Listen to the track to know what it sounds like.

Progression in A Phrygian

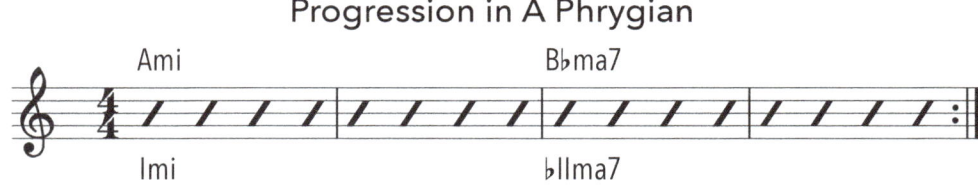

Play the A Phrygian Minor Scale over it. Listen to the demo and watch the transcription provided.

Fretboard Biology — Level 6 • Unit 9: Improvisation

Level 6 Unit 9 • Phrygian Demo 1

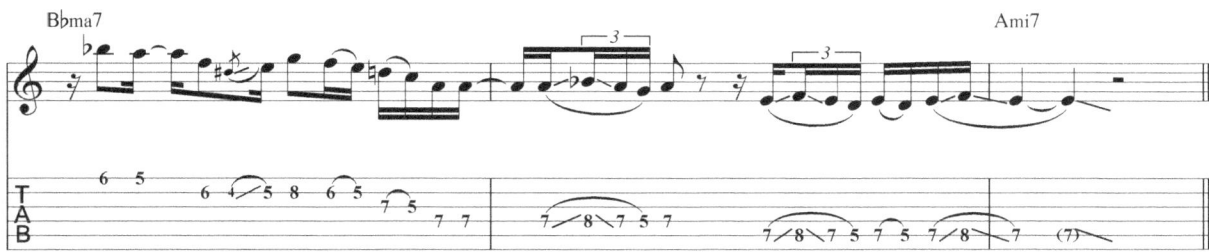

The signature sound in this progression is the half-step move from A to B♭, the roots of the two chords, and E to F, the 5ths of the 2 chords.

Work on this. You are targeting chord tones when you exploit the A to B♭, and E to F. Now listen to the demo and watch the transcription provided.

Level 6 Unit 9 • Phrygian Demo 2

What other chord tones can you take advantage of? It is helpful to see both arpeggios together in-position. On the left is the Pattern IV Phrygian Scale. To its right is Ami7, which is Imi7 and B♭ma7, which is ♭IIma7, all in-position.

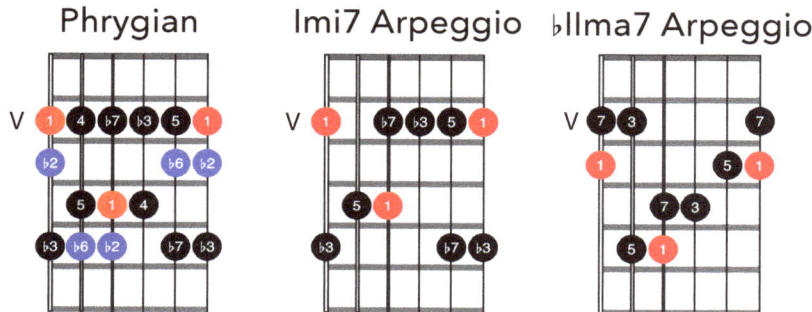

Practice soloing over this track blending the Phrygian Scale and the arpeggio of each chord. What note is common between the two chords? A. That means they can be used on either chord or held over both.

What notes are not in both chords? C, E, and G from the Ami7, and B♭, D, and F from the B♭ma7. Those notes can mark the changes, but don't feel like you need to avoid any scale tone on either chord.

Level 6 Unit 9 • Phrygian Demo 3

Here's another two-chord progression. It is Imi7 to ♭IVmi7.

Now play the A Phrygian scale over it. The signature sound in this progression is the parallel movement of most of the chord tones. Now listen to the demo and watch the transcription provided.

Level 6 Unit 9 • Phrygian Demo 4

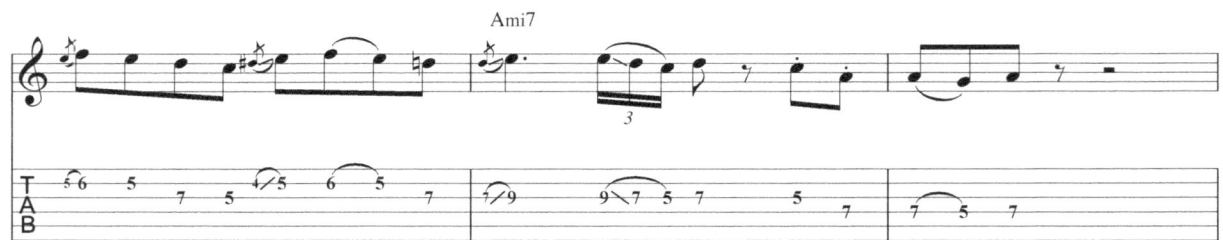

Compare the chord tones and examine the proximity of the Ami7 chord tones to the Gmi7 chord tones. Look at the various ways each chord can move from Ami7 to Gmi7 and then back again.

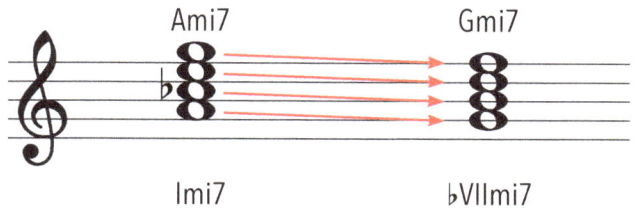

Are there any common tones? Yes, G. That can be exploited by holding it over both chords or building it into a motif that morphs for each chord but includes G for both. Work on this. You are targeting chord tones when you exploit the differences in the chords within the scale. It is helpful to see both arpeggios together in-position. On the left is the Pattern IV Phrygian Scale. To its right is Ami7, which is Imi7 and Gmi7, which is bVIImi7, all in-position.

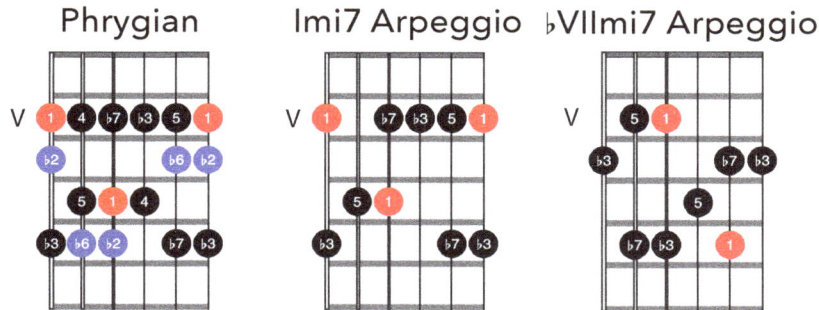

Practice soloing over this track blending the Phrygian Scale and the arpeggio of each chord. What note is common between the two chords? G. That means they can be used on either chord or held over both. What notes are not in both chords? A, C, and E from the Ami7, and Bb, D, and F from the Gmi7.

Those notes can mark the changes, but don't feel like you need to avoid any scale tone on either chord.

Now listen to the demo and watch the transcription provided.

Level 6 Unit 9 • Phrygian Demo 5

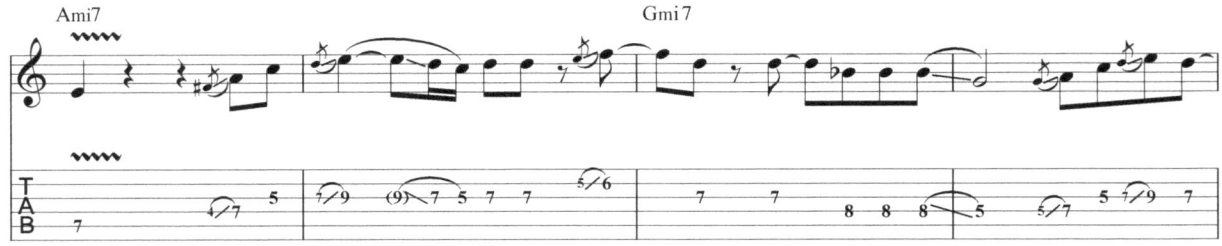

PRACTICE

Theory

- ❑ Learn the common progression fragments in the Phrygian Scale.
- ❑ Learn the important moves of the voices with the common Lydian progression fragments.

Fretboard Logic

- ❑ Know the process of how to derive five patterns of the Phrygian scale from the Minor Pentatonic Scales by adding a minor 2nd and a minor 6th.
- ❑ Become familiar the most common Phrygian chord progression fragments.

Rhythm Guitar

- ❑ Follow the chart and create and record one or more rhythm guitar parts.

Chart Writing

- ❑ Know how to use the various instructive devices to make your chart as clear as possible.

Improvisation

- ❑ Know the personality of each note in the Phrygian Scale when played over a static minor 7th chord.
- ❑ Be familiar with soloing over the common progression fragments from the Phrygian Scale.

UNIT 10

Learning Modules

> **Theory** - Different Kinds of Modulation, Various Ways Modulation is Used in Songs

> **Fretboard Logic** - Deriving Patterns of the Locrian Scale from the Minor Pentatonic Scales

> **Rhythm Guitar** - Creating a Rhythm Guitar Part for a Song in 5/8

> **Chart Writing** - Write a Complete Chart from the Start to Finish

> **Improvisation** - Improvising When There is Modulation

> **Practice** - Continue Practice Routine Development

The tracks for this Unit can be found at the following link:

https://fretboardbiology.com/book6/#u10

THEORY

Modulation

There are many ways to create harmonic interest in a song by using a variation of harmony. Outside of strictly diatonic harmony, you've learned about modal interchange, composite minor, secondary dominants, and modes. These are all tools to make chord progressions interesting. Another important option is to modulate, which means to change the key. Modulation can be subtle or dramatic.

There are two basic methods of modulation:

- Direct Modulation
- Pivot Chord Modulation (or Common Chord Modulation)

Direct modulation is abrupt and without any harmonic preparation or warning. Direct modulation is easy to detect when analyzing harmony because suddenly the chords don't fit in the original key. When several successive chords in a progression do not belong to the original key, a modulation has probably occurred. It's common in pop music chord charts or lead sheets for key changes not to be introduced with a new key signature. If no key signatures are provided for the original key, follow the same rules of analysis we have used before.

When you analyze a progression as an exercise and see that there is direct modulation, bracket all of the chords in the starting key and indicate each chord function below each chord until it is clear the key has changed. Indicate the new key with a new bracket and indicate the function of the following chords relative to the new key, like in the following example.

Progression Example 1

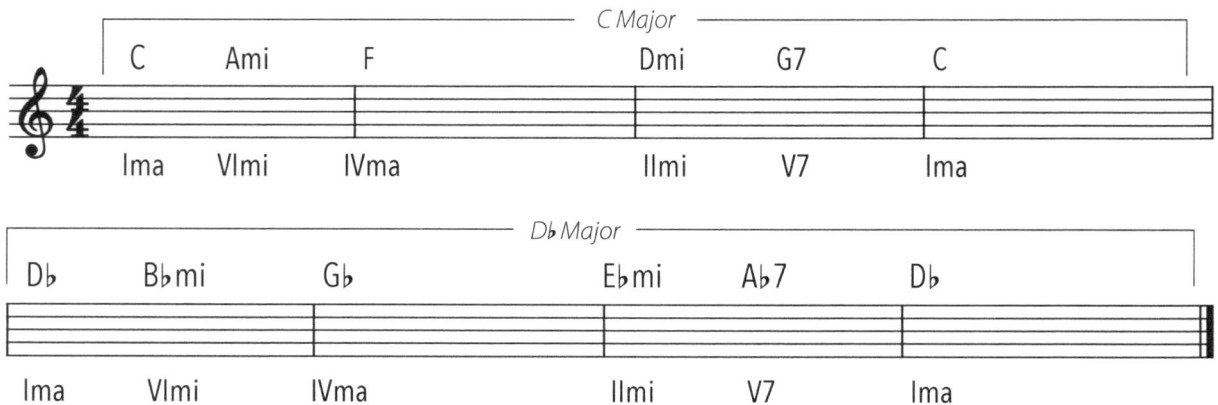

Analyze the next few progressions. Bracket each key and use Roman numerals to indicate the function under each chord.

Progression Example 2

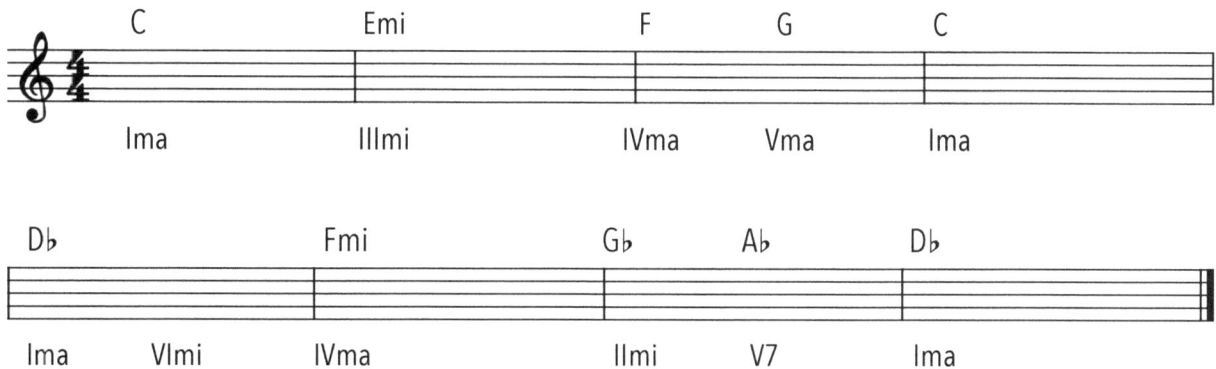

Progression Example 3

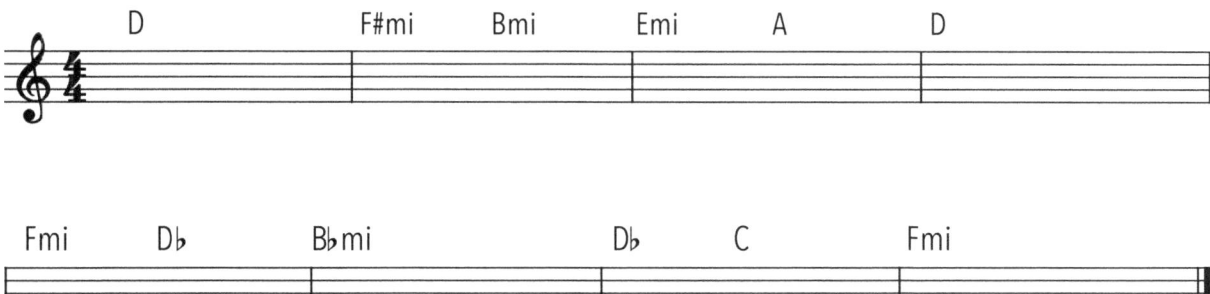

Pivot Chord Modulation

Pivot chord modulation (or common chord modulation) is generally smoother and is accomplished by using a chord common to both the original and the new key as the point of transition. Often the pivot chord is a subdominant chord in the new key. The 'pivot chord' is the 'common chord'; they mean the same thing.

When you analyze a progression as an exercise and see that there is pivot chord modulation, bracket all of the chords that can be analyzed in the starting key and indicate each chord function below each chord until it is clear the key has changed. Indicate the new key with a new bracket and indicate the function of the subsequent chords relative to the new key. The pivot chord should be labeled with two functions: its function in the first key and also its function in the new key. The brackets indicating the keys should overlap at the pivot chord.

Progression Example 4

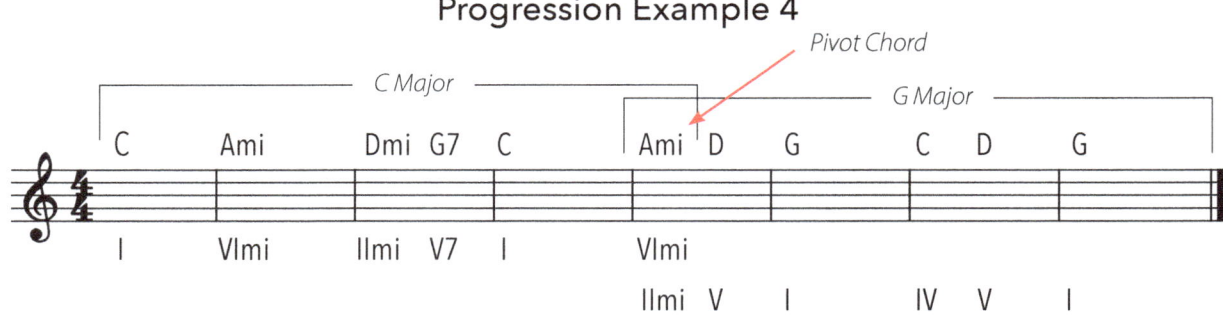

Analyze the following progressions, using brackets for each key and Roman numerals to indicate the function under each chord.

Progression Example 5

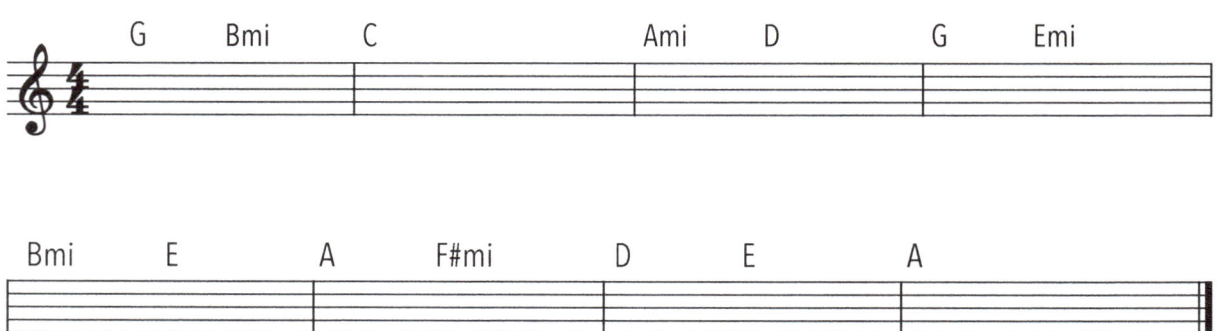

Progression Example 6

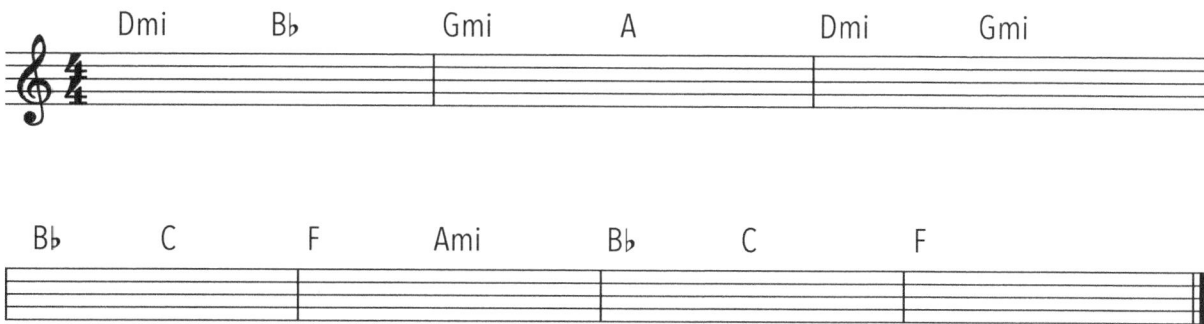

You won't hear that a modulation is direct or pivot chord until it happens, and you could argue that all modulations are direct. After all, even with pivot chord modulation, the melody notes played on the pivot chord are usually from the new key, so you perceive it as belonging to the new key. The point of change has to be somewhere. The pivot chord actually belongs to the new key, but because it also belongs to the previous key, the modulation seems very smooth. That's not the case with a direct modulation. The first chord in the new key is not part of the original key and the shift is decisive and dramatic. So for lack of a better term, the 'value' of a pivot chord modulation is that it is smooth and not jarring.

Within the worlds of both direct and pivot chord modulation, there are many ways modulation occurs in a song:

- Songs can modulate more than once.

- One of the most common modulations is up a half step. This can energize a progression in a final push to a big ending.

- It's also common for there to be multiple modulations up a half step in a song that builds. This energizes a progression with each upward change of the key.

- It's very common for progressions to modulate from a major key to its relative minor. This is very smooth and the shift is so subtle that it's sometimes hard to define exactly where it occurred. The shift is subtle because relative keys have all of the same notes.

- Songs may modulate from section to section. For instance, the A sections of a song may be in one key and the B sections in another. Bridges or solos are popular places for a song to modulate, too. A modulation from section to section sharply defines the section boundaries.

- There are instances where a song might modulate for a series of chords in the middle of a section.

More About Modulation

This next section has a lot of information that is very interesting and useful, but I would not consider it highly critical. It explains something that happens in many songs, and knowing it will help you understand the inner-workings of a song. Once you learn about it, you'll recognize it when you see it. And if you're a songwriter, too, understanding it will be another writing tool in your bag. Songs can modulate to literally any key from any key. Songwriters can choose to be subtle and smooth or dramatic and shocking. There is a clever category of modulations that is worth mentioning:

**Many modulations, especially the temporary ones,
are to the 'keys of chords in the original key'.**

Eventually, the song will work its way back to the original key following a modulation and perhaps even end there. Think about that statement again. Repeat it a few times before we go on.

Let's examine this idea in both major and minor scenarios.

If a song is in C major, it would be common for it to modulate to D minor, E minor, F major, G major, or A minor. Why those keys? Think again about the statement above: Many modulations are to keys of chords in the original key. This usually feels smooth because of the big-picture relationship between the original key, the chords of the key, and the temporary modulation to the key of this related chord.

Let's look at each one and understand that most of the time in these instances, the song returns to the original key.

- In the key of C, Dmi is the II chord. It's common for a song to modulate temporarily to the key of a chord that's in the original key. A song in C major might modulate temporarily to D minor. There's a close relationship.
- In the key of C, Emi is the III chord. A song in C major might modulate temporarily to E minor. It feels smooth because there's a close relationship.
- In the key of C, F is the IV chord. A song in C major might modulate temporarily to F major.
- In the key of C, G is the V chord. A song in C major might modulate temporarily to G major.
- In the key of C, Ami is the VI chord. A song in C major might modulate temporarily to A minor. And of course, this is the relative minor.

Modulating to the key of the VII chord in major is not so common. You'll recall that the VII chord is built on a diminished triad and is considered to be an unstable sound. You may also recall from our discussion of secondary dominants that we didn't consider a V7/VII for this very same reason.

Now let's examine modulations for a minor key. If a song is in C minor, it would be common for it to modulate to E♭ major, F minor, G minor, A♭ major, or B♭ major.

In the key of C minor, D diminished is the II chord. Modulating to the key of the II chord in minor is not so common. The II chord is built on a diminished triad and is considered to be an unstable sound. You may also recall from our discussion of secondary dominants that we didn't consider a V7/II in a minor key for this very same reason.

- In the key of C minor, E♭ is the ♭III chord. A song in C minor might modulate temporarily to E♭ major. And remember, that's its relative major.
- In the key of C minor, Fmi is the IV chord. A song in C minor might modulate temporarily to F minor.
- In the key of C minor, Gmi is the V chord. A song in C minor might modulate temporarily to G minor.
- In the key of C minor, A♭ is the ♭VI chord. A song in C minor might modulate temporarily to A♭ major.
- In the key of C minor, B♭ is the ♭VII chord. A song in C minor might modulate temporarily to B♭ major.

Let's now take a look at modulations from major to keys of chords from their parallel minors.

- If a song is in C major, it would be common for it to modulate to E♭ major, F minor, G minor, A♭ major, or B♭ major.
- In the key of C major, E♭ is the ♭III chord from the parallel key. It's common for a song to modulate temporarily to the key of a chord that's in the parallel key of the original key. Therefore, a song in C major might modulate temporarily to E♭ major. There's a close relationship.
- In the key of C major, Fmi is the IV chord from the parallel key. A song in C major might modulate temporarily to F minor.
- In the key of C major, Gmi is the V chord from the parallel key. A song in C major might modulate temporarily to G minor.
- In the key of C major, A♭ is the ♭VI chord from the parallel key. A song in C major might modulate temporarily to A♭ major.
- In the key of C major, B♭ is the ♭VII chord from the parallel key. A song in C major might modulate temporarily to B♭ major.

These modulations to keys of chords in the key tie the multiple keys that are possible in a song together harmonically. The notes you choose have to fit the harmony of the moment. So whether or not it's an 'official modulation', your note choices need to fit the key and chords happening at that moment.

FRETBOARD LOGIC

The focus in this Module will be on the Locrian Mode. You know how to create the modes by adding notes to the pentatonic shells.

The goal in this Module is to learn all of the patterns of the Locrian Mode by adding two notes to the five Minor Pentatonic shells. You will also need to alter the 5th.

To create the Locrian Scale from a Minor Pentatonic shell, add a minor 2nd and a minor 6th. The 5th needs to be lowered one half-step as well.

Locrian as a Derivative of the Minor Pentatonic Scale

Minor Pentatonic	1		mi3	P4	P5	mi7
Locrian Mode	1	mi2	mi3	P4	D5	mi6	mi7

It's important to have a clear understanding of the correlation between the following shapes: the Minor Pentatonic and Locrian Scales and the chord and arpeggio built on the 1st scale degree.

Pattern I

Let's look at Pattern I. The diagram on the left is the Pattern I Minor Pentatonic shell. To its right is the same shell with a minor 2nd and a minor 6th added, and with the 5th lowered one half step. This is the Pattern I Locrian Mode. To its right is the mi7(♭5) chord voicing built on the 1st scale degree and on the far right is the mi7(♭5) arpeggio built on the 1st scale degree.

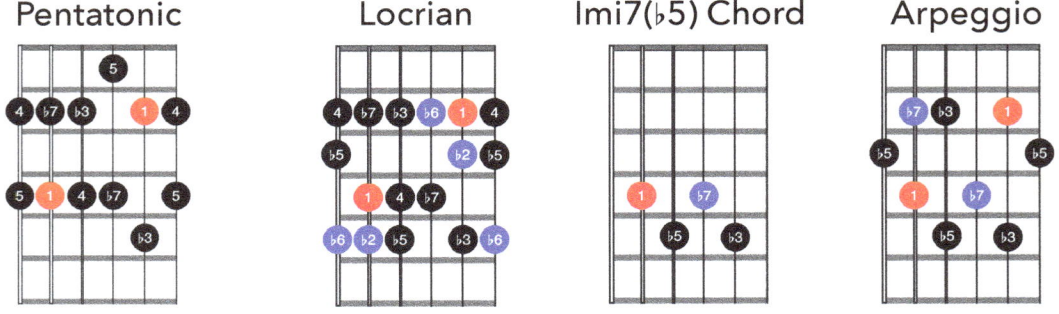

Pattern II

Let's look at Pattern II. The diagram on the left is the Pattern II Minor Pentatonic shell. To its right is the same shell with a minor 2nd and a minor 6th added, and with the 5th lowered one half step. This is the Pattern II Locrian Mode. To its right is the mi7(♭5) chord voicing built on the 1st scale degree and on the far right is the mi7(♭5) arpeggio built on the 1st scale degree.

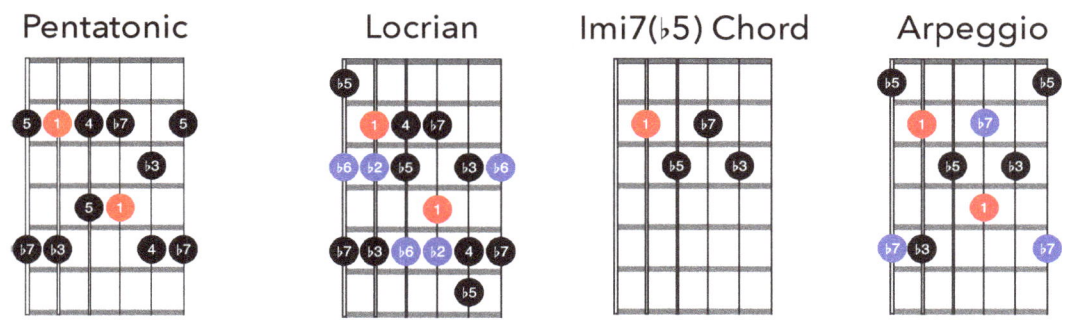

Pattern III

Let's do the same with Pattern III. Add a minor 2nd and a minor 6th and lower the 5th one half step to create the Pattern III Locrian Mode. The mi7(♭5) chord voicing built on the 1st scale degree and on the mi7(♭5) arpeggio built on the 1st scale degree.

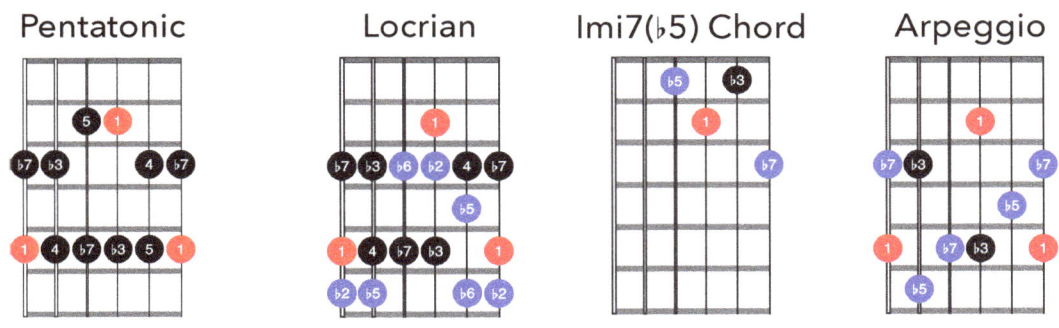

Pattern IV

Do the same process with Pattern IV. Add a minor 2nd and a minor 6th and lower the 5th one half step. The chord voicing and arpeggio are built on the 1st scale degree.

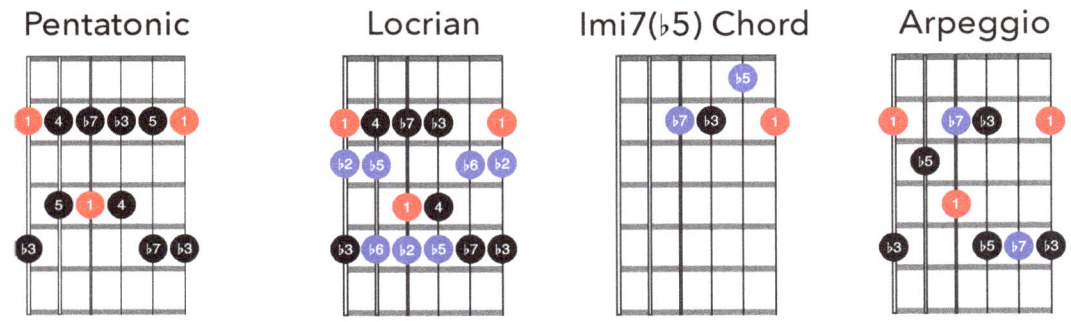

Pattern V

Finally, look at Pattern V. As with the other patterns, add a minor 2nd and a minor 6th to the pentatonic scale and lower the 5th one half step to create the Pattern V Locrian Mode. The mi7(♭5) chord voicing and the mi7(♭5) arpeggio built on the 1st scale degree.

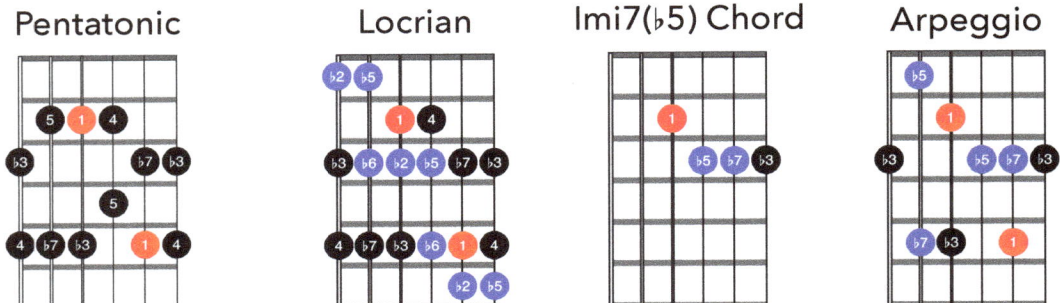

I would not spend much time practicing the Locrian Scale. It's not a commonly used scale, and if you are playing in a Jazz context, there are better options for a chord scale on a mi7(♭5). But you should know how to build one from the Minor Pentatonic Scale or by starting on the 7th scale degree of a Major Scale.

Please relate all of this to the Family Tree. It's important that you keep that connection going!

RHYTHM GUITAR

Creating Parts for Songs in Odd Meter

You studied playing in odd meters in the Level 5 Rhythm Guitar Modules. Because odd meters are used less in popular music, the first order is usually staying in sync with the meter. Regardless, good feel is the essential ingredient in music.

We covered a variety of odd meters in the odd meter Rhythm Guitar modules. In this Module we'll work with the most common, which is 5/8.

First, let's take a look at the road map in the following page and use your Chart-Reading Checklist.

Chart-Reading Checklist

1. Look at the top left corner where all the preliminary information is: Key signature, Time signature, Style
2. Note the Tempo
3. Scan the form
4. Seek out any figures that need to be played
5. Scan the chords for the ones that are new or difficult for you
6. Seek out more detailed instructions like dynamics, accents, and expression markings

Follow along with the chart while listening to the 5/8 track provided in the link for this Module.

As with the other genres, listen to the track and think like a producer. Listen for a part that fits with the meter and mood of the track, and consider the instrumentation. Pay attention to how busy or sparse you should be and also the kind of voicings you should use, and in what register.

Because odd meters may be less familiar to you, strive to create a part that stays in a lane and feels good. Record your part and judge it from the perspective of a listener. Ask yourself, "would I want to hear this part on a recording?"

If you're comfortable, add a second or even a third part.

No matter how simple you may need to make a part so that you can stay with the 5/8 groove, strive to make it feel good. Remember that feel is not about complexity. It's more about how a part fits into the fabric of the rhythm section.

Odd Meter Song Chart

This is the last Level 6 Rhythm Guitar Module. This was a very different series of Rhythm Guitar modules than the others. You had to use knowledge and vocabulary you acquired in earlier modules, and hopefully in real world settings. Real-life environments always present unique challenges, so be ready to adapt.

In nature, it's not the smartest, fastest, biggest, or strongest species that endure. It's the most adaptable. So how does that relate to you and your rhythm guitar playing? Know the basics of each of the primary genres you've studied thus far in the Fretboard Biology program, and you will begin to realize the wonderful world of adaptability. It's so much fun to 'get into character' for each style of music!

Genres, at an emotional level, are about attitude, feel, and vibe. Part of all that is an intangible thing called musicality. But, part of it can also be broken down into tangible elements that can be studied and practiced.

Ultimately rhythm guitar parts are all about being part of the texture of a rhythm section. Keep that front of mind at all times.

CHART WRITING

Now You Do It!

Throughout all the Chart Writing Modules, you learned the best practices for creating chord charts that are easy to read and perform. Now, chart another song from start to finish, but this time, all in one unit.

This will be a shorter and less complicated song, but it will be helpful for you to go through all the steps in fairly rapid succession. Follow all the steps that were discussed starting in Unit 1. Listen to the track for this Module. Work your way through creating a chart on your own and when you're finished, compare your version with the version shown below. It would be best to not peek! Try it all by yourself and see how close you come to my version.

Steps to Create Your Own Chart

1. Listen to the song and make your form chart
2. Count and write out blank measures for each section
3. Figure out chords and write them above the measures
4. Identify where there are rhythm figures and riffs
5. Look for opportunities for 1- and 2-bar repeats
6. Look for opportunities for start and end repeats
7. Look for opportunities to use jump marks
8. Transfer everything to staff papaer

Listen to the track for the module and work your way through the song. Like the lyrics say in the song we charted in Units 1-8, writing a chart makes gigs go better. And writing a chart can make learning and rehearsing go better, too. Band rehearsals are efficient if everyone does their homework. Homework is easier for everyone if they are thinking of the road map the same way, which is what a chord chart will do for you and the band.

The more you chart, the better and faster you get. You will constantly encounter new challenges because every song is different. Some charts will write themselves and others will be incredibly frustrating. That's just how it is, but keep at it. Make chart writing part of your routine when learning new songs, especially if you are playing in a band.

Your guiding principle when writing a chord chart is to keep the musician's focus on playing the music well and not on deciphering what you wrote.

Sample Song

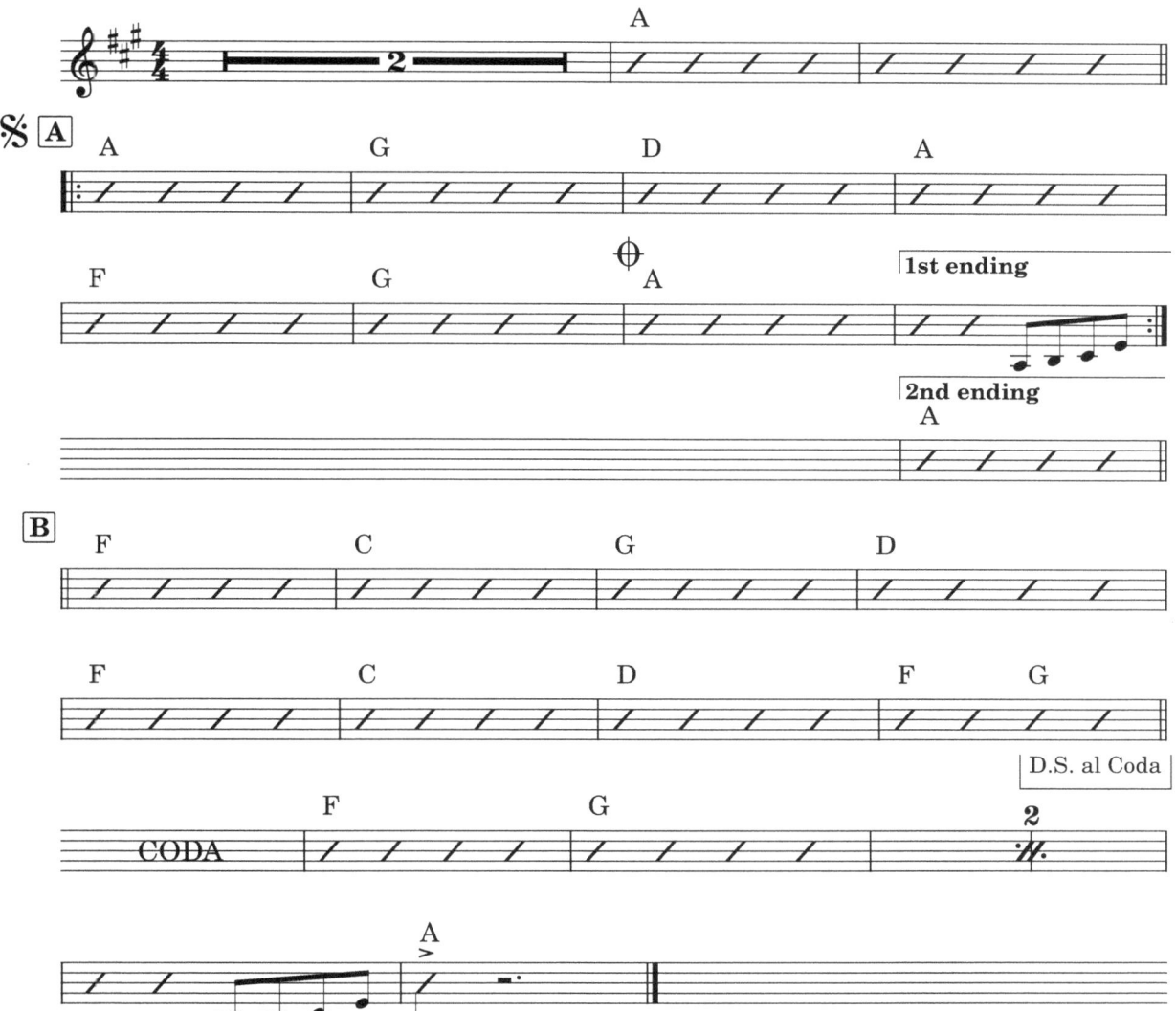

IMPROVISATION

Modulation

The Level 6 Improvisation Modules have taken you through a lot of involved information. You've learned about playing though modes and Composite Minor.

The subject in Unit 10 is quite different. In the Unit 10 Theory Module you learned about modulation. While understanding how modulation affects an improviser seems obvious, there are some important points to be made that you may not have considered.

But first, let's review the ways modulation occurs in a song:

- Songs can modulate more than once.
- One of the most common modulations is up a half step. This can energize a progression in a final push to a big ending.
- It's also common for there to be multiple modulations up a half step in a song that builds. This energizes a progression with each upward change of the key.
- It's very common for progressions to modulate from a major key to its relative minor. This is very smooth and the shift is so subtle, it's sometimes hard to define exactly where it occurred. The shift is subtle because relative keys have all of the same notes.
- Songs may modulate from section to section. For instance, the A sections of a song may be in one key and the B section in another. Bridges or solos are a popular places for a song to modulate, too. A modulation from section to section sharply defines the section boundaries.
- There are instances where a song might modulate for a series of chords in the middle of a section.

One thing is constant: Modulation catches the listener's attention, regardless of how or where it's used. The number one obligation when soloing is to play notes in the new key when a modulation occurs.

If you listen closely and/or transcribe solos you'll find that soloists will often start the transition to the new key before the band does. They'll play a line that leads the listener's ear to the new key. This telegraphs the modulation to the listener because they hear the notes that don't belong, even if for just an instant. This builds anticipation, and when the rest of the band arrives in the new key, there's a sense of relief and resolution, and a lot of new energy injected into the music.

There's no rule about how early you can play notes of the new key before the band. It really depends on the flow of the music, tempo, and other undefinable factors. The earlier you start, the more tense it will feel because the clash of tonalities happens for a longer time until all the musicians are in the same key.

Here is a progression that starts in the key of C. After eight bars it modulates up a half step to the key of D♭. Follow along with the chart as you listen to the track.

Progression in C

246 Level 6 • Unit 10: Improvisation

Work on this moving to the new key two ways:

1. Start playing notes of the new key at exactly the point where the key change occurs with the rest of the band.

Level 6 Unit 10 • Demo 1

Fretboard Biology — Level 6 • Unit 10: Improvisation — 247

2. Start playing notes of the new key at a little ahead of the point where the key change occurs with the rest of the band.

Level 6 Unit 10 • Demo 2

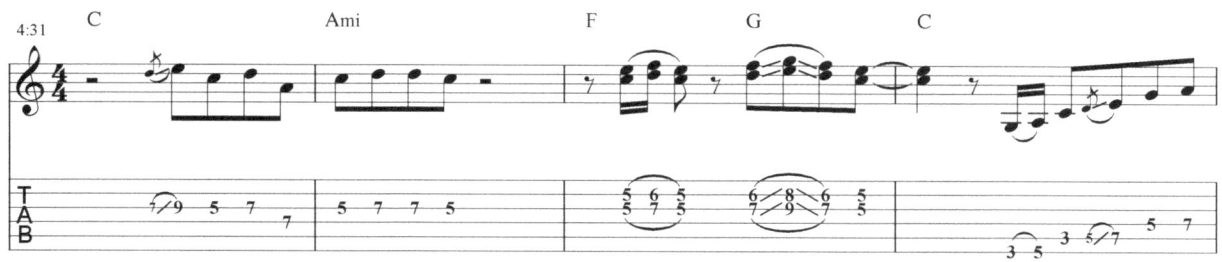

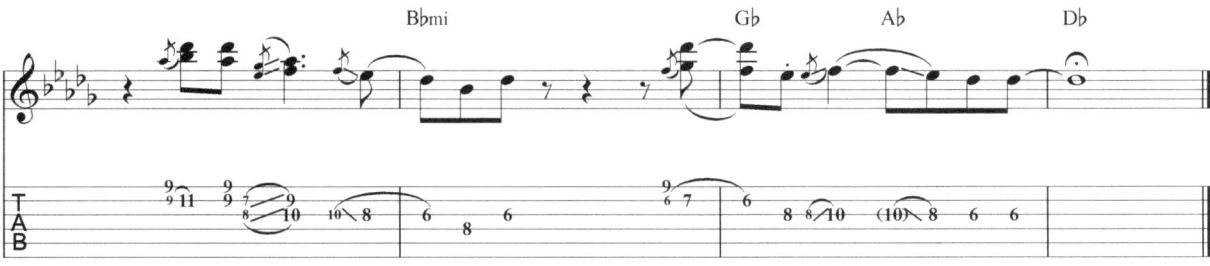

Consider the difference and what effect it had on you. Be adventurous and on subsequent passes gradually enter the new key earlier and earlier until it just doesn't sound good to your ear. How comfortable you are with how early you enter the new key is up to you. But I suggest you experiment and push the boundaries so you know.

How about the opposite. Can you wait a beat or two to change keys and be late? You would then in effect be catching up with the band and modulation. Based on my experience and listening, that's a bad idea. Don't be late for a modulation! It just sounds wrong. It just sounds as if you've been caught off-guard. Try that with the track as well.

The list above shows ways modulation happens in songs that are related to the form, meaning there's a modulation between sections.

A solo can really be set apart by being in a brand new key. Songwriters often set the solo apart from the rest of the song by modulating just for that section. As a soloist who has learned about storytelling, know that the new key is a huge gift to you as you create an interesting solo. Holding on to one note in the new key at the beginning of a solo can be powerful, especially if that note is not in the previous key.

But the opposite is true, too. If you can find a note common to both keys and anticipate or lead into the new key with that note, it'll have a powerful effect on the listener.

Here's a little more about the last way modulation can happen in a song from the list above. There are instances where a song might modulate for a series of chords in the middle of a section. Particularly in Jazz, there are often temporary modulations within a section. Often this is for a really short time, like a measure or two. The idea about telegraphing the new key applies here, too. And it can apply to the quick modulation back to the original key as well.

PRACTICE

Theory

- ❏ Know how to recognize both direct and pivot chord modulation.
- ❏ Know the various ways modulation is used in songs.

Fretboard Logic

- ❏ Know the process of how to derive five patterns of the Locrian Scale from the Minor Pentatonic Scales by adding a minor 2nd and a minor 6th and lowering the 5th a half step.

Rhythm Guitar

- ❏ Follow the chart and create and record one or more rhythm guitar parts.

Chart Writing

- ❏ Know how to use all of the steps learned in this level to create a chart from start to finish.

Improvisation

- ❏ Know how to improvise when there is a modulation.

Appendices

> **Appendix 1** - Octave Shape Family Trees
> **Appendix 2** - Table of Inverted Intervals
> **Appendix 3** - Shell Voicings
> **Appendix 4** - Root Maps
> **Appendix 5** - Chord Charts
> **Appendix 6** - Modes

Pattern I Family Tree

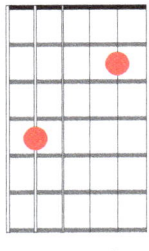

MAJOR

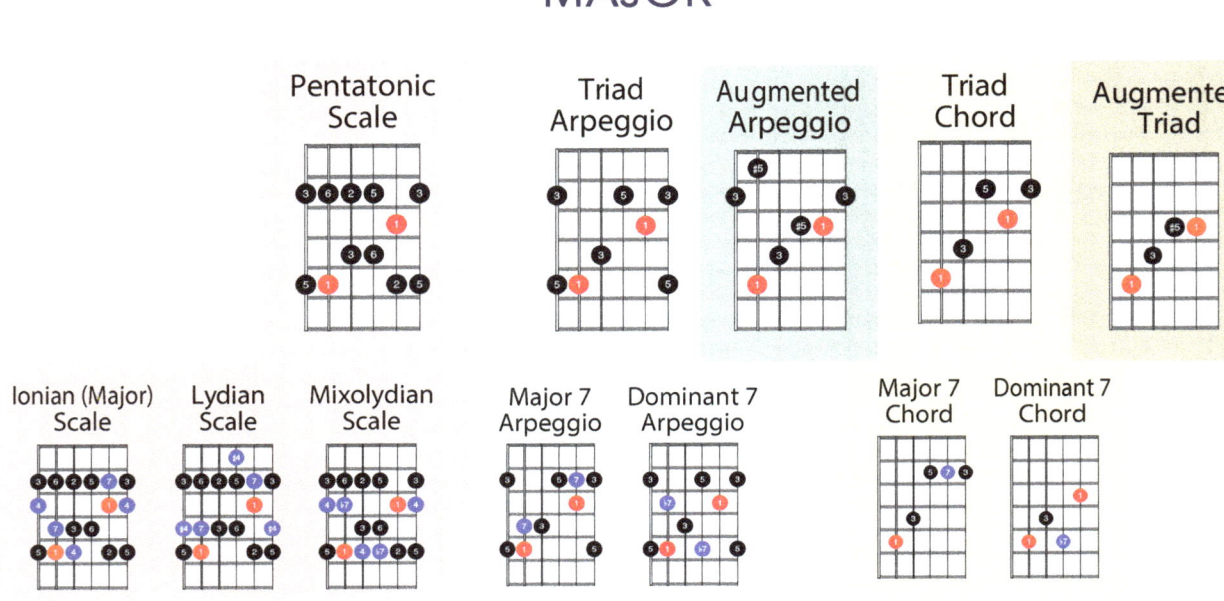

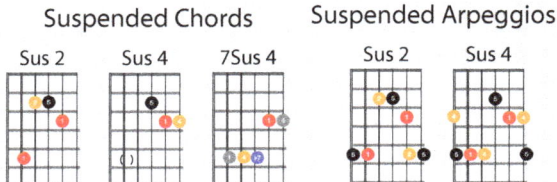

Pattern I Family Tree

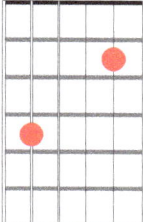

MINOR

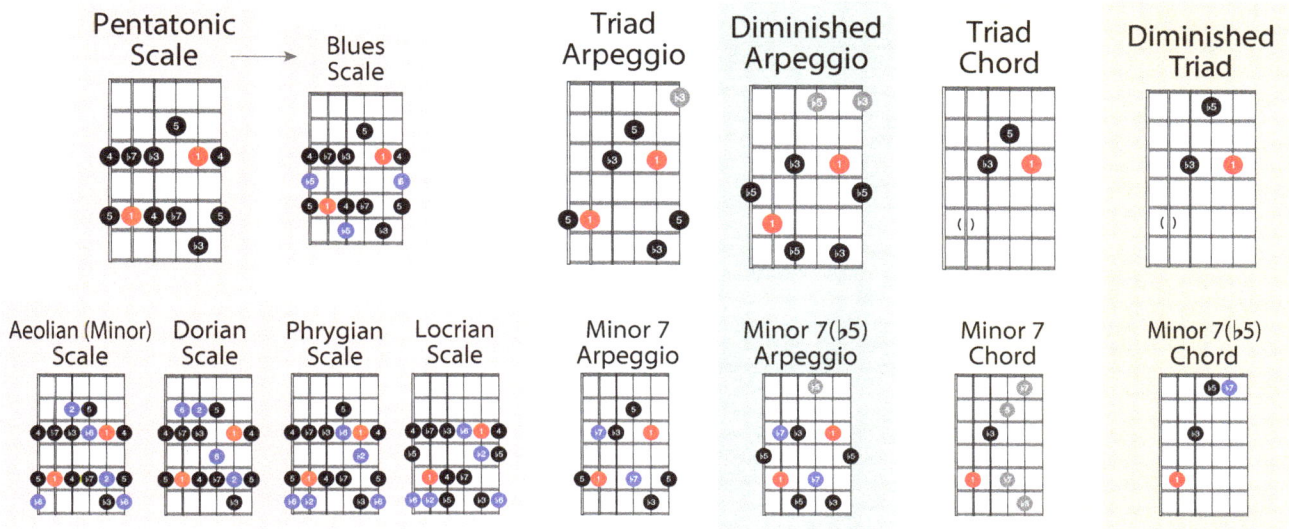

Pattern II Family Tree

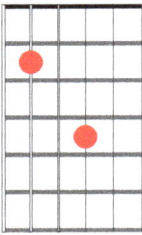

MAJOR

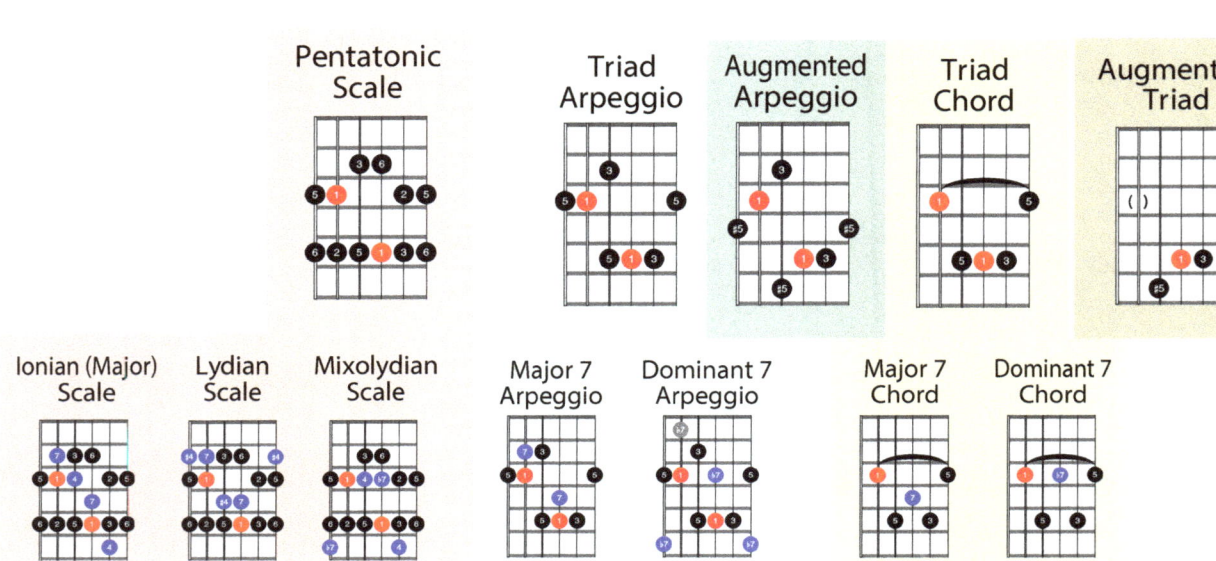

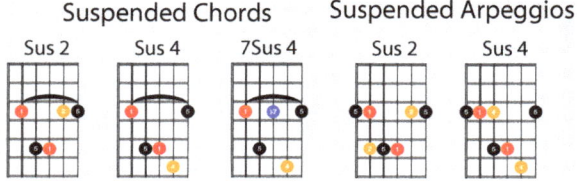

Pattern II Family Tree

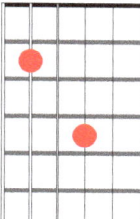

MINOR

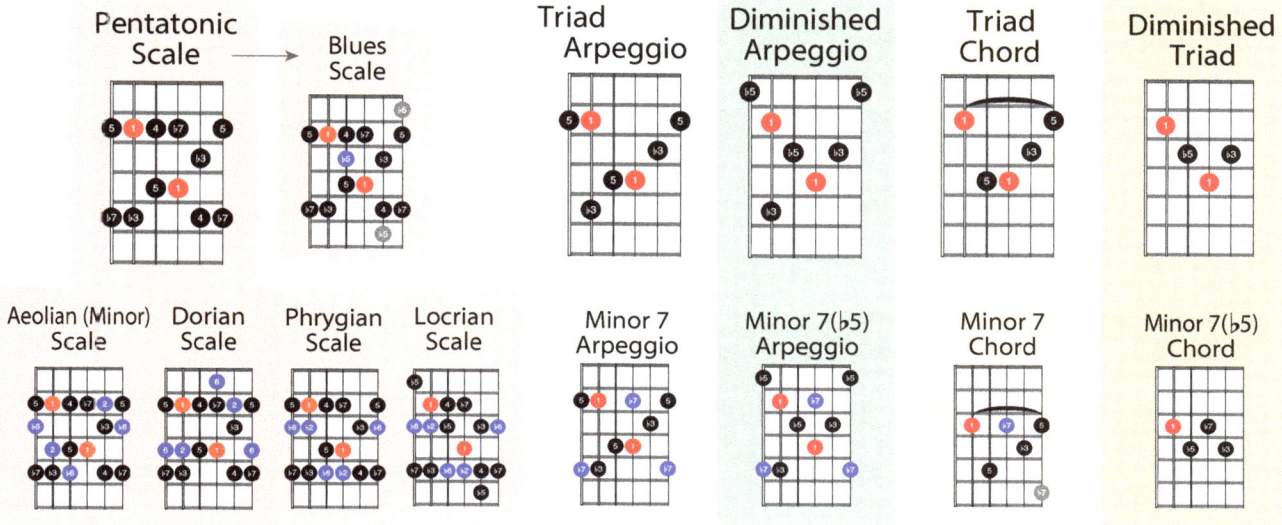

Pattern III Family Tree

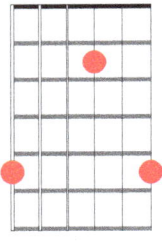

MAJOR

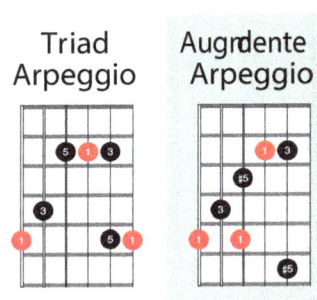

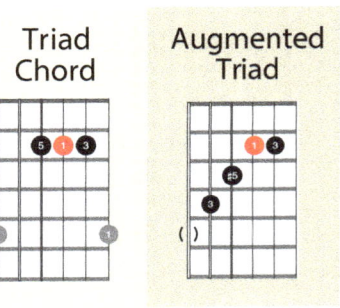

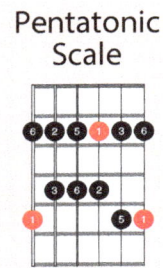

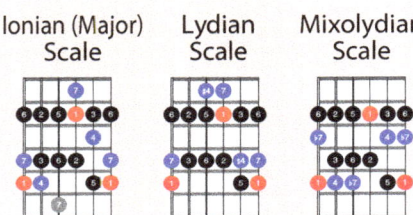

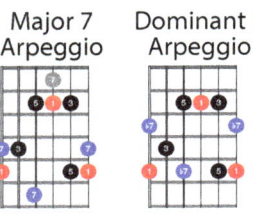

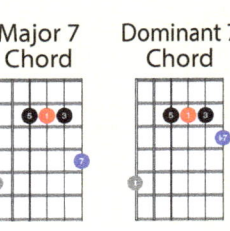

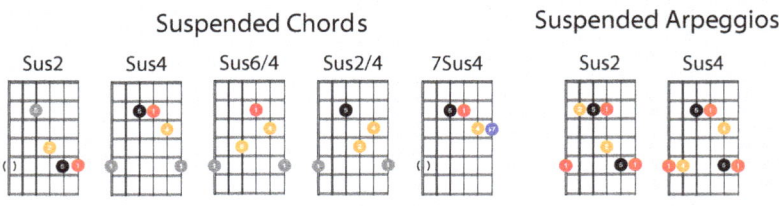

Pattern III Family Tree

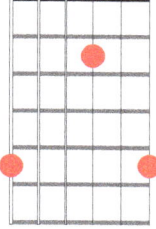

MINOR

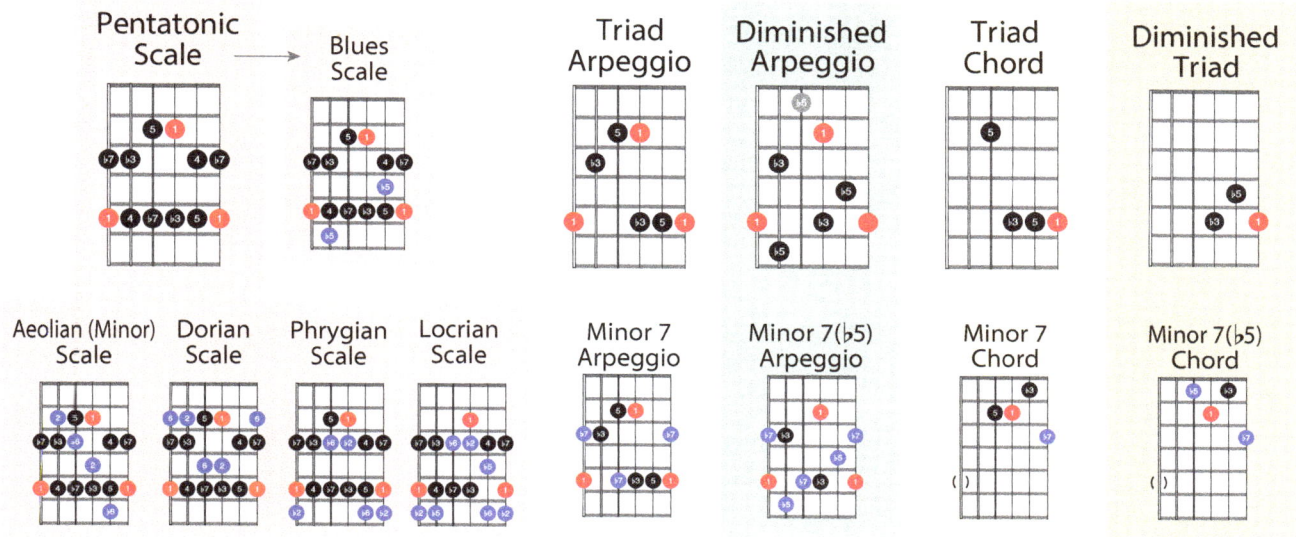

Pattern IV Family Tree

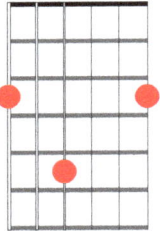

MAJOR

| Pentatonic Scale | Triad Arpeggio | Augmented Arpeggio | Triad Chord | Augmented Triad |

 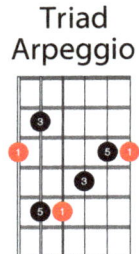 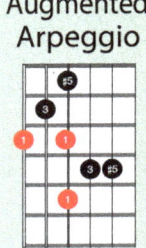  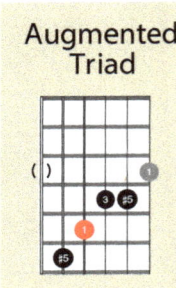

| Ionian (Major) Scale | Lydian Scale | Mixolydian Scale | Major 7 Arpeggio | Dominant 7 Arpeggio | Major 7 Chord | Dominant 7 Chord |

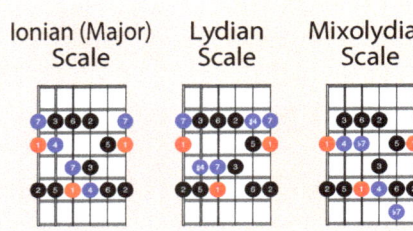 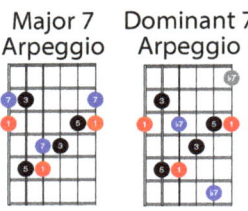 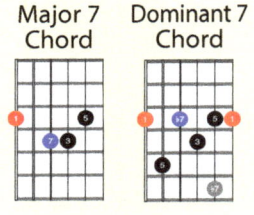

Suspended Chords   Suspended Arpeggios

Sus4   Sus6/4   Sus2/4   Sus2/4   Sus4

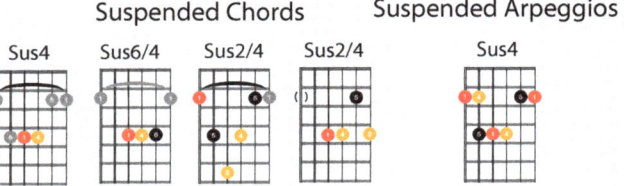

Pattern IV Family Tree

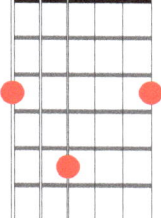

MINOR

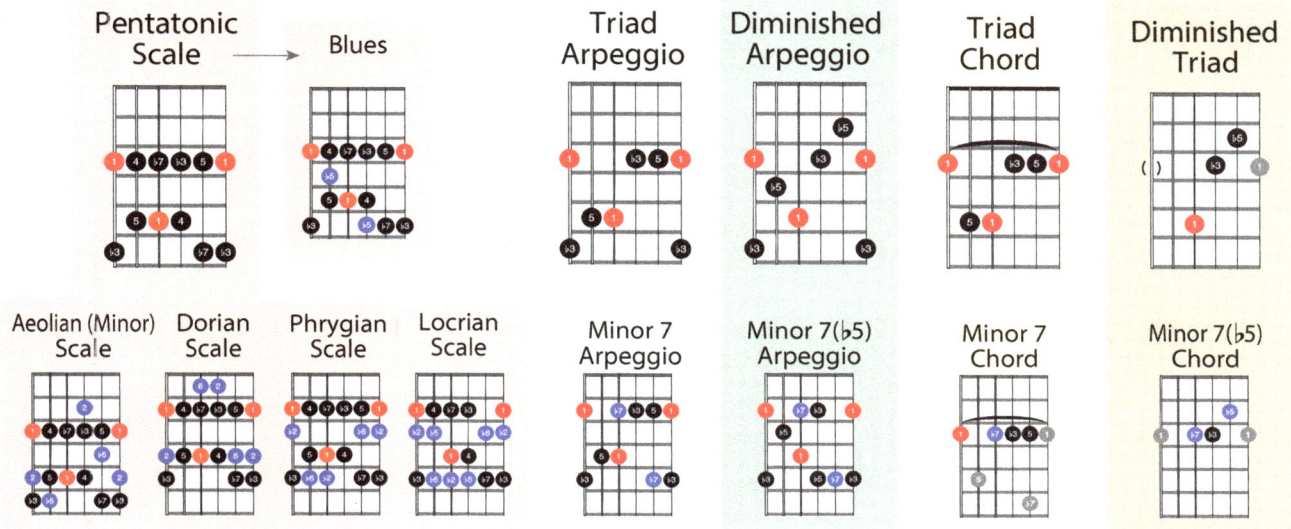

Pattern V Family Tree

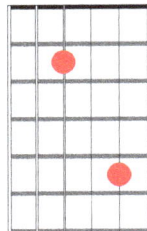

MAJOR

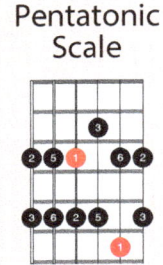
Pentatonic Scale

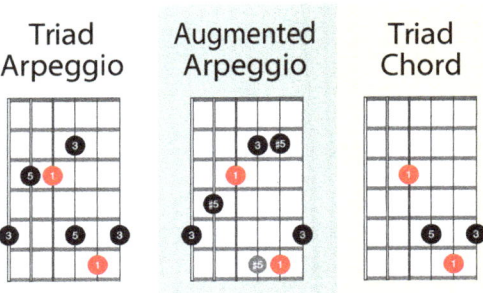
Triad Arpeggio • Augmented Arpeggio • Triad Chord

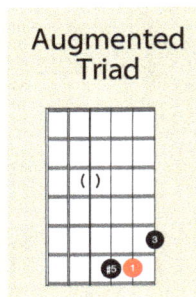
Augmented Triad

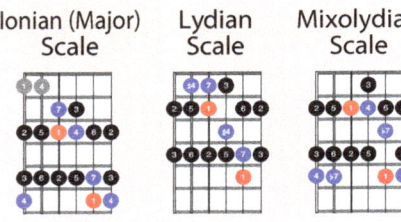
Ionian (Major) Scale • Lydian Scale • Mixolydian Scale

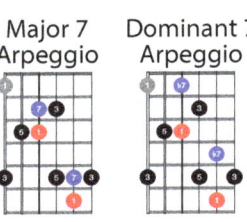
Major 7 Arpeggio • Dominant 7 Arpeggio

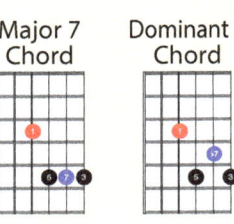
Major 7 Chord • Dominant 7 Chord

Suspended Chords — Sus4, Sus2

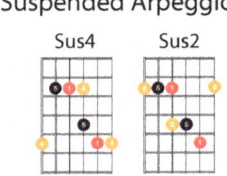
Suspended Arpeggios — Sus4, Sus2

Pattern V Family Tree

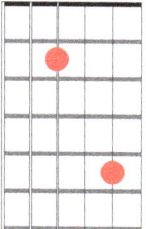

MINOR

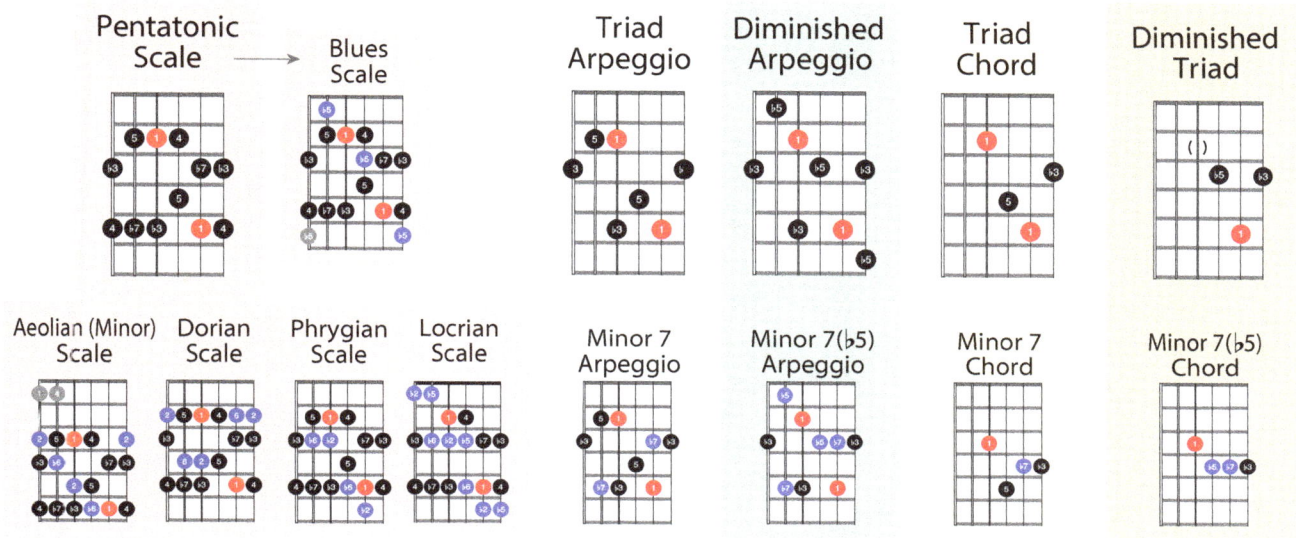

Table of Inverted Intervals

INTERVAL	→	INVERSION
Mi2		Ma7
Ma2		Mi7
Mi3		Ma6
Ma3		Mi6
P4		P5
A4		D5
D5		A4
P5		P4
Mi6		Ma3
Ma6		Mi3
Mi7		Ma2
Ma7		Mi2
P8		Unison

Shell Voicings

Pattern IV (6th string)

Major 7   Dominant 7   Minor 7   Minor 7(♭5)

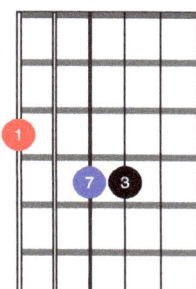 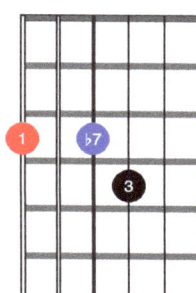 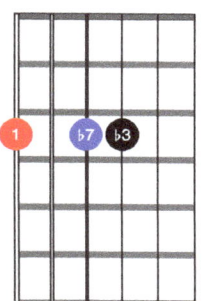 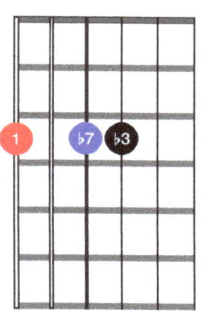

Pattern II (5th string)

Major 7   Dominant 7   Minor 7   Minor 7(♭5)

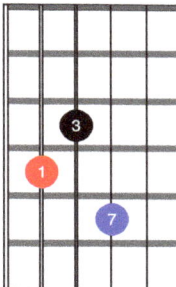 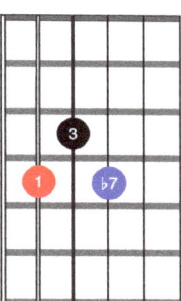 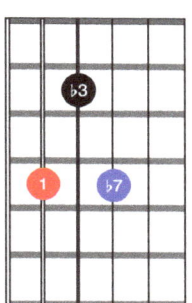 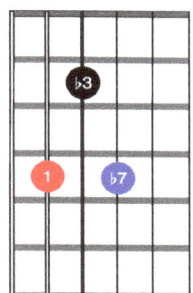

Root Map 1

Root Map 1

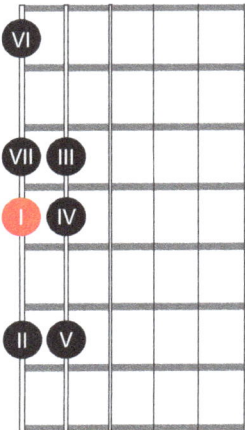

Root Map 1 Shell Voicings

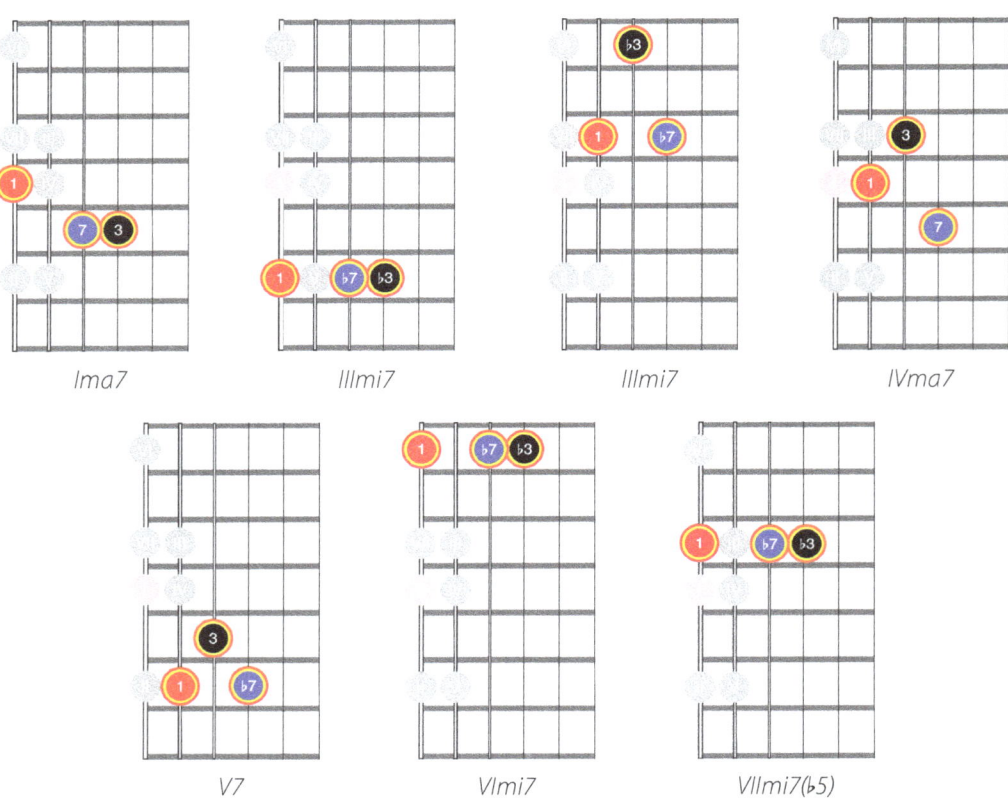

Ima7   IIImi7   IIImi7   IVma7

V7   VImi7   VIImi7(b5)

Root Map 2

Root Map 2

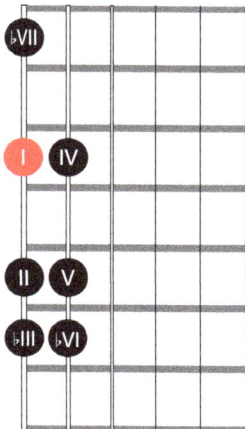

Root Map 2 Shell Voicings

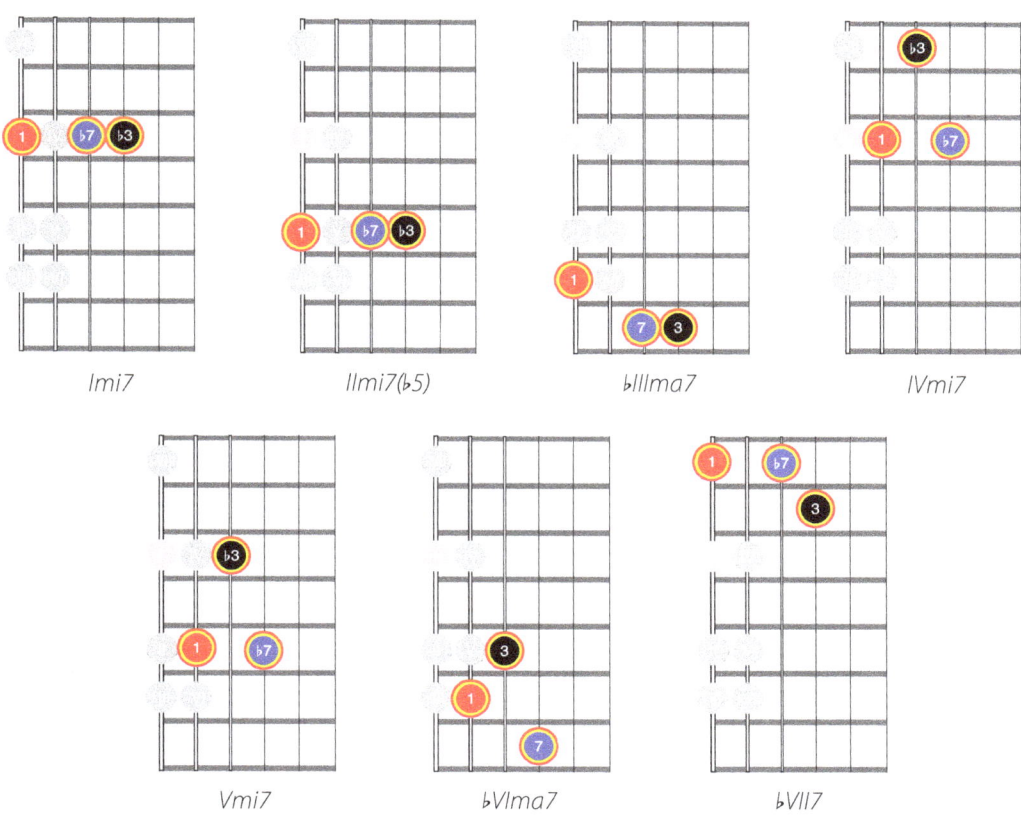

Imi7   IImi7(♭5)   ♭IIIma7   IVmi7

Vmi7   ♭VIma7   ♭VII7

Root Map 3

Root Map 3

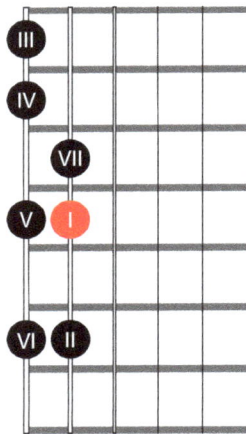

Root Map 3 Shell Voicings

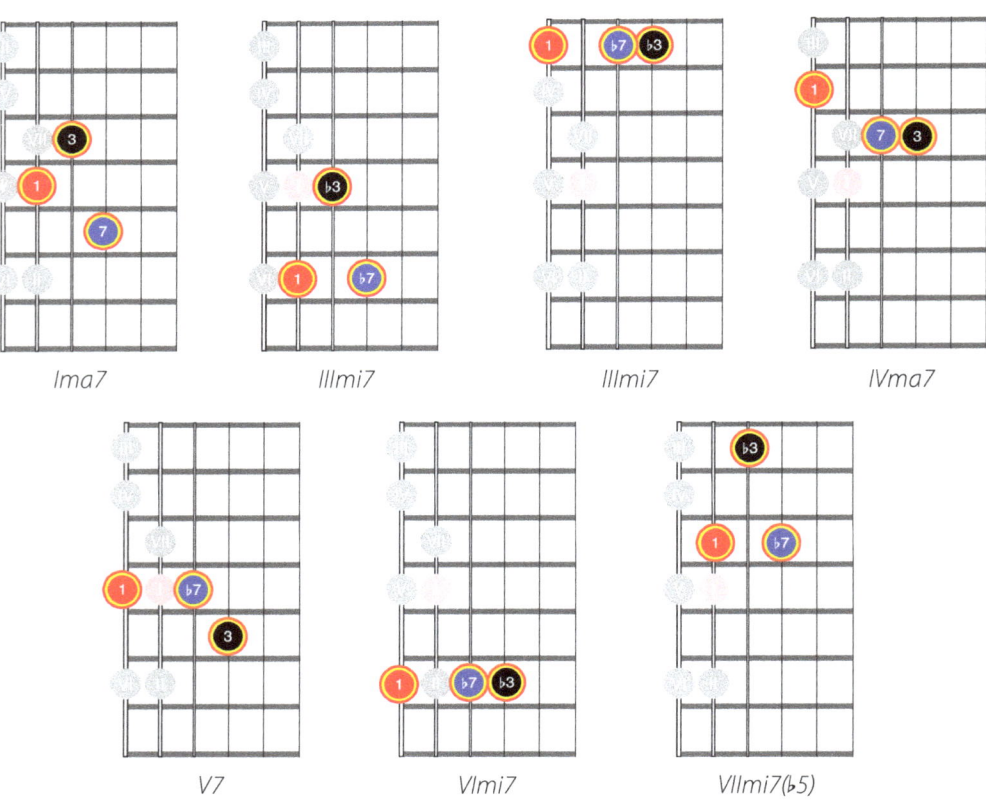

Root Map 4

Root Map 4

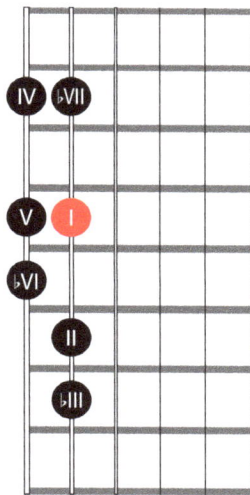

Root Map 4 Shell Voicings

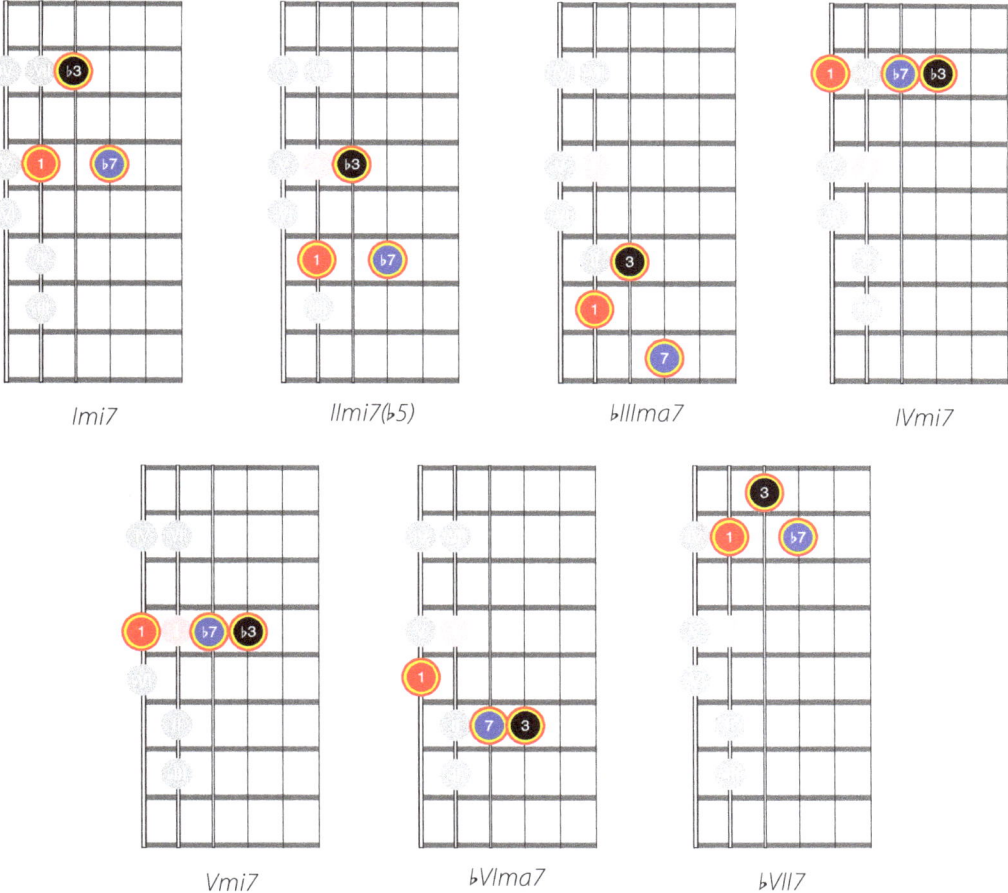

Imi7   IImi7(b5)   bIIIma7   IVmi7

Vmi7   bVIma7   bVII7

Chords

Pattern II and IV Movable / Barre Chords

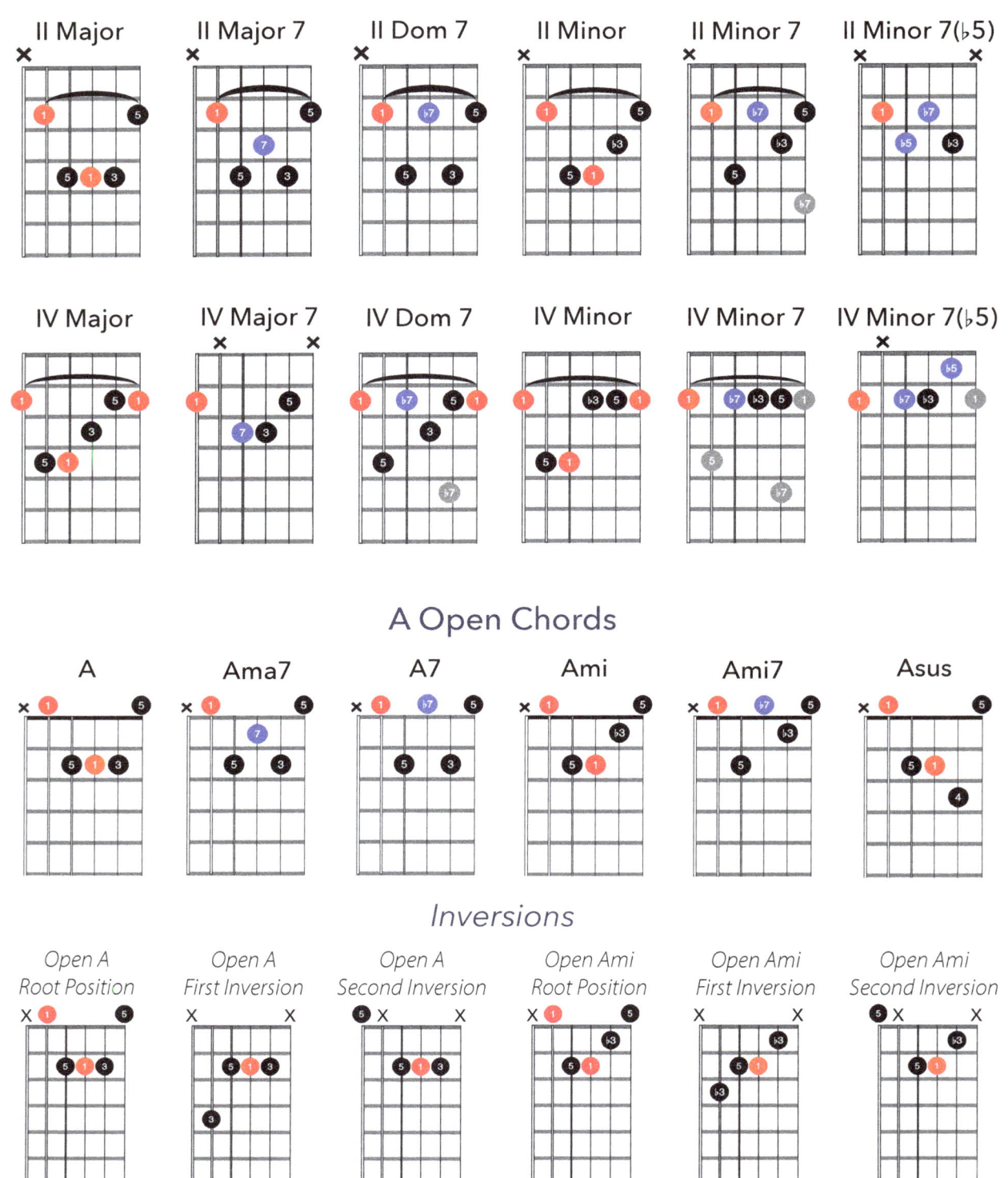

A Open Chords

Inversions

C Open Chords

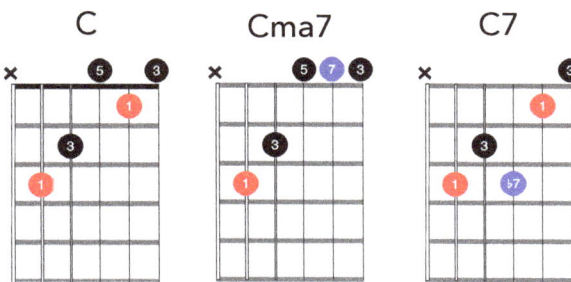
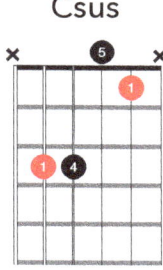

Inversions

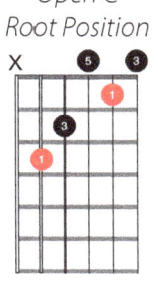
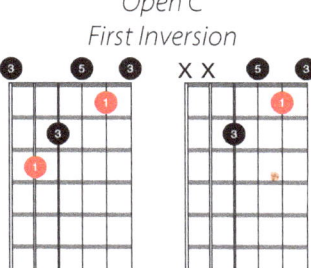
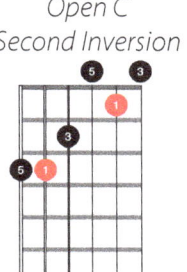

D Open Chords

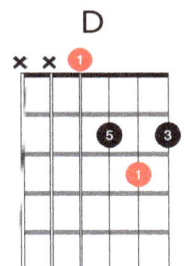
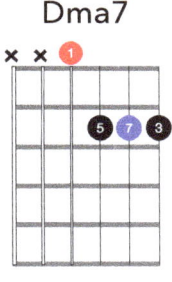
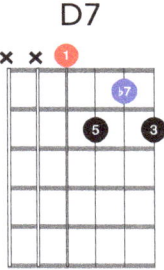
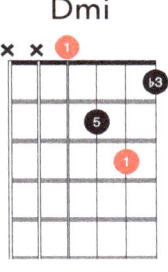
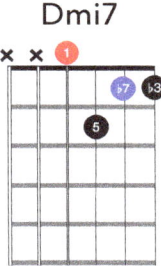
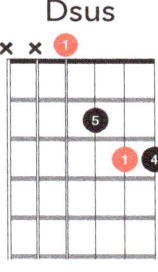

Inversions

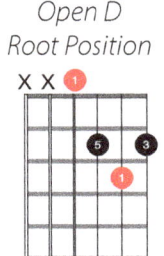
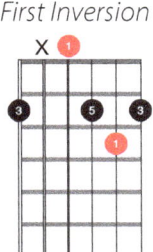
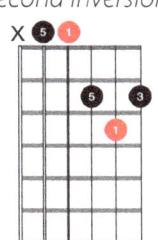
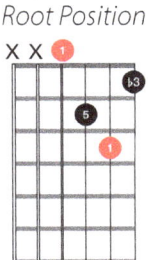
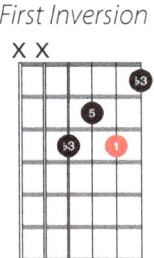
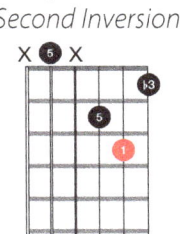

E Open Chords

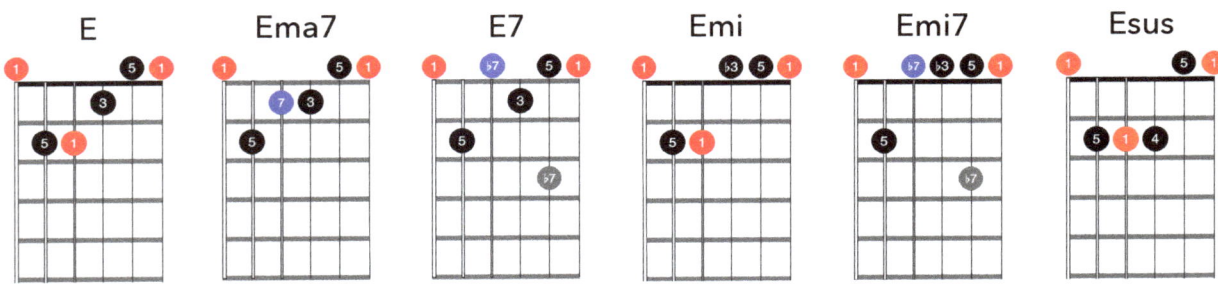

Inversions

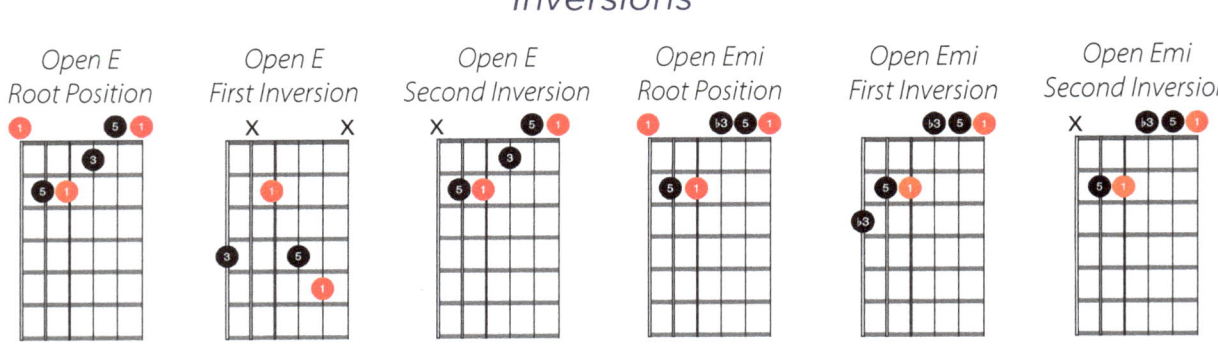

F Open Chords

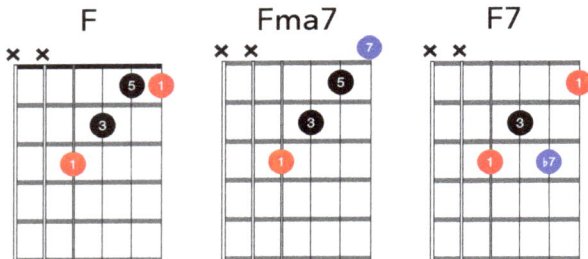

G Open Chords

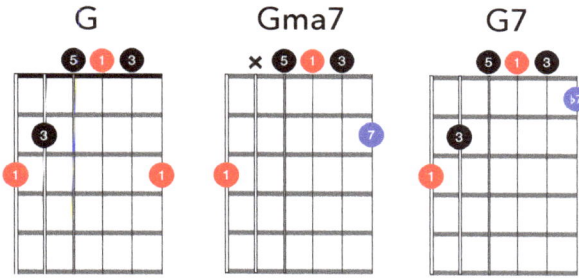
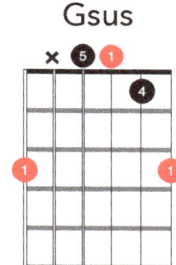

Inversions

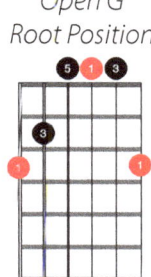
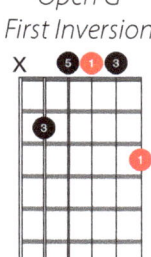
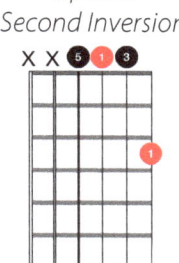

B Open Chords

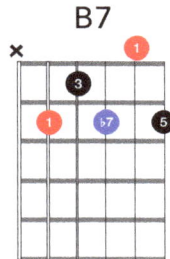

The Seven Modes

Scale Formulas

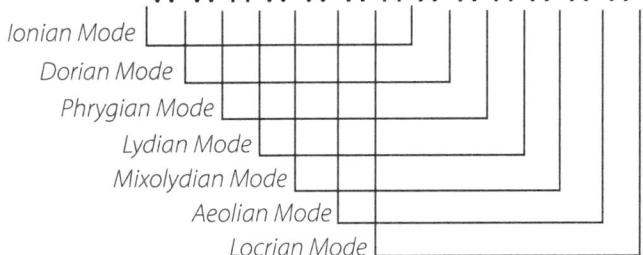

Interval Formulas for the Major Modes

Major Pentatonic	1	ma2	ma3		P5	ma6	
Ionian Mode	1	ma2	ma3	P4	P5	ma6	ma7
Lydian Mode	1	ma2	ma3	A4	P5	ma6	ma7
Mixolydian Mode	1	ma2	ma3	P4	P5	ma6	mi7

Interval Formulas for the Minor Modes

Minor Pentatonic	1		mi3	P4		P5		mi7
Blues	1		mi3	P4	D5	P5		mi7
Aeolian Mode	1	ma2	mi3	P4		P5	mi6	mi7
Dorian Mode	1	ma2	mi3	P4		P5	ma6	mi7
Phrygian Mode	1	mi2	mi3	P4		P5	mi6	mi7
Locrian Mode	1	mi2	mi3	P4	D5		mi6	mi7

Order of Chord Qualities for the Modes

Ionian:	Ima7	IImi7	IIImi7	IVma7	V7	VImi7	VIImi7(♭5)
Dorian:	Imi7	IImi7	♭IIIma7	IV7	Vmi7	VImi7(♭5)	♭VIIma7
Phrygian:	Imi7	♭IIma7	♭III7	IVmi7	Vmi7(♭5)	♭VIma7	♭VIImi7
Lydian:	Ima7	II7	IIImi7	♯IVmi7(♭5)	Vma7	VImi7	VIImi7
Mixolydian:	I7	IImi7	IIImi7(♭5)	IVma7	Vmi7	VImi7	♭VIIma7
Aeolian:	Imi7	IImi7(♭5)	♭IIIma7	IVmi7	Vmi7	♭VIma7	♭VII7
Locrian:	Imi7(♭5)	♭IIma7	♭IIImi7	♭IVmi7	♭Vma7	♭VI7	♭VIImi7

Interval Patterns

Ionian Mode Interval Pattern

Dorian Mode Interval Pattern

Phrygian Mode Interval Pattern

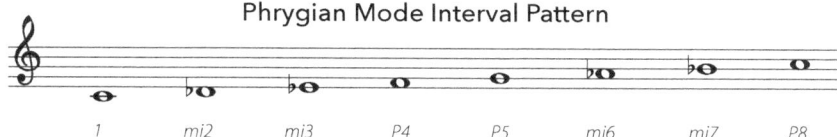

Lydian Mode Interval Pattern

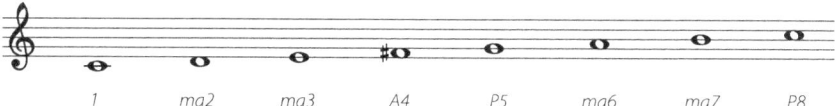

Mixolydian Mode Interval Pattern

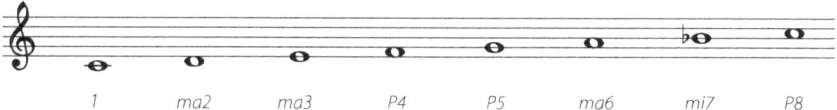

Aeolian Mode Interval Pattern

Locrian Mode Interval Pattern

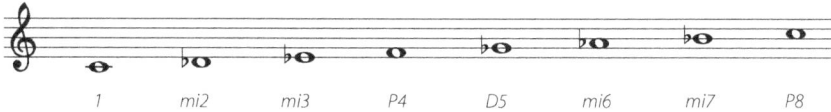

The Major Modes

Pattern I

Pentatonic	Ionian	Lydian	Mixolydian
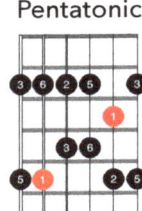	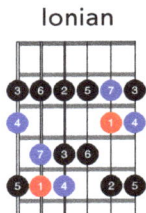	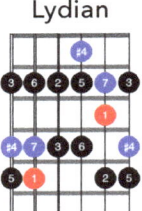	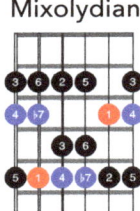

Pattern II

Pentatonic	Ionian	Lydian	Mixolydian
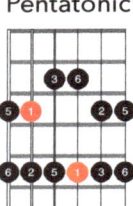	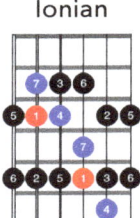	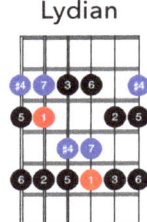	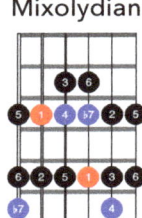

Pattern III

Pentatonic	Ionian	Lydian	Mixolydian
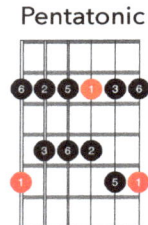	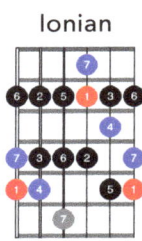	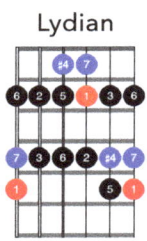	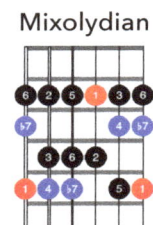

Pattern IV

Pentatonic	Ionian	Lydian	Mixolydian
	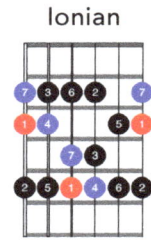	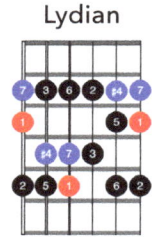	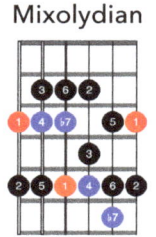

Pattern V

Pentatonic	Ionian	Lydian	Mixolydian
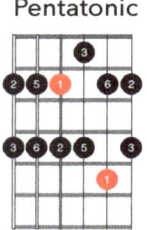	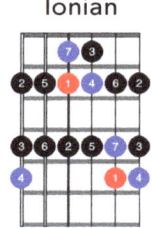	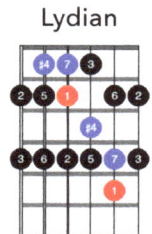	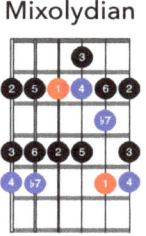

The Minor Modes

Pattern I

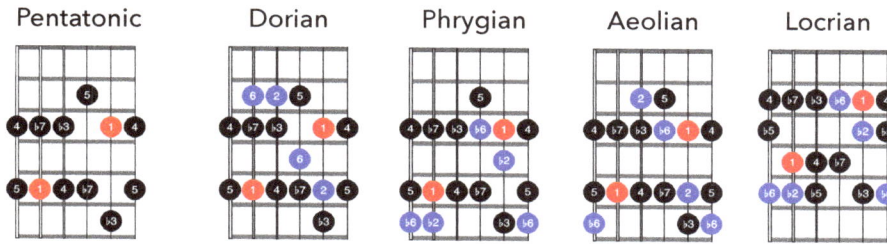

Pattern II

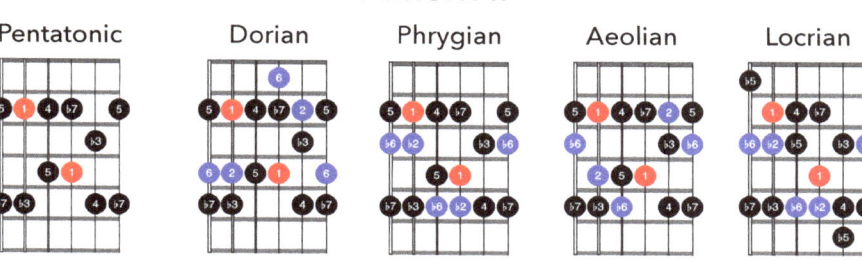

Pattern III

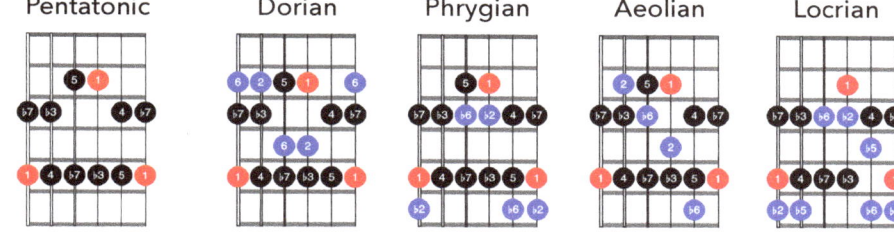

Pattern IV

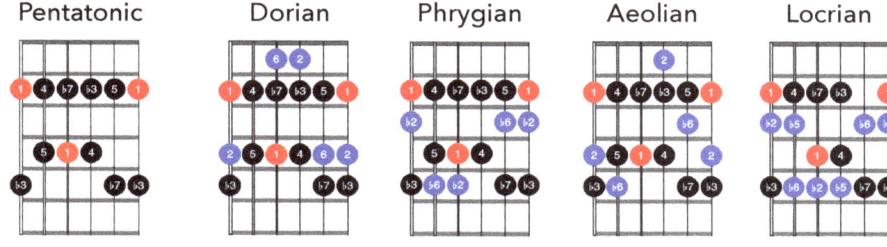

Pattern V

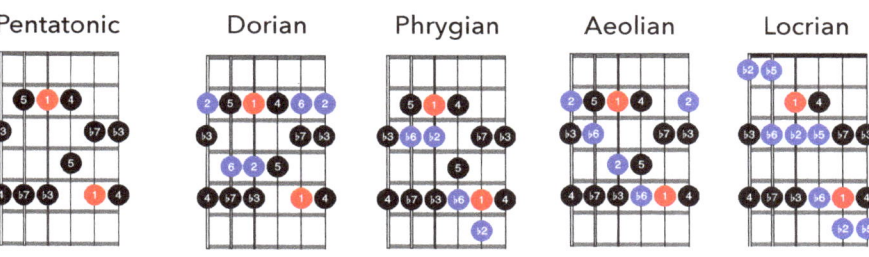

About Joe Elliott

Joe Elliott is an American guitarist, author, composer, and music educator.

Joe's professional experience as an educator includes 23 years of teaching at Musicians Institute (MI) in Hollywood, California, at the Guitar Institute of Technology (GIT). Joe has taught numerous clinics throughout the U.S. While at MI, Joe wrote and edited courses for GIT and MI's Baccalaureate programs. He spent three years as GIT Department Head and nine years as Vice President and Director of Education at Musicians Institute. He spent seven years as the Guitar Department Head and Director of Academic Administration at McNally Smith College of Music in St. Paul, Minnesota. He is currently the co-founder, CEO, and Director of Education of the guitar education website FretboardBiology.com and Music Biology, Inc.

Joe has authored several instructional books for guitar, including *An Introduction to Jazz Guitar Soloing* and *The Fretboard Biology* series of books, and has co-authored *Ear Training* with Carl Schroeder and Keith Wyatt.

Joe has released two solo guitar albums, *Joe's Place* and *Truth Serum*, as well as an instrumental country album, *Country Grit*, is currently a composer for APM Music in Los Angeles, and has composed numerous scores for television and film.

www.ingramcontent.com/pod-product-compliance
Lightning Source LLC
Chambersburg PA
CBHW042357070526
44585CB00029B/2966